Forgiveness

Forgiveness

AN ALTERNATIVE ACCOUNT

Matthew Ichihashi Potts

Yale UNIVERSITY PRESS

New Haven & London

Published with assistance from the foundation established in memory of
Amasa Stone Mather of the Class of 1907, Yale College.

Yale University Press books may be purchased in quantity for educational,
business, or promotional use. For information, please email sales.press@yale.edu
(U.S. office) or sales@yaleup.co.uk (U.K. office).

Excerpts from *Giving an Account of Oneself* by Judith Butler, copyright © 2005
by Fordham University Press, are republished with permission of Fordham
University Press; permission was conveyed through Copyright Clearance
Center, Inc.

Set in Adobe Garamond type by IDS Infotech Ltd.
Printed in the United States of America.

Library of Congress Control Number: 2022934656
ISBN 978-0-300-25985-8 (hardcover : alk. paper)

A catalogue record for this book is available from the British Library.

This paper meets the requirements of ANSI/NISO Z39.48-1992
(Permanence of Paper).

10 9 8 7 6 5 4 3 2

For Colette

Contents

Acknowledgments

I could not have completed this book without the help and support of many friends, family members, colleagues, institutions, and organizations. I am happy and humbled to acknowledge their aid and kindness here.

Dean David Hempton and the faculty of the Divinity School at Harvard University have afforded me generous periods of leave during which I have been able to read, research, and write much of what follows. I am sincerely grateful for the gift of this time and funding, and for my colleagues on the faculty. In particular, I thank Amy Hollywood and Stephanie Paulsell, both of whom read multiple drafts of this book and each of whom offered indispensable advice and counsel for its improvement. I have been working on the questions I investigate here since I was a master's degree student of Stephanie's and a doctoral student of Amy's. In many ways I believe this book to be as much a sign of their teaching as it is of my study, and I hope that it will leave them pleased and proud if that is so.

I also thank my students at Harvard, especially those who enrolled in my classes on forgiveness in the fall term of 2014 and the spring terms of 2017 and 2020. It's a truism that we learn most by teaching, but I guess it's a truism because it's true. Those classes and the challenging conversations they involved helped me immeasurably to develop my thinking about forgiveness. I especially thank my doctoral student and frequent teaching fellow

Mac Loftin, whose close and perceptive engagement with this book and its argument at various stages of development have helped me enormously.

As I was initially drafting this book, the Louisville Institute helped to fund a portion of my research leave through its First Book Grant for Minority Scholars and also graciously welcomed me and other grant awardees into a winter seminar that I found incredibly focusing and fruitful. I am grateful for the institute's programming and its mission, and for having been included in both.

Thank you to Yale University Press, and especially to Jennifer Banks and Abbie Storch, who showed remarkable patience and encouragement as I toiled with this manuscript. Thank you to my copy editor, Jessie Dolch, whose close attention and diligence have corrected and clarified so much of what follows. Thank you to Ann-Marie Imbornoni for stewarding the manuscript through production, to Amanda Wilson for her expert indexing, and to Bob Land for his careful proofreading. Thank you also to my anonymous reviewers for the press, whose gentle yet incisive criticisms and ready enthusiasms have improved this book tremendously.

The first part of the introduction to this book originally appeared as part of a short essay in the journal *Theology* 122, no. 3 (May 2019): 180–87. Thanks to the journal and to Professor Robin Gill for publishing that short piece and for permission to reproduce a small portion of it here.

I'm grateful to Vanessa Zoltan for her patient and thorough reading of this book in its first full draft, for her responsive and helpful feedback, for her friendship, for making me laugh every week during our podcast recording, all over the course of many weeks when this book was (ever and interminably) only almost done.

I offer sincere thanks as well to two Christian churches that I served while writing this book. St. Barnabas Memorial Episcopal Church in Falmouth, Massachusetts, is the church where I learned how to be a priest and learned what it means to love and be loved by a congregation as its minister. Many of forgiveness's problems and much of its promise were made concrete to me in the lives of the people I served and loved at St. Barnabas. All of them, even those now alive only in memory and in the embrace of God, remain close to my heart. I'm especially thankful to St. Barnabas's former rector the Reverend Patti Barrett and to its former interim rector the Reverend Louise Forrest for the support, collegiality, and leave they granted as I drafted this book. Thanks also to the Reverend Deborah Warner, who served as a pastor to my family during a difficult time of transition. My new congregation, the Memorial Church of Harvard University, has been a place of warm welcome and joy since

I took up its pulpit in the final months of writing this book. The congregation has engaged and advanced my ideas for years, and I am grateful that I can finish this book of theology as the Memorial Church's new minister.

Finally, I offer deepest thanks to my family, from whom and for whom I have learned all my most significant lessons about love and forgiveness. In other words, they have given me my theology. Thank you to my wife Colette's parents, Petur, Pat, Dan, and Deb; to Colette's siblings, Jake, David, and Danielle; and to their families, Shelly and Richie, Atticus and Penelope. They have welcomed me as their own. Thank you to my own brothers, Daniel and Thomas, and to their families, Kiwa and Kelli, Stephen and Kensei, whom circumstance and pandemic have made distant but who stay ever close to my thoughts. Thank you to my parents, Daniel and Miyoko, who have shown a depth of love for one another and for their children I hope to emulate in my home, and who have met the challenges of these last years with a patience, a resilience, and a courage that heartens and moves me. Thank you to my children, Camilla, Samuel, and Daniel, who give me all the best stories and who each day pull me headlong into the wide sweep and reach of love. And last, thank you to my wife, Colette, with whom I make that daily fall and for whom I keep falling and falling. Thank you, Colette. This book is for you.

Forgiveness

Introduction

On June 17, 2015, a twenty-one-year-old white supremacist named Dylann Roof walked into historic Emanuel African Methodist Episcopal Church in Charleston, South Carolina, and joined thirteen others for the Wednesday evening Bible study. He sat next to the pastor, Clementa Pinckney, and listened for a while and then bickered with the group over their interpretation of scripture. When the congregants bowed their heads and began to pray at the close of the study, Roof rose, withdrew a concealed handgun, and began murdering the people who had welcomed him into their spiritual home. He killed nine members of the congregation and was quickly arrested. At his arraignment, several (but not all) of the victims' surviving family members offered forgiveness to Roof through a closed circuit television feed to the jail where he had been remanded. "I forgive you," Nadine Collier, daughter of seventy-year-old Ethel Lance, said through tears. "You took something very precious from me. I will never talk to her again. I will never ever hold her again. But I forgive you." Bethane Middleton-Brown, sister of the slain DePayne Middleton-Doctor, said to Roof, "I acknowledge that I am very angry. But . . . [we] have no room for hating. So we have to forgive. I pray God on your soul." Wanda Simmons, the granddaughter of victim Daniel Simmons, also spoke directly to Roof, saying, "Although my grandfather and the other victims died at the hands of hate, this is proof, everyone's plea for your soul, is proof that they lived in love and their legacies will live in love.

So hate won't win."[1] Observing these public acts of forgiveness during an interview, the writer Ta-Nehisi Coates wondered aloud, "Is that real? . . . I question the realness of that."[2]

If forgiveness is real, then it's a real problem. Many philosophers, theologians, and scholars of religion have grown skeptical of forgiveness's value, its reality, or both, and they do so in part because of dramatic and unsettling examples like the one above.[3] Isn't it a moral hazard of some sort when a person who remains entirely unrepentant and absolutely allergic to reparations, who still menaces violence and still threatens victims, is offered forgiveness without any condition at all? Why is it so often people of color and people already marginalized by systemic violence upon whom this forgiving responsibility falls? What unjust purpose might the valorization of such suffering serve? Isn't the offer of forgiveness more of a salve to the conscience of power than an instrument of victims' healing? And isn't it a moral outrage to pressure victims into offering this forgiveness, to mandate that those already subject to loss and victimization assume responsibility for redeeming their offenders? Consider the words of the Reverend Anthony Thompson, surviving husband of the Reverend Myra Thompson, who offered forgiveness at Roof's arraignment but also later said, "If they give [Roof] the death penalty, I'm not going to interfere. . . . As far as I'm concerned he doesn't exist anymore. . . . This is gonna be with us for the rest of our life, but Dylann Roof has no place in that."[4] Or consider the Reverend Waltrina Middleton, DePayne Middleton-Doctor's cousin, who wrote on the anniversary of the Charleston shooting in 2020 that to "insist on a narrative of forgiveness is dehumanizing and violent, and it goes against the very nature of lament. As Christians we celebrate the donning of ashes and sackcloth as a priestly act of lamentation and mourning. Why deny families, in this watershed moment of grief, this right to lament?"[5]

In this book, I both honor Waltrina Middleton's demanding question and reframe Ta-Nehisi Coates's skeptical one. I do so by beginning with these survivors' angry and grief-stricken words while also attending to the forms of forgiveness they say they have offered, forms that reject hate but not anger, that deny superficial healing and forgetting, and that refuse unearned reconciliation. Instead of the narrative of repair Waltrina Middleton rightly recognizes as too easily imposed upon these statements of public grief, I explore the moral status and potential of Christian lament as itself a practice of forgiveness. I believe the Reverend Middleton is correct: Christian forgiveness does too often deny or diminish grief. I therefore want to ask what a Christian forgiveness that rooted itself in grief would look like, and reflect upon the implications for our moral theology. Having observed the lasting grief and anger of these forgiving families, instead of asking "Is that forgiveness real?," I ask, "What if *that* were real forgiveness?"

Forgiveness as it is typically understood definitionally defies our ethical vocabulary and destabilizes our moral foundations. When a law or code demands some recompense for wrong, how can we at the same time obligate or encourage the setting aside of that recompense? Forgiveness resists rationalization. But the adequacy of our moral grammar does not exclusively condition the reality of all our moral acts. Like Theodor Adorno, I assume that moral questions arise only when our moral vocabularies and grammars begin to fail.[6] To wonder about the problematic possibility of forgiveness at all is to presume some limits to our moral language, some gaps in our moral models, and so I am wagering that an adequate depiction or description of forgiveness will depend upon limning these limits and minding these gaps, that it will require the exploration of unsettling examples. I suggest that any "real" forgiveness will and must challenge the assumptions and test the boundaries of our moral instincts themselves. In other words, I suggest in this book that what forgiveness actually reveals when it strains our moral sense is not its own unreality or impossibility but the hidden limitations of our moral reasoning.

In this book then, and in light of these troubling examples, I ask: What if forgiveness were real? What would a just and livable forgiveness look like? What if forgiveness allowed for anger and rage and grief? What if it preserved mistrust and could keep a safe distance for its victims? What if forgiveness acknowledged hurt rather than promising healing; what if it uniquely reckoned with the permanence of a wound, rather than hastily dressing that wound with a thin reconciliation? If forgiveness did these things, then how might we come to understand the forgiving words of Nadine Collier, Bethane Middleton-Brown, Wanda Simmons, or Anthony Thompson, or even the searing lament of Waltrina Middleton? How might our moral grammar have to evolve in order to answer the question of forgiveness? How would our moral theology change as our grammars thus evolved? What is real forgiveness, really, and do the notions and habits that go by its name in our faith and our philosophy, the practices of pardon that have currency in our moral marketplace, really live up to forgiveness's most distressing and pressing demands?

Many of the same worries and incoherencies discomfit Christian theology when it considers the forgiveness of God. The dominant theological model of

God's forgiveness in the Christian West is one effectively interchangeable with the theology of atonement, and the contours of it are largely familiar to most Western Christians. Human beings owe God goodness or honor or holiness or all three, but, having failed to live up to these virtues (so the story goes), they now owe God a debt of some kind. And punishment pays. Moreover, since the goodness for which humans were created is inseparably linked to their very existence as creations of the Father—that is, since we are finite and God is infinite—the punishment required by God's justice is as foundational to our being and it is endless. We owe an infinite debt, by virtue of our existence, that we cannot ever pay; our very being is an obligation. Having betrayed our being itself, how can we possibly be forgiven? The traditional solution to this problem of punishment is Jesus, the Son, himself God and yet also the object of God's judgment, whose punishment can cover our infinite debt, and who (unlike us) may undergo this infinite punishment without it entirely exhausting his being, since he (like his Father) is infinite.

It's simple bookkeeping, really. We owe God more than we can afford to pay. God, in Christ, shares our plight and then pays on our behalf. The accounts once again balanced, we are allowed to enter into our eternal rest. But if we have paid any attention at all, we should have noted on our way into paradise that the cost of settling our accounts has been an astonishing cruelty: the torture and execution of Jesus of Nazareth, the condemnation of a Son by an unrelenting Father, the self-immolation of a brutalized God, and the uncritical valorization of suffering for generations of Christ's disciples to come. God's forgiveness is anything but free on this account. It is paid for, clearly and dearly, in blood. For all the Christian talk about unconditional forgiveness, in this foundational example of divine forgiveness God does not forgive for free. There are conditions and there are costs to God's pardon, and they are steep. Even if we are relieved here of our anxieties about the moral hazard of unconditional forgiveness, we should be horrified by the cruelty of the conditions God has stipulated.[7]

Of course, this is not the only theological story we can tell about the death of Jesus.[8] There are other interpretations of this sordid history, other accounts we can give of our hope in the cross. The outlines that have been carved into this atonement model are so familiar we barely question their necessity, but there is no necessary interpretive frame for the cross of Christ. We may preach Jesus Christ and him crucified, but that doesn't mean we always know what to say or what it means. The metaphor that traditionally grounds this theology is entirely economic, usually given in terms of debt, obligation, and repayment, or sometimes in terms of gift.[9] We owe God goodness, we exist by God's un-ending gift, we are in God's debt, God demands payment, Jesus pays on our behalf through punishment. Sin is debt, punishment pays, and forgiveness is the moral form of God's holy, balanced books. And indeed, the New Testa-ment language around forgiveness—*aphiemi* in the Greek, *remittere* in the Latin—does connote the payment of a debt, an economic exchange that sets the price for a slave's freedom. The unforgiving slave in Matthew 18 has his debts forgiven, and the simple analogy to sin in this parable is difficult to avoid.

But *aphiemi* and *remittere*, the words translated as forgiveness from the Greek and Latin New Testament, concern not debt but distance in their lit-eral etymologies. *Aphiemi* means to send away. To remit, at its root, is to es-tablish a distance. When authority to forgive sin is granted Peter and the disciples, for example, the operative verb is *luo*, to set loose.[10] So New Testa-ment forgiveness is a slippery thing, to say the least. Its metaphorical sense is economic but also spatial. In many cases *aphiemi* appears to require some sort of repentance or implies a reconciliation; in other circumstances it appears to require nothing at all. Often, forgiveness from God seems to depend upon forgiveness between humans: judge not, lest ye be judged, we're told. But then there is also Christ's prayer from the cross in which he asks God to offer forgiveness without condition, a prayer considerably complicated by the fact that Jesus's divinity entitles him to answer his own prayer. All of this is only to admit that *aphiemi* is used in the New Testament without a great deal of consistency and that other verbs—like *luo* in the sense of binding and loosing sin—also seem to carry some of modern forgiveness's semantic weight. I'm not particularly interested in extrapolating from scripture a semantic consis-tency in the usage of these Greek words, though others have attempted some-thing of that sort.[11] As Mark Jordan notes, there "can be no appeal to the simplicity of the Gospels . . . they are not . . . a detailed moral code of any kind. They are contradictory stories studded with paradoxical aphorisms. Every theology that is not written as a life told four ways already departs from the most authoritative model of Christian writing."[12] I therefore take the in-coherencies and contradictions of scriptural forgiveness for granted. Instead of attempting to parse or coerce an impossible consistency, I attempt to read the story of divine forgiveness as it is told four (and more) ways in order to locate modern forgiveness within a broader theological and moral landscape. If I come to soften some of the sharp contradictions of the scriptural witness in so doing, it is ancillary to my goal of articulating what is finally and most importantly at stake in the modern concept.

The governing analogy of sin in the Christian West is economic, and its roots do reach to the New Testament. But there are other ways to read *aphiemi* and thus other ways we might interpret this tradition. Were we to think of sin not as debt to God but as distance from God, and were we then to consider the mission of the Son sent away (*aphiemi*) by the Father to be the crossing of a distance, the opening of a loving space capacious enough to contain sin; if we thought of Christ's work as the journey into a far country, rather than the payment of an awful price, we might find that the typically nifty logic of atonement—that the cost of sin must be paid in full and that only the God-man can pay it—falls away and is replaced by another, perhaps more lovingly tragic, far less cruelly heroic one.[13] If sin is distance, then the Son's obedient estrangement from the Father is a journey already implicated in sin, a mission always and already also a remission. If sin is distance, then God's love will be signaled by the chasm Christ crosses to meet us rather than the torture he bears to win us. If sin is distance, then God's love reaches rather than redeems. If Christian forgiveness could set aside the moral accountancy that structures so much atonement theology, if the penal links of payment between God's love, Christ's suffering, and our sin might somehow be sundered in Christian thought, then the forms of Christian forgiveness that tend to follow human wrong might likewise become self-reflexively less cruel.[14] Forgiveness would set a distance between ourselves and sin, perhaps even between ourselves and other sinners, rather than invite some redemptive suffering to reimburse it, or inflict some imprudent reconciliation to repair it.

In the pages that follow I offer a modest theological defense of forgiveness: a defense, because I insist that forgiveness is real and that it is worthwhile; modest, because I concede that much of what passes for forgiveness in thought and custom should be largely set aside; theological, because I set that all aside due to its complicity with what I see as a misguided theological tradition of interpreting Jesus of Nazareth's death. In other words, I do not just conjure a concept out of thin air; I aim to defend forgiveness by casting off much of what its name connotes while constructing an alternative from the neglected resources of theology. Part of my aim is to show that the intuitive associations among sin, punishment, and forgiveness that so thoroughly undergird our morals also largely pervade Christian doctrine, all the while obscuring other moral and theological possibilities. But when framed differently from the outset, it may be that they imply a radically different form of both divine and human forgiveness.

Consider again the example with which I began: Nadine Collier's insistence that she will never stop missing her mother and so never forget this loss; Bethane Middleton-Brown's persistent anger alongside her determination to forgive; Anthony Thompson's absolute refusal even to acknowledge Dylann Roof's existence. In these examples, wrongdoing cannot be compensated, reconciliation remains impossible, and wounds will never fully heal. Indeed, forgiveness here seems little more than the refusal of retaliatory violence. It is about forswearing vengeance and rejecting retribution. It is about accepting that what has been lost cannot be regained. As such it demands no condition and neither assumes nor expects—let alone aspires toward—any reconciliation. It is (despite the conventional wisdom) more broken-hearted than whole-hearted, full of rage as often as repaired. Forgiveness of this sort is more tragedy than triumph, less miracle than mourning. It is a strategy for surviving an irrevocable wrong. It declines to escrow the life of the future to a past that cannot be changed or to a pain that cannot be compensated. I suspect that what makes unconditional forgiveness incredible—literally unbelievable—in examples like the ones that trouble Coates above is that forgiveness typically comes to us with such hollow confidence. Too often forgiveness callowly promises the impossible in the wake of horrible injustice, right when we are most unready to recognize redemption, just when we are least persuaded by the possibility of miracle. I therefore suggest that the typically triumphalistic tone of our usual language around forgiveness is itself a part of the problem, and that, in fact, forgiveness trucks in much messier and more miserable stuff—as Collier, Middleton-Brown, Simmons, and Thompson know all too well. Forgiveness is difficult and trying and painful and unending, but it can be real perhaps, and holy sometimes too.

To elaborate a bit, allow me to suggest the following. First, forgiveness is not about feelings. We should feel restored or at peace when we forgive, we are told. We believe that when we forgive we should have moved on or, at least, should have put aside our wrath and our resentment. Indeed, for some a primary purpose of forgiveness is its use as a tool for self-transformation, so that one can allow oneself to move away from damaging or negative emotions such as rage and rancor in the aftermath of wrong.[15] Recently, psychological literature has complicated this picture, distinguishing, for example, the decision to forgive (which wills a behavioral change or commitment) from emotional forgiveness (which signals a change of heart or affect).[16] But I argue that forgiveness has no necessary relation to positive affective change. If forgiveness is simply about what one does—or rather, about what one restrains oneself from doing—then one's feelings needn't enter into it at all. On the contrary, the emotions that follow trauma are always volatile and often remain so for long periods of time. Restraint from revenge likely will mean struggling with bitterness and anger. Emotions are always fleeting; one cannot expect victims of injustice or trauma to feel permanent equanimity after a single, momentous decision to forgive. Instead, one should expect that victims and survivors will feel all sorts of emotions in the wake of their trauma, whatever their decisions about forgiveness. Rather than a determination never again to feel rancor or resentment in perpetuity, forgiveness is simply a promise not to act with retaliatory violence when those painful emotions and vengeful desires inevitably and repeatedly arise. What matters with respect to forgiveness is not how I feel about the person who has wronged me, but how I measure and temper my interpersonal response to that wrong.

Second, and relatedly, forgiveness is not reconciliation. We presume that forgiveness requires welcoming an offender back with open arms, with restored relation between two parties, even if only momentarily.[17] Indeed, we often use the language of forgiveness and reconciliation interchangeably, but restored relation is, strictly speaking, the work of reconciliation, a work I characterize as crucially distinct from forgiveness.[18] This is for practical as well as theological reasons. Reconciliation can be a good and honorable goal, but it may demand certain concessions or actions between parties that my version of forgiveness—restraint from revenge—need not. Conditions can and should of course be met before a perpetrator and victim establish, transform, or restore their relationship. At minimum, the safety of all concerned should be assured. But if all forgiveness demands is the forswearing of vengeance, then it need not carry any specific conditions, not even these basic ones. To be sure, there is a voluminous commentary in both philosophy and theology about the necessity of various conditions, if any, required for a felicitous offer of forgiveness.[19] But I find that these mostly depend upon a collapsing of the distinction between reconciliation and forgiveness. Forgiveness may in some cases prove a first step to reconciliation, or it may simply occasion a lasting nonretaliatory estrangement. Some may object that a restraint which lacks the desire to reconcile wants the moral bravado of self-sacrifice so often canonized in Christian thought and practice. But we should be wary of such valorizations and their manipulations by power, I think, for moral and theological reasons. Christians are commanded to forgive, it is true; but it's also clear that full and final reconciliation is ultimately the eschatological work of God in Christ (Col 1:20). When bodies and lives are at risk, it seems to me mere restraint is quite saintly enough. We will love our enemies as much as we can with our broken human hearts, but that may not be much—perhaps just enough to keep us at a safe distance. God can love our enemies (and us) the rest of the way to reconciliation if and as God so chooses. In fact, there may be a commendable spiritual humility in declining to collapse forgiveness into reconciliation, because restraint from violence while full and final reconciliation is left to the eschaton can theologically signal the limits of one's own love while recognizing the infinite reach of God's.[20] God loves those we do not or cannot love. And so we intend God's children no harm, we refuse to exact vengeance even when they deserve it, even when we might wish it upon them, for God's sake, and then we keep our peace as we wait for God's infinite love to bridge the painful chasm sin has opened in our lives. It seems to me that the additional step of requiring fully achieved human reconciliation—that is, fully restored relationship as opposed to a cautious and estranged nonretaliation that need neither strive nor even hope for reconciliation in this life— misreads the theological tradition in significant ways, and with troubling moral consequences. It replaces Christ's work with our own. Earthly reconciliation beckons intimacy, right or wrong, and in this fallen creation it is often obviously wrong, or at least carries unjust dangers and demands. Forgiveness as I describe it, meanwhile, can turn its cheek while also keeping a safe distance as it does.

Third, forgiveness happens in time. This is obvious, perhaps; what act does not occur in time? What I mean to emphasize here is that forgiveness not only obeys those laws of irrevocability and irreversibility that the physical passage of time imposes upon us, but that forgiveness is furthermore an act expressly responsive and suited to these chronological constraints. That is, forgiveness rejects retaliation precisely because of the futility of vengeance with respect to the irrevocability of time. Much of the popular and scholarly discourse around forgiveness implies that it can either undo, restore, or erase the past. But the common delusion that an act in the present can somehow rectify a wronged past is in fact the hallmark of retribution's magical thinking, not of forgiveness's realist grief. It is part of why the language of moral debt is so ill-suited to sin and forgiveness. If you take five dollars from me, you can give five dollars back, with interest even, depending how we define repayment. But if you kill my brother, no act can restore what has been lost. This restorative penal fantasy, and retributive punishment's constant conceptual linkage to forgiveness, skews our moral reflections upon these issues. I seek to sever this linkage and suggest that whereas punishment too often attempts vainly to will backward in time, forgiveness should in fact seek to do exactly the opposite, to be available to a difficult future. Forgiveness reckons unflinchingly with a past that cannot be undone. The futility of retribution's urge to turn time backwards is precisely what forgiveness understands and works against.

This, then, is why throughout this book I characterize forgiveness as akin to mourning. Forgiveness seeks to live in the wake of loss. It accepts that what has been lost cannot be restored, and then it aims to live in and with the irrevocability of wrong. If forgiveness is a moral good, then it is good only in the sense that mourning might be construed a social or psychological good—not because mourning itself is a wonderful and enjoyable thing, but because it is the way we learn to struggle with and through and in a loss we cannot redeem. On this account, once again, forgiveness is more tragedy than triumph, less miracle than mourning, more resignation than redemption. And in this sense, forgiveness's theological provenance becomes clarified too, as it is I think better understood as a habit of Christian nonretaliation than as the spiritual regulation of posttraumatic emotion or as the coerced companion to an injudicious reconciliation. Christian forgiveness, as certain corners of the theological tradition will evince, is thus an expression of love for one's enemies, though—when understood in this way—it may also transform our expectations of what Christian love requires. Forgiveness is the habit of nonretaliation; or better, it is the judgment nonretaliation renders. We cannot forgive virtues. We forgive only sins. But as it issues its condemnation of sin, as it resolutely names a violation that cannot be undone, forgiveness also accepts that past as unalterable and so imagines what possibilities for the future its battered history might bear.

If forgiveness is more mourning than miracle, a manner of living with rather than magically fixing a broken past, then its posture is paradoxically forward facing. Since forgiveness addresses the past so unflinchingly, it also necessarily and paradoxically sets itself honestly toward whatever future can actually come to be in the wake of that past. In attempting to find the past's wrongs livable even if irrevocable, forgiveness requires and inspires imagination. To refuse the retributive attempt to undo the past is to accept that past and to be open to the only possible future that can follow from it. The urge to live with loss is still an urge to live, and so forgiveness will be, even if only reluctantly, a stance of openness toward the future. It is a future some parts of which we may dread, a future which might demand that we daily face down sorrow, anger, and anguish. But just as the realism of mourning involves an acceptance of a future bereft of one's beloved, forgiveness's refusal to forget its wrong imagines what a wronged life lived well might be. It does not vainly try by violence to restore a life that has been permanently destroyed. It refrains from a retaliatory attempt to rectify an irrevocable wrong. It looks with grief toward what life really must become going forward, and then it faces that future with a grim will and survives. It is precisely because forgiveness refuses the retributive fallacy of fixing the past that it is freed to move—slowly, painfully, even perhaps like Christ with permanently open wounds—into the future.

This is a book of theology, but it is also a book of literary interpretation. Another way of saying this is that I am writing theology in the margins of literary texts. In some sense, of course, theological writing has always been marginal. Theology has always operated as a commentary upon scriptural and other authoritative (ecclesial, liturgical, devotional, historical) writings. But from those margins, theology has aimed to give life to these writings, to unearth their subtleties and relevance to readers' lives. This book aims to perform the same normative, theological writing in the margins mostly of literary (but also of theological and philosophical) works to unearth their subtleties and relevance to readers. And even if these works themselves make no obviously dogmatic or explicitly theological claims, I will. I want to be clear, however: this is not a work of literary history or of literary criticism in the usual sense. I am not interested here to give an exhaustive account of how forgiveness has been articulated across time in a particular literary culture, or by a single major writer. Several works of this type already exist, some of them quite excellent and important.[21] Although I depend upon and note others' critical scholarship where necessary, neither is my aim to review the readings of others or to discern how a particular set of literary texts regards forgiveness. Rather, I use these texts to make my own argument about how Christians in particular ought to do so. I expect this approach may discomfort both some literary critics and some theologians, but I'm convinced that my readings and my strategy here are methodologically sound and uniquely appropriate to this project.

To do this, I undertake in this book extended readings and analyses of a novel by each of four contemporary writers: Kazuo Ishiguro's *The Buried Giant*, Marilynne Robinson's *Gilead*, Louise Erdrich's *LaRose*, and Toni Morrison's *Beloved*. Of course, forgiveness is a common problem in human life and a frequent topic of literature across time and place. One might reasonably ask why I chose these particular authors to aid in my argument, or why these four of their many novels. To answer the first question, it is clear to me that these authors have persistently engaged with a wide range of moral issues deeply related to forgiveness throughout their work. Ishiguro has explored questions of memory, apology, and remorse in all of his books. Robinson's early first-person novels invite useful reflection upon confession while her later novels give way to the complications of love and reconciliation. Erdrich's recent work especially has unsettlingly rendered dilemmas of revenge, justice, and atonement. And healing from the violence of the past while making a way into the present is a constant concern across Morrison's fiction. But it's not just that these four writers often focus on forgiveness; other authors obviously do so too. I have selected these four in particular because I believe their literary explorations complicate the problem of forgiveness in exactly the way I think Christian theology has often failed to but manifestly ought to. Ishiguro's early novels, set as they are in Nagasaki, not only examine issues of apology and remorse; they also raise questions about guilt, blame, and the annihilating consequences of modern war. These themes resonate throughout his work and should inform any adequate theological account of forgiveness. Robinson reflects upon our relation to past wrongdoing in all of her novels. But situating interpersonal and familial forgiveness within the context of nineteenth-century American abolitionism and twentieth-century American racism as she does in the Gilead books reveals how the interpersonal and familial can obscure broader political concerns about justice and obligation. A theology of forgiveness that hopes to address both the political and the interpersonal should do likewise. In her justice trilogy of *The Plague of Doves*, *The Roundhouse*, and *LaRose*, Erdrich repeatedly explores issues of revenge, community, redemption, and atonement. But in setting these explorations under the colonial conditions of contemporary Ojibwe life, her novels unsettle European moral assumptions in a way that a Christian theology of forgiveness eager critically to engage white supremacy, including its own, must welcome. And though Morrison's works do often depict habits of personal and social healing among Black communities in the United States, the forthrightness and candor with which she documents the scale of their violations prevent any forgiveness she suggests from appearing to be an easy remedy or a simple solution. A theology that hopes to offer forgiveness as an answer must also ask the most difficult questions, and Morrison's novels always do.

Why then these four novels? In truth, the answer is partly personal: they are my favorites. I find each quite difficult and beautiful and moving, and it has been easy to spend many hours of study and reflection in their company.

My reasons are also practical: for the sake of my writing and your reading, four novels is enough. But the main and most important reason is more substantive. I have selected these four books by these four essential writers because each story is singularly preoccupied not only with forgiveness, but also with grief. *The Buried Giant* is about war and retaliation and punishment, but it's also about an old couple mourning the death of their son while coming to grips with a terminal illness. *Gilead* is about abolition and racism and the return of a prodigal son, but it's also about the complications of dying while trying to love the dead. *LaRose* is about building community under colonial conditions and about what repair remains possible beneath the weight of a genocidal history. But it's also about two families reckoning with the death of a young child. And while *Beloved* is about living both with and beyond the burdens of memory and the traumas of horrific violence, it's also about being haunted by loss and living with unending grief. As I have said above, I believe forgiveness can be usefully framed as a habit of grief and a practice of mourning, and indeed I believe framing forgiveness this way might transform not only our understanding of it as a Christian practice but also our approach to Christian morals more generally. These novels, insofar as they begin and end in grief, thus provide ample and inviting margins in which to write this moral theology.

Part of what I argue in this book is that the effort to live loss into the future, to wrestle a habitable life from the anguish of our grief, will usually involve some engagement with language and will always oblige imagination. Indeed, I suggest that to engage loss with language at all—even despairingly, even if all we can bring ourselves to say is that there is nothing whatever to be said—is to attempt to place our faith in the possibility of meaningful relation mediated through fallible words in the aftermath of harm.[22] Why cry out that we have no words unless we wish our wordlessness to be heard by others? Language may only frailly or imperfectly facilitate meaningful relation, but even when—especially when—it is self-conscious of its limits, all its fragile failure can still mediate relation and signal an embarkation upon the future.

This is how I read the New Testament writings compiled and shared in the aftermath of Jesus of Nazareth's death. His friends and students, traumatized by his death and haunted by his resurrection, took up the types and tropes of their time and place and essayed to imagine a future with(out) their friend and teacher. But just as the survivors of his death used the tools and frames at hand in their time and place—the religious culture of ancient Judea and the traditions of Hellenistic philosophy and the oppressions of Roman authority—to read and write the meaning of Jesus's life and death into cross and communion, into ministry and mission, I also see those who continue to mourn Jesus's death today as engaged in a similar struggle. That is, to mourn Jesus in at least one sense is to seek some habitable meaning for and from his death in our own world. This is not necessarily to undermine those Christians who would set their firm faith in Christ's resurrection against my exhortation toward mourning. It is only to suggest that the aim of understanding how the crucified one still lives in our own lives is an urge largely congruent with the movements of everyday mourning and grief, even if we believe the circumstances in Christ's case to be supremely and supernaturally unique. Modern Christians may also be traumatized by Jesus's death and haunted by his resurrection. And while it's true that scripture bears a unique authority for us modern-day mourners, just like those ancient saints before us we take up the language of our time and place, with all our own types and tropes, our own habits and traditions and privileges and oppressions and scriptures, and attempt then to read and write the meanings of this death into our lives. This is and always has been the method of theology.

None of this is to deny that early Christian scriptural writing is still quite different from contemporary fiction, or that the biblical witness can and should carry unique authority for Christian theologians. But the manner of doing theology is the same, whatever margins we write that theology in: we have a loss and the story of a loss, and a given language by which to note our meanings in the margins of that story. Whether in the first or twenty-first century, we have the death of Jesus and the call to discipleship, and a world around us through which and of which to make these diremptions and demands more livable.[23]

To put this all more simply and more to the point of this book: I do not find that the theology of the Christian West, historically and in general, has always grappled convincingly with the problems of forgiveness, mostly because those problems are linked to deeper confusions I see in the theology of atonement already internal to Western Christendom. But contemporary literature wrestles with forgiveness most admirably, in a way that mimics scripture's similar complexities. Literary fiction, and these fictions in particular, allows forgiveness to be a problem, it is unsurprised by how forgiveness confounds and confuses, it doesn't aim to clean up the mess forgiveness leaves. Literary fiction doesn't expect to speak conclusively of forgiveness, it only wishes to speak at all. It looks for—but does not ever conclusively find— meaning in its fraught scenes of forgiveness, and in so doing it in fact mimes the meaningful movements of forgiveness itself, which is also provisional and fragile, a habit of continued survival rather than a conclusive feat of sanguine understanding or triumphant resolution.

Of course, this is the nature of literary language: it succeeds insofar as it opens rather than closes meanings, insofar as it speaks of something inexpressible and, in so doing, allows that much more still needs to be said. Indeed, it is because literary language only provisionally asserts its significance, because it knows it is frail and fragile and still cannot but speak, because it knows it must fall short in crucial ways, because even (or especially) the Bible will remain open to interpretation and available for misuse and misunderstanding, that I attempt to include the literary in my theology. Literary writing is writing that has become a question, writing that self-consciously recognizes its own provisionality and frailty, even as it steps into the void and makes its semantic stand; it is writing which knows that it cannot ever say quite enough but resolves to speak meaningfully anyway.[24] One might be tempted here to say that this provisional frailty is also one foundational to Christian theology's understanding of itself and of its own object, of the Word made flesh who is given to us in unstable signs, in word and sacrament. The fragile movement of mourning into provisional meaning that is exemplified by the New Testament writings is also one that literary writing embraces and the incarnation, perhaps, establishes. That Christological claim can be argued more fully elsewhere, but at this point at least, in apology of this theology written here from the margins of literature, let me finally simply say: it is because contemporary literary fiction so frequently and so beautifully presents the problem of forgiveness, and because Christian moral and systematic theology so often fails to, that literature offers a unique opportunity for a theologian like me to critique and reconstruct Christian forgiveness on more careful, subtle, tentative—in other words, on forgiveness's own—terms.

As it is to most people, forgiveness is personally important to me. The desire to forgive and to be forgiven has arisen in all of my significant relationships. Since we cannot forgive without implying something about the nature of justice, it may be that every personal forgiveness is political too. So the politics of forgiveness is also deeply personal for me. Issues of war, peace, wrong, and repentance have structured my family history and my identity in essential ways. My father is white from the United States and my mother is Japanese. My grandfathers served on opposing sides of a war in which Japan committed horrendous atrocities throughout Asia, in which U.S. aerial bombardment targeted Japanese civilian noncombatants with fire and atomic bombs, and in which the U.S. government employed racist policies to authorize the internment of its citizens and the seizure of their property. After its surrender and under the supervision of Allied occupation forces, Japan renounced war and committed never again to establish armed forces in its 1947 constitution. Since then, Japan has wrestled with recognizing and apologizing for its war crimes. The United States, meanwhile, has also struggled to reckon with the impact of its atomic bombings, though it has paid reparations to survivors of internment since the late 1980s. My father met my mother in Japan while serving in the navy during the United States' own misguided incursions into Southeast Asia, and while stationed at a naval base meant to provide Japan the defense it could not constitutionally provide itself. I also served in the U.S. Navy, at that same naval station, on a ship already notorious for having killed 290 innocent people in 1988 because of a mistaken missile strike on a commercial airliner. I eventually departed naval service as a conscientious objector. I am a Christian who aims to take with absolute seriousness Jesus's instructions to repent and forgive and love my enemies. But taking these commandments seriously means acknowledging the staggering challenge of their demands. It means grappling with what they could possibly mean under the complicated and conflicted conditions of our world, conditions of racism, colonialism, war, and atrocity, the conditions out of which my family has somehow managed to arise, even while so many others have perished. It means wrestling with the reality of loss and the possibility of life beyond it. This book is one attempt to do that.

The first part of this book takes up the question of accountability, and the second part, of atonement. The first part asks the question, If we forgive a wrong or a wrongdoer, how can we hold that wrongdoer accountable to their wrong? In Chapter 1 I consider how the inclination toward retaliation, the compensation of harm through proportional punishment, is institutionalized in law, and how these legal models—and the forms of extralegal forgiveness they imply—depend upon a problematically violent model of sovereignty. Through readings of Kazuo Ishiguro's novel *The Buried Giant* and analyses of Friedrich Nietzsche, Vladimir Jankélévitch, Jacques Derrida, and Hannah Arendt, I articulate a form of forgiveness that rejects compensatory schemes of justice and instead attempts freely to initiate the risks of a new future while remaining knowingly beholden to the wounds of its past.

In Chapter 2 I turn toward issues of repentance and confession, meditating upon the compensatory logic of customary forgiveness through readings of Michel Foucault and Martha Nussbaum, showing how confessional sincerity and narrative accountability function as currencies for transactional models of punishment and forgiveness. Following Judith Butler, I articulate a form of narrative accountability that is grounded on the impossibility of full self-articulation rather than on its necessity. From this critique I turn to Marilynne Robinson's novel *Gilead* in order to explore the threat that an ethic of explanatory self-justification poses for theology. In further readings of Judith Butler on the use of violence, and explorations of both Dietrich Bonhoeffer and the Japanese philosopher Tanabe Hajime around issues of guilt and justification, I offer a reading of Robinson's novel that exposes the profound moral and racist failures of its central characters and propose a model of forgiveness as a twofold commitment to both persistent penitence and retaliatory restraint.

In the second part, I focus more explicitly on the implications of these questions for Christian theologies of atonement and vice versa. Informed by traditional atonement models that emphasize God's anger, in Chapter 3 I first explore the affective dimension of forgiveness and uncover in both the eighteenth-century bishop Joseph Butler and the contemporary philosopher Charles Griswold a conceptual tie between our preoccupation with anger appeasement and the sovereign exceptionality of forgiveness. I link this preoccupation to the fragile anxieties of white supremacy and then turn to Louise Erdrich's novel *LaRose* in order to develop a different theological posture toward anger in atonement from the colonial setting of an Ojibwe reservation in North Dakota. Using the theological analyses of Paul Fiddes and John Milbank, with attention to the atoning work of love in the theology of Julian of Norwich and others, and keen to incorporate indigenous perspectives on relation and kinship, I discern in the novel a love that self-consciously exceeds the bounds of the personal and necessarily invites politically significant relationship, a love that forestalls any too easy reconciliation for the sake of honoring both history and victims' anger. In other words, I reveal a love that can bear rather than bury, endure rather than erase, human sin.

In Chapter 4 I continue exploring what it would mean for love to bear and endure our deeply broken histories rather than to bury and erase them. To do so, I consider Jeffrey Blustein, Paul Ricoeur, and Miroslav Volf on the role of forgetting in forgiveness. I critique the inclination I see in much Western thought to impose an unearned resolution—or even a happy ending—upon our histories, a resolution intended primarily to assuage or curtail the pain and anger of our grief. In a reading of Toni Morrison's novel *Beloved*, I explore the dangers of this unearned resolution and question the degree to which conventional Christian understandings of resurrection might be held in sway to them. Turning to Rowan Williams, Michel de Certeau, and M. Shawn Copeland, I suggest a theology of resurrection that unrelentingly insists upon the reality of loss, and then I explore how writing and imagination can emerge into the space of that loss. Following Julia Kristeva and Jacques Derrida, I suggest a mourning that insists on speaking of the past's irrecuperable losses while simultaneously insisting on the absolute inadequacy of our speech. Forgiveness as mourning thus emerges at the end of this book as a persistent practice of writing, speech, and critique.

PART ONE

Accountability

Retaliation

How should we respond to wrongdoing? Whatever else forgiveness may be, it is a way we address and reckon with past wrongs. Our attitude toward forgiveness will therefore depend at least in part upon how we think about the past and upon how we think about wrongdoing. Much of what follows in this book approaches these difficult realities—the past and its brokenness— from multiple literary and theological angles. In this first chapter I draw the possibilities of forgiveness into greater relief by considering another way of responding to wrongdoing: retaliation. I argue that retaliation may be understood as forgiveness's opposite, that in fact forgiveness might usefully be defined as the commitment to forgo retaliation. But our retaliatory impulses run deep, both conceptually and culturally. It may be that forgiveness only ever makes any sense if we are willing to abandon not just the right of retaliation but also the logic that underlies that right. Forgiveness could help us reconceive our forms of justice away from any fantasies of recompense.

Retaliation moves within a matrix of related words and meanings. In our common speech, it seems more well-reasoned than revenge but less controlled than retribution. If I seek vengeance, I act with abandon; if I seek retribution, I move with calculation. When I retaliate, I do something of both; I lash out but in a measured way. Etymologically, retaliation is fundamentally rooted in the idea of careful proportion. The English word "retaliation" traces its roots to the *lex talionis*, the law of talion, or literally, the law of like for like rooted in Exodus and Leviticus and more remotely related to Hammurabi's Code. Retaliation assumes a justice meted out as an eye for an eye and a tooth for a tooth. The proper way to respond to a wrong, retaliatory logic suggests, is to respond in kind. There is virtue in this logic, because a law of like for like presumes a condition of equal status and equal regard. The rich man's eye is worth no more or less than the poor man's, and so a like for like compensation can inscribe this equality into law and upon bodies. Of course, even in this law there are limits to equality of status and regard, since in Exodus and Leviticus, not to mention in the law's Babylonian and Roman analogues, these protections were in place only for men and only for men within specified social categories. Nonetheless, we can understand how we might read the law of like for like as fundamentally concerned with equity and justice. Over time, Jewish scholars and teachers interpreted this law away from literal mortification so that my neighbor's loss could be calibrated to a standard financial compensation. Thus I might pay a fee rather than lose my tooth. This presumption of compensatory damage deeply structures our moral instincts and expectations; we believe crime demands punishment, and I argue that our assumptions about forgiveness are constrained by this retaliatory frame. We tend to think about what wrongdoing and wrongdoers owe, we perceive moral failures as debts, and when we do, we come to think less clearly about what forgiveness is and does.

In this chapter and the ones that follow, I argue that in fact forgiveness posits a different sort of response to wrongdoing, one that questions the prudence of returning past pain in kind. Forgiveness turns away from retaliation, not only because it rejects the satisfaction of its own understandable desire for vengeance, but also because it denies the possibility of eradicating its own pain. The loss it has suffered is so grave and irredeemable that it can only accept the ineradicability of its loss while turning away from any customary or compensatory satisfactions. In this chapter, I pay close attention to our ethical urge toward retaliation, toward the law of dealing like for like, toward trading suffering for suffering and paying for pain in pain. To do so I explore the novel *The Buried Giant* by Kazuo Ishiguro and its depictions of remembrance and revenge, as well as introduce considerations from a range of thinkers on retaliation and its relation to the law. I suggest that a clear-eyed approach to irrevocable wrong might help expose the potential moral misreadings of the *lex talionis*, while coaxing us not only toward a more useful form of forgiveness, but also toward a more challenging model of justice.

SATISFYING JUSTICE

Kazuo Ishiguro's novel *The Buried Giant* appeared in 2015 as something of a departure from his other work.[1] Ishiguro's novels tend to share a patient, reflective pace and a disposition toward loneliness and loss, even if they do exhibit a consistent willingness to pursue new forms, mix genres, and explore unfamiliar literary territories. Though Ishiguro's early novels resemble each other narratively, since *The Remains of the Day*, they have seemed self-consciously to differ from one another in important formal, if not thematic, ways. The Arthurian fantasy underlying *The Buried Giant* marks the largest such departure in his body of work. Ishiguro sets his novels mostly in the present or near-present, even if these worlds are sometimes dystopically or psychologically refracted in disarming ways. But *The Buried Giant* is set in a linguistically stylized and self-consciously fabular Britain, at some time during the settlement and conquest of the Saxons, when the memory of Arthur remains fresh among the people and his knights still patrol the land. The novel flirts with the genre conventions of fantasy, and indeed it received some awards for fantasy fiction, but it was also poorly received by some readers who thought it employed the conventions of fantasy and allegory awkwardly.[2]

My own sense is that the novel is both beautiful and important, and if the Arthurian allegory provokes discomfort, it is mostly for the difficult questions it raises. The novel's plot is fairly straightforward, if shrouded deliberately in a fog of mystery. The story opens with an elderly couple, Axl and Beatrice, living in a warren of dirt hovels among a community of Britons. We are given the sense that the two are somehow marginal to the community; they are treated with dismissiveness and disdain. But they understand neither the reason for their marginalization nor the general aggression and unkindness that surrounds them, and this is largely because almost nothing among the Britons can be remembered. Axl and Beatrice cannot recall conversations or the previous day's events. Children go missing from the warren but searches for them disband in confusion after a few hours. The emotions around minor arguments remain even if the claims and contents of those arguments are lost. Beatrice comments to her husband that the forgetting is like a sickness that pervades the whole land, an amnesiac plague afflicting all the peoples of Britain (*Buried Giant*, 17). But even this lament over lost memory is fleeting. Mostly, we're told, it simply doesn't occur to these oblivious villagers to think about the past (7).

Axl and Beatrice share some unstated, unremembered, and nonetheless obvious sense of loss and sadness. Beatrice surmises that a visit to their son's village will relieve this sadness, and although Axl opposes this journey for some time, he cannot remember why. The novel opens with Axl relenting to Beatrice's wishes, and they finally leave the cruel exclusions of their warren to embark upon a journey across open country to a village whose name and location they cannot recall.

We soon discover that this affliction of forgetting affects not only Axl and Beatrice and their community, but all the people of the land. Beatrice suffers from an undiagnosed pain in her side, so she and Axl start their journey by visiting a nearby Saxon village to seek advice from the Briton healer Ivor who lives as an alien there. There is a constant threat of violence as they travel— the Saxons are on edge because of a nearby ogre attack, for example—but this nervousness also manifests as mutual suspicion between Britons and Saxons and an aggressive tension among peoples. Forgetting makes people uneasy and suspicious of strangers. Ivor hides Axl and Beatrice upon their arrival at the Saxon village, to guard their safety amidst the village's suspicion and disorder. While lamenting and reflecting upon the forgetfulness that has descended on their land and peoples, Ivor recounts to Axl and Beatrice the visit of a stranger the previous year who had speculated that the pandemic of forgetting might also afflict the divine, that perhaps God's own mind might no longer have access to the past. And a past eradicated from the mind of God would have no chance of memory in the minds of mortals. But Beatrice recoils at this idea, finding it inconsistent with God's love. "Can such a thing be possible?" she asks Ivor (64). If God loves each of us dearly as his own child, could "God really forget what we have done and what's happened to us?" (65). Beatrice worries that God's love must keep its memory for it to be infinitely loving, a concern to which we shall return later on.[3] But after they have left the village and Beatrice has had more time to reflect upon the affliction of their forgetfulness, she wonders in a quiet moment with Axl whether God might indeed choose to forget their pasts. If God were sufficiently angry or ashamed, she speculates, then perhaps a divine forgetting would be necessary in order to eradicate those affects and accommodate God's love. Axl's response, however, is curious. Even if God's anger were so substantial, Axl wonders, "why doesn't [God] punish us" and satisfy that wrath, rather than consign the world to foolishness and confusion (76)? At first, with Ivor, Beatrice refuses to believe a loving God could forget. But when she considers the anger or shame memory might occasion, she thinks again. Axl here reacts differently. If God's memory gives rise to anger or shame, then God would or should most reasonably expiate that divine affect through punishment. And indeed, that expiating punishment would serve a mnemonic function for the sinning people as well, as opposed to letting them "forget like fools" (76). Axl suggests that punishment would be preferable to forgetting, and indeed might serve as an aid or instrument of memory.

All of this introduces a dilemma central to the plot of *The Buried Giant*, the relationship between love and memory, because on their journey to their son's village, Axl and Beatrice become concerned that they will not be able to remain together unless they can somehow prove their love through a shared memory of their past, a proof I further reflect upon shortly. Ivor recommends that Beatrice travel to a nearby British monastery for further examination of her ailment, and for their protection he sends the elderly couple on their way with an itinerant Saxon warrior named Wistan, who slew the attacking ogres and rescued from them a Saxon child named Edwin. The travelers are soon also met on their way by an aged Sir Gawain, who roams the land hunting the dreaded dragon Querig. Gawain accompanies the small band to the monastery. Upon meeting Gawain, the Saxon Wistan asks the Arthurian knight how Arthur managed to heal the deep wounds of war between Britons and Saxons so quickly, and with barely a trace of conflict remaining (111). The answer, we find, is that the dragon Querig's breath is enchanted with amnesia, that the mist Querig exhales shrouds both the land in fog and the minds of the people in forgetting (154).

Querig's breath quells memory, and with it the anger that might give rise to violence. What gradually emerges from the novel's fog of forgetting is that the dragon's breath is the historical work of King Arthur and his knights. Mired in a forgotten war between Britons and Saxons, caught in an escalating cycle of reciprocal violence, Arthur could see no escape from Saxon retaliation and no avenue for future peace other than through a wholesale forgetting and occlusion of the past. But his technologies of forgetting are sometimes cruel and sometimes conjured. He partners with Merlin to trap Querig and enchant her breath with amnesia, but he also commands the massacre of children so they will not grow to remember and avenge their fathers. We eventually learn also that Gawain is not Querig's hunter but her guardian, and that his mission since the days of Arthur's reign has been to protect the land's pacific amnesia from Saxon avengers like Wistan, who might seek to lift the mist and uncover the truth of their past sufferings, thus stirring anger and a cycle of retaliation once again. This leads to a final confrontation between Wistan and Gawain late in the novel during which moral questions of vengeance and punishment arise in much the way they did between Axl and Beatrice.

Facing one another with swords drawn before Querig's lair, Wistan and Gawain wax theological, speculating upon God's opinion of the land's forgetting. Against Wistan's accusations of forgetting as sinful, Gawain protests that whatever God's disappointments, Arthur finally brought peace to the land, and therefore Wistan's and Gawain's gods alike should bless the enchanted dragon for ending the intractable war. But in an echo of Axl's earlier pondering of divine punishment, Wistan protests, asking, "What kind of god is it, sir, wishes wrongs to go forgotten and unpunished?" (285). Punishment is here once again associated with memory, perhaps even collapsed into it, so that retribution might be seen as a mnemonic, itself as a moral practice of memory. Gawain persists in pleading for patience, arguing that a year or two more of the forgetting fog may prove sufficient an amnesiac erasure to guarantee lasting peace. But Wistan remains unconvinced by Gawain's pragmatism and asks the old knight how a wound infested with maggots could ever heal or a peace built upon slaughter could ever hold. Wistan also notes how Gawain's pragmatic peace cynically obscures his own complicity in sin while undergirding British power (286). Gawain and Arthur's pious devotion to peace cannot be separated from their avoidance of any responsibility for the violence Querig's magic quells. The past is covered but not erased, Wistan argues, and it demands a just remembering, a form of memory that arises uniquely as retaliatory punishment.

VENGEANCE TO BE RELISHED

This association of memory with punishment is not novel to this fictional depiction of late ancient Britain. It is deeply rooted in our moral instincts. In *On the Genealogy of Morals*, Friedrich Nietzsche excavates the roots of our moral intuitions when he asserts that if "something is to stay in the memory it must be burned in: only that which never ceases to *hurt* stays in the memory."[4] Pain is a mnemonic, Nietzsche argues, and because of this it naturally incorporates into human systems of power, religion, and conflict. According to Nietzsche, humans "could never do without blood, torture, and sacrifices," and religious rites of obligation and mortification in particular, when attempting to establish ineradicable memories since "pain is the most powerful aid to mnemonics" (Nietzsche, *Genealogy of Morals*, 61). But this recourse to pain, for Nietzsche, all begins in the human capacity to make promises. Because humans are will-driven creatures, they intend and sometimes are able to effect a future, and they articulate their plans for that intended promise among others. But because the future is uncertain, some of their promises will fail, and pain (on Nietzsche's account) becomes a tool of promissory enforcement. To "inspire trust in his promise to repay," therefore, and to guarantee the "sanctity of his promise," the indebted promiser pledges to his creditor "his body, his wife, his freedom, or even his life" as collateral or substitute "if he should fail to repay" what is owed (64). Nietzsche thus theorizes pain as a mnemonic: in substituting something of value for the broken promise, it reminds debtors of what they owe, and of what they have failed to repay. What's more, the threat of punishment can inspire others' obligations to us to be met. Punishment is, for Nietzsche—as it is for Axl and Wistan—an expression not only of memory, but of the imposition of that memory on others. In exacting punishment, we force others to remember; we declare not only "I remember I was injured," but also "you will never forget that you injured me."

But the mnemonic of pain gives rise to some corollary benefits too, Nietzsche argues. As soon as he assigns a memorial function to punishment, Nietzsche also explores the satisfactions of retaliation. To "see others suffer does one good," Nietzsche writes, "to *make* others suffer even more" (67, emphasis added). The one who exacts punishing vengeance soon finds that retaliatory acts serve not only as a reminder to the other, but as a compensation to the punisher. According to Nietzsche, suffering can "balance debts and guilts" because to make another suffer is "in the highest degree pleasurable, to the extent that the injured party exchange[s] for the loss he ha[s] sustained . . . an extraordinary counterbalancing pleasure: that of *making* suffer, a genuine *festival*" (65). This is a claim many would rightly challenge, but Nietzsche's emphasis here on the putative pleasure of punishment nonetheless exposes an irrationality internal to the law of talion. Because there is in fact no eye for an eye. No one can remove my tooth for use in your mouth. Taking my eye or my tooth after I have injured you provides no replacement. Payment does come, but it comes in another form. A currency has been exchanged. Recompense comes through "a kind of *pleasure*—the pleasure of being allowed to vent [one's] power freely upon one who is powerless, the voluptuous pleasure '*de faire le mal pour le Plaisir de le faire*,' the enjoyment of violation" (65).[5] The law of talion, for Nietzsche, is not a case of like for like, but of pleasure for pain.

Nietzsche perceives that the relationship between wrongdoing and punishment is neither natural nor necessary. Punishment is a social construction, not an expression of a wrongdoer's debt but a compensating pleasure to the wronged. Punishment is not what crime naturally or necessarily merits or deserves; it is simply what anger wants. But "this anger is held in check and modified by the idea that every injury has its *equivalent* and can actually be paid back, even if only through the *pain* of the culprit" (63). In other words, there is a limit to anger's expression; not all acts are authorized by anger. As human behaviors and interactions are increasingly socialized in more established communities, the responsibility for punishment transfers from the individual to the larger society. It is not the individual but the community (represented by law) that has been violated by wrongdoing, and it is the community (once again, mediated by law) that is satisfied by punishment. Under these circumstances, an economy develops, wherein crime carries a price, and anger is allowed by penal convention to be expressed in the correct proportion. How else, for example, might we have come in the contemporary United States to tabulate aggravated robbery as "like" a sentence of five to ninety-nine years of incarceration, or marijuana possession as "like" a sentence of three? How could or do we rationally reconcile years to acts as like for like or roughly equivalent? Like the Jewish and Christian interpreters of the *lex talionis* before us, conventions of punishment have been constructed to balance out crime and satisfy the demands of justice, however irrational these demands and conventions might be. In the end, Nietzsche argues, these balancing satisfactions manifest as a festival of cruelty. The law of talion pretends toward equivalence, it plays at a common currency in pain; but in fact what retaliation offers the wronged as payment for their suffering exchanges one currency for another one. A tooth is not really given for a tooth; like is not given for like. Instead, pleasure is given for pain, even when it is institutionalized within a system of legal justice. What compensates for suffering is not equal suffering, and certainly not the replacement of a lost good, but the satisfaction of seeing wrongs visited upon the one whom we resent.

These Nietzschean insights are elaborated in contemporary defenses of retaliation, retribution, and vengeance. Jeffrie Murphy, who writes at length defending revenge on moral grounds, defines vengeance as "the infliction of suffering on a person in order to satisfy vindictive emotions or passions."[6] But this satisfaction is more than just an affective phenomenon of human hurt. It grounds, for Murphy, a moral response to harm. Though legal punishment inspired by vengeance "may accidentally serve deterrence or retributive purposes," these "are not its goals," Murphy writes. Vengeance's goal, he continues, "is simply to provide vindictive satisfaction to victims," even if their satisfaction demands "something other than what is necessary to control crime or what wrongdoers deserve."[7] The benefit of vengeance in this case is quite clear, and closely follows Nietzsche. There is no like for like; or rather, the compensation given to victims is not the return of a lost good, but a pleasure given in response to and through pain. It has to do neither with the desert nor the deterrence of offenders. Rather, vindictive satisfaction is simply what victims are owed in the wake of offense. It is how they are compensated for their losses. Murphy warns that we should be careful to take too much offense or become too morally squeamish at a notion of justice that resembles Nietzsche's festival of pain. Though "vindictiveness is often condemned by the educated, the privileged, and the sheltered" as an urge "found mainly among . . . uneducated rednecks or other assorted trailer trash," in his opinion this merely reveals the elitist prejudices of academics like moral theologians or philosophers.[8]

This latter claim seems unfair at least and racially obtuse (or worse) upon further reflection. It goes without saying that the vindictiveness Murphy wants to defend rears its head most powerfully not in trailer parks but in federal, state, and local governments, under whose systematizations of vengeance poor people, mostly but not only of color, are repeatedly and oppressively subject to excessive sentencing practices that serve little to no deterrent purpose. The sentences we assign and the prisons we build in the United States to sustain our vindictive satisfactions do in fact generate a lot of money, though, and for some fairly privileged people, too. The elite don't just condemn vengeance; they profit from it richly.[9] If Nietzsche imagines how the satisfactions of cruelty can be regulated and institutionalized as law in a civilized society, he does not predict how they might be twisted and weaponized in a racist one. A glance at America's criminal justice system can immediately remind us, Murphy's admonition notwithstanding, that vindictiveness is not down and out in the United States. On the contrary, it is poor people, and especially Black and brown people, who in our prisons and on death row bear the quantifiable and staggering brunt of our desire for penal vindication.

Even apart from all this, however, another moral problem immediately arises. If what compensates for offense is the victim's pleasure, then the pain to be inflicted as payment upon the offender must always be paid in a different currency. In other words, like is not actually given for like when pleasure is given for pain. The amount of suffering required to satisfy a victim's desires will never be an identically corresponding or even roughly consistent tabulation. If your tooth is not equally given for mine, then how much of your suffering should serve my pleasure? When and how much should victims be pleased to see their offenders in pain, and what punishments will qualify as either appropriately pleasurable or excessively cruel?

If there aren't easy answers to these questions, it is because there is no rational standard for how much pain pays; there is no going rate for punishment. But Murphy's concern is not just to toss potshots at academics. He has a more robust moral claim, too. For Murphy, vindictiveness has a crucial moral relevance, because it benefits the self-worth and self-assertion to which each human is entitled and which is so often compromised in the wake of violent harm. What is required in the wake of wrongdoing is the victim's self-restoration and self-validation. And Murphy argues that vengeance—both felt and enacted—can accomplish this.

Robert Solomon also argues that we need our anger and our resentment to help us recognize the injustice of the world and to inspire us to respond adequately to it. The desire for vengeance on this account is about satisfying the desire to pay back the offender. It carries "immense pleasure, and aesthetic satisfaction" to answer wrong with violence as a means of "getting even, putting the world back in balance."[10] For Solomon, to eschew retribution is to undermine justice and to give moral license to iniquity in our world. Trudy Govier summarizes Solomon's argument saying that when "bad things happen, our anger and resentment lead us to a sense of injustice and the desire to act to make things right, to get a kind of balance by bringing harm to the one who harmed us."[11] On this account, justice isn't just associated with retribution. The concept of justice itself depends upon and requires retribution. However "problematic its current role in justice may be, there is no doubt" for Solomon "that vengeance is the original passion for justice."[12] In the Hebrew scriptures and in Homer, justice "virtually always refers to revenge," and throughout history justice has been almost entirely concerned "with the punishment of crimes and the balancing of wrongs."[13] Again, however, we cannot but observe an encroaching inconsistency. On some metaphorical scale of justice, my tooth may weigh as much as yours, but does my pleasure balance the scales against your pain? In any case, Solomon defends the desire for revenge therefore on moral grounds, arguing that the quest for revenge is never, as such and in itself, illegitimate. "Getting even is just an effective way of being angry, and getting angry typically includes a lively desire for revenge."[14]

But in Solomon's argument there is a curious collapse between affect and action. Is vengeance a feeling or an action? Or a feeling that demands satisfaction in action? To have the desire is to demand and to deserve its satisfaction, he asserts. But having a passion for justice that arises as the affective experience of vengeance can and should be morally differentiated from the expression of that passion through acts of revenge. Govier, for example, concedes that it may be that seeking "revenge is one way to reassert ourselves, to attempt to get relief from the hurt and humiliation of being wronged" and that when "we seek revenge, we *seek satisfaction by attempting to harm the other (or associated persons) as a retaliatory measure.*"[15] But even if we "expect to feel better" when we "express our negative feelings in actions," Govier reminds that "the desire for revenge" cannot be read as "deeply 'natural' in the sense of being an elemental, culturally independent feature of human nature."[16] And even if "revenge were to be natural in that way, such naturalness would not constitute a moral argument in its favor."[17]

Be that as it may, it is around these lines of necessary self-assertion that impulses originating in anger eventually move through revenge and finally mature into systems of retribution in the philosophical literature and in law. Theorists who are less comfortable than Murphy and Solomon with a robust defense of vengeance and its pleasures, or who worry like me about how they might be standardized in a moral system of justice, nonetheless can still articulate a carefully adjudicated account of retribution when and if they perceive wrongdoings to be primarily mistakes of moral valuation, acts of social injury. Jean Hampton argues that what retribution accomplishes is a reversal of the helplessness victims suffer when they become victimized.[18] When a victim is wronged, what that wrong signifies socially is that the offender devalues the victim; that victim's social status has been compromised and their dignity diminished. In retributive punishment, then, the victim's vanquishing of the wrongdoer, whether directly or through the agency of the state, "symbolizes the correct relative value of wrongdoer and victim."[19] What constitutes this symbolic defeat as retributive punishment "is not the objective painfulness of the experience, but the fact that it is one the wrongdoer is *made* to suffer and one which represents his *submission* to the punisher."[20] Here we see Hampton eschewing the compensating pleasure of others' suffering. Instead, what is important is to assert the equal dignity of the victim through the subjection of the offender. In this case, it is the power I assert in making you suffer, rather than the pleasure I feel in doing so, that compensates for my pain.

In other words, it is no longer the wrongdoer's pain but the victim's mastery that satisfies. To harm a wrongdoer in a fashion similar to his wrong, eye for eye and tooth for tooth, is "to master him in the way that he mastered the victim. The score is even. Whatever mastery he can claim, she can also claim. If her victimization is taken as evidence of her inferiority relative to the wrongdoer, then his defeat at her hands negates that evidence."[21] Hampton is careful, like Murphy, to note that deterrent and desert are not primary concerns for retributive punishment, because in the case of both deterrent and desert the focus is on the perpetrator when it should be on the victim. The purpose punishment should rather serve, they claim, is to restore the status of the wronged. Retribution "isn't about making a criminal better; it is about denying a false claim of relative value."[22] Hampton thus carefully distinguishes the disrespectful and immoral aims of the "vengeful hater," who is concerned purely with self-elevation over and against the offender, from the careful and ethical retributivist, who attempts only to annul any evidence of the wrongdoer's superiority. Thus the restrained "retributivist is interested in asserting a moral truth; hence he is always mindful of, and respectful towards, the value of his wrongdoer."[23] But the expression of that moral truth is singularly satisfied through mastery and the imposition of suffering.

But is mastery of another the best, most effective, or most moral way to establish and express self-worth? The use of other people, even offenders, as objects by which one's own status might be restored is usually read as inherently contrary to human dignity and valuation, because it casts people as means rather than ends. Trudy Govier maintains that the "suffering of a person or persons to satisfy oneself is morally objectionable, because it amounts to the treatment of the wrongdoers as means only, failing to respect their human worth and dignity."[24] Martha Nussbaum argues, therefore, that while lowering the "status of the wrongdoer by pain or humiliation" does indeed elevate the victim relatively, such an exclusive or obsessively narrow focus on status "is something we ought to discourage" in our morals.[25]

What's more, the argument for retribution as a form of dignity restoration assumes that status can be recovered only through the same means by which it was taken. In fact, it must be true that dignity and humanity can be elevated through means other than the infliction of violence, even—perhaps especially—when dignity has been denigrated by violence. Indeed, in response to public ambivalence around the acts of forgiveness witnessed in Charleston (see the Introduction), James Cone has described forgiveness as precisely this sort of dignified moral act, an act whereby victims assert their humanity not in offering like for like, but in denying the possibility of any compensatory economy entirely: "It's victory out of defeat. It is the weak overcoming the strong. It's 'You can't destroy my spirit. I have a forgiving spirit because that's what God created me to be. You are not going to destroy that.' When they forgive, it is a form of resistance, a kind of resilience. It is not bowing down. That is misunderstood by a lot of people, even black people, and even some black ministers. It's part of that tragic experience of trying to express your humanity in the face of death and not having any power."[26] Or as Trudy Govier has again written, "Seeking and achieving revenge against an offender is not the only way to show one's power."[27] In other words, though Hampton's and others' arguments are sensible, they are not necessary. While it is surely true that victims' dignity is affronted through wrongdoing, it is not at all obvious that such dignity may be restored *only* through retributive or retaliatory acts, or that such acts therefore constitute the only possible form of an adequate justice. What they do promise, instead, is satisfaction. Revenge, retaliation, and retribution seek to satisfy a desire, whether that desire be for cruelty, status, or mastery. But the desire they satisfy is not for the restoration of an irredeemable past or the erasure of an irreversible trauma. The past cannot be undone or traumas unlived. These desires must remain unsatisfied.

The problem with all this argument about payment as a moral paradigm or framing metaphor is that all too often no payment is actually possible. A law of like for like falls apart before the singularity of loss. There is nothing uniquely alike to the wound I bear or the trauma I carry. What is lost cannot be bought back. Strictly speaking, no *lex talionis* is possible. Retributive punishment does not give like for like, but pleasure for pain. Though retaliation offers some satisfaction, it satiates the wrong desire. Perhaps what we really most want is to remember, and we have been tricked by custom or instinct into believing pain will be our best mnemonic. In fact, however, to remember the past rightly would be to admit that no payment is possible, that what is lost is really lost, in which case grief rather than retaliation should be the outcome or partner of our anger. It is not that we must force the other to remember through imposing suffering, nor even that we must be persuaded of their good memory by the severity of their penance. It's that the fullest, truest memory of the past would acknowledge and address that past's irrevocability, the irrecuperability of its wrongs and wounds.

This fundamental irrecuperability is no surprise to philosophy. Ideas "of payback have deep roots in the imaginations of most of us," but these are cultural, not necessary or rational, roots.[28] Our intuition that "lowering [the perpetrator] through pain and even humiliation will right the balance" is only that, an intuition. It does not follow any rational necessity.[29] Put more frankly, Martha Nussbaum flatly states that "doing something to the offender does not bring dead people back to life, heal a broken limb, or undo a sexual violation."[30] There are certainly financial crimes like theft that we might construe as potentially compensable, but even these become messy when issues of human dignity or status are considered and demand the additions and manipulations of interest payments in order to better recover complex and enormously particular variables such as lost opportunity or investment. One undertakes acts of retaliation, Nussbaum writes, *"because of and as a way of assuaging or compensating for* one's own pain"; however, she cannot help but wonder why "an intelligent person [would] think that inflicting pain on the offender assuages or cancels her own pain." There is a "magical thinking" at work in this, Nussbaum argues, since "harsh punishment to the offender rarely repairs damage."[31] Nussbaum is not wrong here, but I think she oversimplifies the desire of the "intelligent person." It's not that inflicting pain upon another cancels one's own; it's that it brings its own separate and singular pleasure. Still, that pleasure is separate and singular. It does not offer adequate compensation, and true payback remains impossible.

Charles Griswold, whose study of forgiveness is examined more closely in Chapter 3, also admits that "the past cannot ever be changed, and it is a sort of metaphysical delusion to imagine otherwise. Violence directed at the agent of injury will certainly not undo the effects of the past deed."[32] Punishment does not really compensate; the eye and the tooth I give you are of no real use to you other than to please you with my suffering. To be clear, punishment may have purposes other than payback, but our philosophical justifications of retribution and our penal practices of justice tend especially, as Solomon argues above, to cling quite firmly to the idea that payback is crucial and primary. Nussbaum therefore reasonably wonders why these ideas persist and what purpose they serve. The desire for recompense mistakenly assumes that the "suffering of the wrongdoer somehow restores, or contributes to restoring, the important thing that was damaged." Though she acknowledges these beliefs as ubiquitous, she also insists they are "false and incoherent," derived from "deep-rooted but misleading ideas of cosmic balance, and from people's attempt to recover control in situations of helplessness."[33]

In the end, it seems these ideas serve largely the purpose with which I began in Nietzsche and Murphy: to satisfy the natural feelings of rage and resentment that arise after wrongdoing, to give victims pleasure at others' suffering. But even this well-argued position for vindictive satisfaction cannot claim necessity or universality. Traumatized people often "imagine that revenge will bring relief, even though the fantasy of revenge simply reverses the roles of perpetrator and victim"; but in practice, satisfaction "may never come. . . . Avenging the self can be too costly emotionally, by stoking fires of hatred."[34] Indeed, it may be that the illusion of compensation—or better, the confusion in satisfying one desire to stand in for the satisfaction of another, like eating when you're thirsty—can contribute further moral injury to those who have already been injured. Strong evidence suggests that "people who actually commit acts of revenge, such as combat veterans who commit atrocities, do not succeed in getting rid of their post-traumatic symptoms; rather, they seem to suffer the most severe and intractable disturbances."[35] According to Judith Herman, the fantasy of revenge can thus become a horrible form of self-imposed torment that can be escaped only when the survivor "comes to terms with the impossibility of getting even."[36]

It seems, then, that however the penal or penitential relation is structured, what is at stake is always payment. Wrongdoing (quite obviously) costs something. Suffering takes a toll. And sufferers are conditioned to seek compensation in the wake of that loss. But what we also discern is that this compensatory intuition is constructed and conditioned, not natural or necessary. It allows an unrealizable desire to stand as necessary or natural. Indeed, haunting all this reflection upon what must be given and what should be paid in order to justify either punishment or its withholding is the blank admission in the philosophical literature that some losses—perhaps most, and certainly grievous ones—are not really recoverable. Indeed, that's what makes them grievous. Any attempts to recover those irreparable losses—whether they operate under the language of punishment or pardon—are misguided at best. This concession reaches back at least to Nietzsche, who, though seeming to relish punishment's glories in *On the Genealogy of Morals*, in *Thus Spoke Zarathustra* regards revenge, retribution, and punishment as irrational urges of the will.

"It was": thus is called the will's gnashing of teeth and loneliest misery. Impotent against that which has been—it is an angry spectator of everything past.

The will cannot will backward; that it cannot break time and time's greed—that is the will's loneliest misery. . . .

That time does not run backward, that is its wrath. "That which was"—thus the stone is called, which it cannot roll aside.

And so it rolls stones around out of wrath and annoyance, and wreaks revenge on that which does not feel wrath and annoyance as it does.

Thus the will, the liberator, became a doer of harm; and on everything that is capable of suffering it avenges itself for not being able to go back.

This, yes this alone is *revenge* itself: the will's unwillingness toward time and time's "it was."

Indeed, a great folly lives in our will; and it became the curse of all humankind that this folly acquired spirit!

The spirit of revenge: my friends, that so far has been what mankind contemplate best; and wherever there was suffering, punishment was always supposed to be there as well.

For "punishment" is what revenge calls itself; with a lying word it hypocritically asserts its good conscience.[37]

The will's "loneliest misery" is its inability to alter the past. Revenge, for Nietzsche, is nothing more than the will's refusal to accept the intractability of time. Retaliation is a sort of magical thinking, an irresistible urge to undo a past that has escaped the reach of our will.

In most of these examples from moral philosophy there is an assumption echoed in Axl's and Wistan's comments above. Forgetting has an alternative: punishment. Even in these last lines from Nietzsche, the thrust is that the past is something to be left behind rather than either remembered or redeemed by revenge. And when the philosophers expound upon the compensating pleasures of exacting the pains of vengeful memory upon our enemies, we find that this too resounds in the Arthurian landscape of Ishiguro's Britain. All over that war-torn landscape are strong impulses toward revenge, retribution, and repentance, which slumber fitfully under forgetting and arise and stir up with memory. In *The Buried Giant* we can recognize each of these impulses as varieties of retaliation, as attempts to satisfy a law of like for like, the *lex talionis* of eye for eye and tooth for tooth. What the amnesiac survivors of *The Buried Giant* seek to balance is an unwieldy ledger book of suffering. But what the novel and its characters finally reveal is that certain forms of loss, the ones that perhaps most want forgiveness, are exactly those that defy any economy, the ones for which no recompense or recovery or satisfaction is ever possible.

A GREAT KING LIKE GOD HIMSELF

The central characters of *The Buried Giant*, Axl and Beatrice, are on a quest to find their son's distant home, but as noted above, they are also anxious that their faded memories will leave them unable to prove their mutual love at some crucial moment to come. Early in the story Axl and Beatrice happen upon the ruins of a Roman villa. They take shelter there from the rain and find inside an unsettling scene. A boatman also shelters there, claiming that the villa is his childhood home, but he is being accosted by an old woman who gently strokes a rabbit while holding a small knife against its throat. The woman bears a grudge against this boatman because he once failed to carry her, together with her husband, across some faraway waters to a mysterious island. Since then she has been left alone. Convinced that the boatman has swindled her of companionship, and recalling the boatman's offer of a rabbit for her supper on the evening of her loss, she now visits the boatman routinely and always brings "with her a rabbit, or some such small creature," in order to kill it and then scatter its blood around the villa (Ishiguro, *Buried Giant*, 37). Axl and Beatrice intervene and exhort the woman to leave the boatman in peace, which she does, though she vows to return and warns the elderly couple to distrust the boatman. Axl and Beatrice are curious about this passage to the island and ask the boatman about the conditions required for a couple to journey together. He tells them that passage for two across the water is difficult but not impossible, and that to cross together a couple needs only to prove that their love for one another is indubitably true. The boatman warns that love is difficult to discern and often disguises itself as different urges. Indeed, the boatman claims that the rabbit-woman was left alone not because she was cheated but because she wrongly credited her marriage as truly loving.

Axl and Beatrice's journey is to find their son. But they also seek healing for Beatrice, and as she weakens and slows, they expect eventually to encounter the boatman's test and they worry over it more and more. Because the amnesiac fog has obscured their pasts, they share no memories and so they do not know how they can prove their love even as they are desperate not to be left alone. Thus when they learn of Wistan's mission to kill Querig and to rid the land of forgetting, they join it. Late in the novel, in an eerie scene that unsettlingly recalls the boatmen's passage and his test, Axl and Beatrice attempt to navigate a small stream in some wicker baskets because no boat is available to them. As they cross the reedy, shallow water in their tethered baskets, they meet an old woman traveling in a rowboat of her own. She is motionless and pleads to Axl for help getting rid of "them." We are told that something about the woman tugs at Axl's memory, but he is perplexed by her request and her helplessness, so he peers skeptically into her boat. In its stern, he sees a long-handled hoe lying among the fishing nets and a lidless basket filled with skinned rabbits (229–31). When he lifts his eyes from the piled carcasses, Axl suddenly sees dozens of pixies crawling all over and around the woman's body and everywhere throughout the boat. Immediately, the pixies leap onto and overrun Beatrice's wicker vessel too and try to steal Axl's wife away. Axl takes up the hoe from the strange woman's boat and uses it to hack and sweep at the sprites. Once Beatrice is free, she and Axl flee the rowboat and leave the still pleading woman drifting in the stream.

In this novel of hazy memory, very few references or associations are entirely clear. But in a novel of so few characters, it is not hard to link these two women with their rabbits to one another. A third scene hints at an additional, and perhaps more consequential, association. In a short first-person passage during which Gawain reflects upon his own culpability for the violence that preceded Britain's pervasive forgetting, and his complicity in that erasure, he remembers one particularly savage battle from the recent war that his Britons had won. In the midst of the fighting, a young British woman seeks Gawain's help on the battlefield, and Gawain, believing her in need of rescue or repair, chivalrously agrees to aid her. As it happens, her desire is not for rescue but revenge. She tells Gawain that her dearest prayer is that a particular Saxon lord has survived the battle, because she wishes him to die at her hands to pay for the suffering he inflicted on her mother and sisters. She tells Gawain that the hoe she carries is meant for this work. "It breaks the ground of a winter's morning," she reasons, "so it will do well enough on this Saxon's bones" (209).

When the battle is won and the combatants largely cleared, Gawain escorts the woman through the carnage and they find the Saxon lord lying wounded and set for death. There the woman stands above him, and she pulls the hoe against the man's flesh with slow, torturous prods, the way she might carefully search "for potatoes in the soil" (211). Gawain begs the woman to finish her work more quickly and mercifully, but she calmly thanks him for his service and invites him to depart as she scrapes the dying man's flesh from his bones.

The memory of this young woman with her vengeance and her hoe is old; like Gawain and Axl, she should be an aged woman at the time of the novel's action. Indeed, it's an old woman matching her description who meets privately with Beatrice early in the novel and sets them off on the journey to find their way to their son and to seek healing. I don't want to overread these few scenes or force associations that might be too strained, but the forgetful fog Ishiguro renders leads the reader to look for and perhaps impose meanings where they would likely dissipate. These scattered encounters and linked memories of a hoe-wielding, grudge-bearing, rabbit-slaying woman are not likely accidental. I believe we are meant to read these characters as the same, that the young woman Gawain aids in mutilating a war criminal is the same woman who later haunts the boatman's house and sacrifices rabbits on his hearth, the same woman who warns the couple of the test they will face in their passage, the same who lies motionless in a drifting rowboat while being overrun by relentless pixies, the same who speaks in private with Beatrice and sets them on their journey. And though it's difficult to give a clear reading of the ties between these various encounters, we can recognize in this figure a tragic and troubled character, one who should spur us to reflect further upon our desire for revenge and retribution, as well as upon the pleasures and the memories of punishment.

Our reflection should not marginalize her reactions, however. This peasant woman's desire for vengeance is neither unique nor unexpected, as other examples from the novel show. Midway through the novel, at the monastery where Beatrice seeks healing, Wistan discerns the compound's past as a military outpost specifically designed to cause extreme and gruesome enemy casualties in the case of a hopeless siege. In a situation where the Saxons could not win, the fort was designed to massacre as many attacking Britons as possible. Interestingly, Wistan justifies the Saxons' preemptive vengeance as a sort of deposit on payment in punishment, a way for doomed Saxons to collect in advance some of the satisfaction they will have earned by their eventual suffering and defeat once the fort has fallen. Wistan imagines his people at the end of a terrible journey, huddled in this final and temporary safe haven, having seen their loved ones massacred and their communities destroyed. Knowing that they must be overrun by the Britons in time, Wistan envisions his people cherishing the first days of the siege during which at least some Britons would have paid an awful price for all that Saxon suffering. As Wistan tells Axl, it would have been "vengeance . . . relished in advance" by those who would not survive to retaliate after the fact (141–42). Importantly, the cruelty here is not repayment for past acts, but prepayment on acts they expect will occur. The value of vengeance is based here primarily in the pleasure of satisfying one's anger. As with Nietzsche and Murphy, for Wistan the anger to which memory gives rise demands satisfaction, it wants a compensating pleasure that only vengeance offers. The problem, at least as Arthur has identified it, is whether and how this cycle of retaliatory violence may be broken. If there is, in fact, no exactly corresponding like for like, then the satisfactions of violence can never produce a closed loop of hermetically contained retribution. The pain I exact for pleasure will necessarily exceed the narrow bounds of a single incident or event, the discrete fee of an eye or a tooth, and expand outward.

As noted above, Nietzsche describes how the individual pleasures of exacting vengeance are eventually abstracted from their economic origins and institutionalized into law and the prescriptions of just punishment. But he also argues that, as societies and social institutions become more established and powerful, the transgressions of individuals can become less significant to those societies, since they are progressively less "dangerous and destructive to the whole" (Nietzsche, *Genealogy of Morals*, 72). The more established and powerful a community, he writes, the less any individual harm threatens it and the more possible it becomes to "treat every crime as *dischargeable*" (72). The end result might be a community so conscious of its own power "that it could allow itself the noblest luxury possible to it—letting those who harm it go *unpunished*" (72). That is, the transferential movement of law that displaces individual vengeance with penal convention ultimately undoes its own original aims. It ends up "winking and letting those incapable of discharging their debt go free" (73). At the summit of its power, the law no longer requires retaliation but overcomes itself and transforms into "*mercy*; the privilege of the most powerful man, or better, his—beyond the law" (73). It is the supremely powerful man, the one untouched and unconcerned by others' actions, who can act beyond the law and its parochial concerns. "What are my parasites to me?" he might say. "May they live and prosper; I am strong enough for that!" (72).

One of the secrets that hides in all the lost memory in *The Buried Giant* is the legal mechanism by which its forgetting arises. This secret hides along with the identity of Axl, who in the end we learn was an ambassador or bureaucrat of sorts for King Arthur. It was Axl who brokered a special peace in which war between Britons and Saxons was executed with restraint. A sort of late ancient Geneva Conventions were agreed to: no attacks on innocents or noncombatants would be made. Gawain recalls his uncle Arthur, the king, as a man who earned even his vanquished enemies' deep respect because of his constant piety and humility in seeking God's moral guidance (Ishiguro, *Buried Giant*, 111–12). Indeed, Gawain recalls, Arthur commanded his warriors to spare all innocents and to offer sanctuary to "all women, children and elderly, be they Briton or Saxon" (112). These treaties and truces, Gawain claims, helped build trust between enemies despite violence. Note here that Arthur's kingship, his sovereignty, is said by Gawain to arise from his resolve on behalf of restraint. Because Arthur sets himself humble before God and commands his knights to give sanctuary to innocents, all wish for his kingship. But Axl's treaty, Arthur's great law, eventually falls apart, and it does so because Arthur worries it will be insufficient to curb retributive vengeance and retaliatory violence. As Gawain explains to Axl, however noble the truce, it could not end the war. A conflict that began over land and religion had become instead about avenging "fallen comrades, themselves slaughtered in vengeance" (273–74). Gawain laments a hopeless situation in which infants would be inevitably raised into warriors through escalating cycles of violence. The violence is deeply layered and predetermined; even babies are already guilty of a vengeance they cannot but exact in adulthood. The shift in time here is subtle but crucial. Because of fallen fathers, infants are already enemies, their futures set in advance toward vengeance. Morally, Gawain is making a calculation analogous to Wistan's at the ancient Saxon fort. Vengeance must be paid in advance. One can shortcut an inevitable retributive cycle by preemptively punishing the innocents who will avenge what has been (or will have to have been) done. The moral calculus here is neither unfamiliar nor especially fictional. I can't help but note Ishiguro's own family origins in Nagasaki. In Japan during World War II (as elsewhere, including at the hands of the Japanese), innocents, women, children, and the elderly were targeted for annihilation. And in Hiroshima and Nagasaki in particular, the moral rationale for their utter destruction was decidedly preemptive, since nothing else (it was argued) could ostensibly have prevented the relentless and avenging violence with which these women, children, and elderly people would have met an otherwise necessary ground invasion.[38]

Desperate to break the reactionary responses of revenge, Arthur breaks his own law and orders his knights to slaughter the Saxons: infants, children, women, and all. And in this, Arthur reveals the true power of his sovereignty. He is not the sovereign, as Gawain claims, because he wins his enemies' hearts by establishing the wise and reasonable rules of his good truce. He is the sovereign, rather, because he decides when those rules will apply and when they won't. In this fictional ancient Britain, Carl Schmitt echoes: sovereign is Arthur, who decides the exception.[39] And not just any exception, but a violent one that establishes a new order: "For Schmitt, the sovereign performs a sacred violence in the state of exception, and that sacred violence grounds or renews the social order."[40] Arthur's decision is beyond the law. In a reverie of memory, as he recalls the British ambassador Axl's insubordinate chastisement of Arthur for his betrayal of the peace and the rule of law, Gawain argues that his king's aim was always peace, even when he turned away from legal restraint for the sake of royally authorized slaughter. Watching the hoe-wielding woman torture that Saxon lord, Gawain regrets that the small Saxon boys they have slaughtered would inevitably have grown to avenge their fallen fathers; that the small girls' wombs are surrounded by lament and must give birth to future warriors. Only pious, regal Arthur, Gawain cries, could recognize their one cruel chance to "sever this evil circle"; only Arthur had the courage to act where others faltered, and his boldness, Gawain insists, demands reverence (213).

The slaughter that the Britons perpetrate is simply an additional technology aimed at forcing a forgetting, at erasing any memory of violence by erasing the lives of the violated. But, crucially, the breaking of this particular law exposes the law's foundations outside of or beyond the law, its basis in that which is already radically heterogeneous to the law. Arthur's legal authority is proved by his willingness and ability to break his own treaty. As Gawain protests to Axl, a "great king, like God himself, must perform deeds mortals flinch from!" (275). Note how Gawain, who once described Arthur as humbly subjecting his sovereignty to God, now regards his king as exceeding the limits of human morals. Again, Arthur's greatness and kingship are established precisely because he determines the reach and limits of his own law. He is unaffected by the parasites, in this case the innocents he determines to have slaughtered. And indeed, the reach of Arthur's sovereignty and the limit of his law as violence is reinforced in its obverse, in a corresponding show of mercy: when Axl insubordinately decries and condemns the king for betraying the truce, Arthur deigns not to punish his counselor and instead bids him merciful peace (273).

Ishiguro's example here is troubling, bloody, and revealing, for in this brutal exception the law is broken while the violence that upholds it is exposed. But forgiveness is also often read as an exception to, rather than a fulfillment of, the law. As Nietzsche suggests, punishment stands in for lawful justice in Western thought; retributive desert is conventionally and legally demanded. To eschew it is to stand beyond the law. Sovereign therefore is the one who decides to forgo retributive justice. But this sort of sovereignty has its price. The philosopher Gillian Rose, in observing (not Ishiguro's but the legendary) Arthur's dilemma when he discovers Guinevere and Lancelot's infidelity, notes that whatever "King Arthur chooses, whether to overlook the betrayal or to prosecute the crime, the choice is not the issue. For, one way or the other, the King must now be sad."[41] Here sovereignty takes the form of sadness; the law cannot meet the complex demands of the world, but it also cannot be simply abandoned or overthrown. It will be perpetually dissatisfied, always unfulfilled, forever at a loss. "Betrayed or avenged," Rose writes, "sadness is the condition of the King. Whether action is taken in the spirit of the law, or whether its requirements are ignored, the law will rebound against [Arthur's] human weakness so as to disqualify itself."[42]

Ishiguro's novel is heartbreakingly sad, but neither Arthur nor Gawain ever appears particularly sad in it. At novel's end, however, the warrior Wistan is rueful at least, even sad, at an unmistakable loss. In this land of forgetting, hatred is a memory, it is a way to recall the losses one has suffered. But because Wistan cannot separate the act of remembering from the act of visiting vengeance, or the feeling of vengeance from the act of revenge, he regards retaliation as tragic yet necessary. He repeatedly instructs the Saxon boy Edwin, when "the hour's too late for rescue, it's still early enough for revenge" (Ishiguro, *Buried Giant*, 243). Indeed, the same desire for retaliatory satisfaction inspires the rabbit-woman. That they stand on opposing sides of this conflict signals the ceaseless and irredeemable reciprocity of their desire. Vengeance and its pleasures are positioned as an alternative to rescue, as a compensatory and satiable desire. But as the novel ends Wistan acknowledges that his books cannot truly balance, even if he—like Robert Solomon or Jeffrie Murphy—is unable to imagine any other possible form of justice. Out of concern for his enemies, Wistan urges Axl and Beatrice to flee west as quickly as possible, because ruthless Saxon armies are approaching to mete out "justice and vengeance" to the Britons, "for both are much delayed" (296). But Wistan's repeated language of preemption and delay here—too early, too late—betrays the time-bound impossibility of any adequate response. When Axl anticipates that "quick-tongued men" will make "ancient grievances rhyme with fresh desire for land and conquest," he sees that revenge will only metastasize into the future since it cannot reach back into the past, and Wistan agrees. "The giant, once well buried," Wistan allows, "now stirs" (297). The wakened memories of war will lead to massacre and mutilation of innocents once again: men will burn their neighbors' homes and hang children from the trees. Wistan wishes he could delight in this delayed vengeance since, as he says, it will be a justice achieved at long last. But his many years among the Britons and his friendship with Axl and Beatrice leave him uncomfortable with his hatred. Ashamed of his affectionate weakness before his British friends, Wistan commissions the boy Edwin, whose will is "cleaner," to exact the violence he cannot bear to (297). He will pass along through memory a hatred he no longer holds, for the sake of a justice he no longer esteems but cannot cede. None of the war crimes the Saxon warrior here anticipates sounds much like justice, not even to Wistan himself, who can take no delight in them. A broken past remains, entirely uncompensated if finally recollected. Satisfaction and compensation are illusions. Only a broken future lies in wait, inevitable and ruthless in its promise. Whether Wistan achieves the full pleasure of his retaliation or not, the depth and irreparability of his loss must mean that this vengeful warrior will remain sad, even though a floridly and gruesomely realized vengeance quickly approaches. The pleasure he receives from his enemies' pain will prove poor payment indeed, an inflated currency in an unfair exchange, since all that suffering will satisfy only his desire for revenge but not his need for rescue. Come what may, Wistan will grieve.

LAW AND FREEDOM

Punishment, Nietzsche writes, compensates for broken promises. The Saxon warrior Wistan extracts a gruesome promise from his young charge Edwin in *The Buried Giant*. Though Wistan has been raised by Britons and remains fond of Axl and Beatrice even after all their memories have been restored, he nonetheless sees no remedy for his grief other than vengeance. He tells young Edwin that while there may be Britons who tempt friendship or love, a deeper commitment to duty must always overwhelm those personal affections. It is their duty as Saxons, he says, to "hate every man, woman and child of their blood," and should that hatred ever "flicker or threaten to die," Wistan makes Edwin promise to tend the fire of that hatred well, to "shield it with care till the flame takes hold again" (242). Edwin agrees and gives his promise, but at the end of the novel as he is rushing toward the approaching war, the boy hears Beatrice call out to him, begging him to remember them and their friendship in the war-torn days to come. As he hears them, Edwin recalls the promise he made once to Wistan and wonders if that duty to hate could possibly "include this gentle couple" (301). He pushes the thought aside, however, increases his pace, and runs on, eager to exact revenge. What will bind Edwin to this promise in the years to come, and how free will he be to keep or to break it?

I now want to think in particular about the problem of the law and its relationship to forgiveness, and also of forgiveness's relation to freedom. Though a literature I later consider takes pains to set the conditions for any potential offer of forgiveness (see Chapter 3), in general forgiveness is also simultaneously and paradoxically understood as operating outside the constraints of law. How could we ever mandate that a victim forgive, for example? If we legally impose forgiveness, haven't we violated something basic to the nature of the act, its freedom, its logic, or both? The best it seems we can do is to describe the optimal conditions under which one might freely choose to forgive. And though the social norms that govern these conditions can often feel as binding as law, even those who insist upon formal conditions for forgiveness do usually want to preserve the moral instinct that forgiveness should be free. Law cannot fully determine justice because, as Ishiguro has shown, it is founded on violence and covertly perpetuates it. But another inadequacy of the law is revealed when Edwin remembers the old couple's friendship: its inability to provide the conditions for forgiveness.

I argue that in expressing the simultaneous insufficiency and exceptionality that grounds human justice, forgiveness reveals, as Gillian Rose has written, that "sadness is the condition of the king," that a fundamental mourning haunts any human justice, and it is upon this irrevocable grief rather than the illusion of its avoidance that both freedom and forgiveness might establish themselves. In order to make this argument, I introduce the thought of Vladimir Jankélévitch and complicate his polemics against the prescriptibility of forgiveness, and then follow Jacques Derrida's critique of Jankélévitch toward a model of mourning and impossibility that any and every necessarily imperfect act of forgiveness must betray. Finally, I turn to Hannah Arendt to explore what constructive posture forgiveness might take toward the impossibly irrevocable and suggest the form of freedom that might remain available to a politics of forgiveness and as an alternative to Arthurian violence.

Jankélévitch's 1967 work *Forgiveness* is an indispensable analysis of forgiveness as a moral act.[43] Like other twentieth-century French thinkers, Jankélévitch engages in a sometimes gleefully confounding and aporetic rhetoric in this volume. Though this difficulty can weigh down the prose, his repetitive, circular, and hyperbolic rhetoric does serve a deliberate and needful purpose. For Jankélévitch forgiveness is and must remain a fundamentally unthinkable, irrational action. This does not necessarily mean forgiveness is undesirable or impossible, only that it definitionally defies the logic of our moral grammars, that it exposes us to the limits of our moral language. Jankélévitch's insistence upon forgiveness's unthinkable quality here links him to others in suggesting that moral questions arise only and exactly where our moral vocabularies fail.[44] But raising the problem of forgiveness's impossibility need not be only to assert its nonexistence. It might also be to highlight and reveal the limits of the moral frameworks in which forgiveness is conceived or described. Forgiveness thus can serve a heuristic purpose in our reflection and be a way of diagnosing the limiting frames of our moral reasoning. Where forgiveness is impossible, every attempted description of it will endeavor to mind the gaps in our moral grammars, which is what Jankélévitch undertakes in his book. So, however much his work exoticizes or hyperbolizes forgiveness, the difficulty of Jankélévitch's book is meant to show the limits not of forgiveness as a human practice, but of human attempts to think about or conceptualize forgiveness.

The irrational dilemma Jankélévitch poses is fairly straightforward and also insurmountable. As noted above, there has been, for example, a significant discussion in the recent philosophical and theological literature on forgiveness about its various and necessary conditions. Many claim, for example, that unconditional forgiveness—that is, a forgiveness that does not exact some price, either of penitence, reparation, apology, or amendment—is morally suspect at best, a hazard at worst. Much scholarly reflection, then, concerns how much expiation, how sincere a repentance, how elaborate an apology is required for forgiveness. I discuss these worries further in Chapters 2 and 3, but for Jankélévitch, forgiveness requires only one thing: sin. As Jankélévitch states quite bluntly, forgiveness "is born on the occasion of the misdeed or of the offense" (Jankélévitch, *Forgiveness*, 122). If there were no wrong, there could be no forgiveness. Thus any diminishment or erasure of the establishing wrong would undo forgiveness's logical foundations. The purest forgiveness would require only wrongdoing, because any other requirement that might meliorate or expiate offense would synchronously sweep the legs out from forgiveness. If you have never actually wronged me, or if your wrong has become erased through explanation or indifference, then I could not rightly forgive you for your nonoffense. For Jankélévitch, then, forgiveness definitionally defies reason because it has no reasons. If one discerns a good reason or receives a strong justification to forgive, then what we will have offered when we offer forgiveness will not be pure or "authentic" forgiveness. Since forgiveness arises with the wrong, insofar as that wrong is reduced or erased—whether by expiation, explanation, remediation, restoration, reparation, or atonement—forgiveness will be reduced or erased as well. Without any wrong, forgiveness will search in vain for its object. When there is "no longer an offense, an offended person, or an offender; there is no longer sin or sinner" and therefore nothing and no one left to forgive (59). Instead, all the lengthy philosophical consideration of its necessary conditions notwithstanding, forgiveness "finds its use when the injury remains unexpiated, the mistake remains uncorrected, and as long as the victim is not paid damages for the damage" (10). If people earn our forgiveness in some manner and we grant them the pardon they have come to deserve, then all we will have really rendered them is their due; what we will have given them is simply justice. Once again, forgiveness has no good reason. It is, on Jankélévitch's account, a free act of grace, given without cause. When it is justified, it is merely justice—the granting of what we are obligated to offer. This is not to assert that it is immoral or undesirable in its "impure" form. Quite the contrary; Jankélévitch suspects that no pure form of forgiveness ever actually arises in human life except as an idea that undergirds our acts. What he's interested in is how that idea's provocations can help us think through what is finally at stake in our acts and our morals.

This then is why Jankélévitch denies the usefulness of understanding or explanation for any accounting of forgiveness or as a rationale for it. A wrong that has warrant, a sin one has been justified in committing, is neither a wrong nor a sin. A crime I was warranted in committing is no crime and does not solicit forgiveness.[45] Any forgiveness offered in exchange for an excuse or a justifying explanation, therefore, will be "reduced to the simple admission that there never was an offense" to begin with (60). To forgive in this instance is thus, paradoxically, "to recognize that there is nothing to forgive. The obstacle called misdeed was the contradictory condition of forgiveness. In obliterating the obstacle, we get rid of forgiveness itself" (60). In other words, when we understand and accept an offender's justifying rationale, we intellectually overcome the wrongdoing. It no longer exists to be forgiven. The wrong is no longer wrong but right, having been morally justified. Our sympathetic understanding thus "takes the place of forgiveness and renders forgiveness useless" (68). But when "the atrocity of . . . crime and the overwhelming evidence of . . . responsibility" resist all explanation, when there are "neither mitigating circumstances, nor excuses of any sort" and the "hope of regeneration has to be abandoned," then forgiveness not only rises into possibility, it remains the only possibility left (106). In other words, for Jankélévitch, forgiveness does not right any wrong. It responds to a wrong that cannot be made right. It manifestly and emphatically does not overcome wrongdoing. Forgiveness answers a wrong that refuses to be overcome. But, as Jankélévitch wisely notes, this should not necessarily prevent our practice of forgiveness, even if it confounds our reasons for it. In this, it is not unlike love, since the deepest and most gracious form of love would not be one that overlooks or erases wrong, but one that acknowledges a wrong as real and irrevocable and yet loves anyway. In fact, this is why Jankélévitch calls forgiveness a form of love. Forgiveness, like love, has no reason or rational justification. It can only be freely offered, never earned (144). If the misdeed is erased by explanation or expiation, then so is the grace of love and forgiveness. After such erasure, one forgives another because the misdeed has vanished and so risks loving that other only because they have been made lovable, rather than for love's or the beloved's own sake.

This is also why Jankélévitch demands that forgiveness is a form of memory. In the loss of memory he sees wrongdoing mitigated or reduced. Because insofar as an act of forgetting—whether as wholesale erasure or selective obscuration—erases or lessens the reality of a wrong, it also for Jankélévitch diminishes the constitutive grace of forgiveness. Especially in cases where forgetting merely marks the passing of the years, in cases when time gradually heals all our wounds, Jankélévitch cannot countenance that normal intellective decline as expressive (let alone constitutive) of forgiveness. A forgiveness rooted in the amnesiac erasure of the past's errors would reduce forgiveness to "a senile weakness and a poverty, a phenomenon of deficit, a headlong flight of consciousness, a letting go of memory and of the will" (29). To forgive and forget, for Jankélévitch, is not to forgive at all. Since the pain of injury lessens with time, so also its root of wrongdoing fades, and this compromises forgiving's sole condition. According to Jankélévitch, "the time that soothes the wound must render forgiveness less true, less authentic, less meritorious. There is almost nothing left to forgive, therefore nothing is really forgiven" (41–42). The purest forgiveness, therefore, would be one granted in utter haste, perhaps offered as the crime is being committed, before any instant of mitigating decay or explanation or apology or expiation could have even come to pass. "Father, forgive them, for they know not what they do" (Luke 23:34). In a similar way, even any "offense that is rendered insensitive and painless, . . . that is transformed into an indifferent memory," will merely cause forgiveness to "resemble a mediation that integrates the antithesis into a higher synthesis" (26–27). This final phrase is frustratingly obtuse, but what Jankélévitch refers to here is the narrative incorporation of past pains, our telling of our stories such that the failures or sufferings we have borne can be read as necessary steps on the path toward a greater good. He's talking about crafting and curating our memories of past pains toward a happy ending. To diminish or obscure difficult memories so that they become mere details in an ultimately triumphant story, for Jankélévitch, is also to diminish and obscure the wrongs we have committed or suffered, as well as to diminish and obscure the forgiveness we have offered or received in response.[46] Once again, when our reason or failed remembrance erases wrongdoing, the possibility for real forgiveness disappears as well.

To be clear, once again, Jankélévitch is primarily concerned with forgiveness as a moral concept, not with forgiveness as a practical, personal, and political act. With a sort of Platonic flair, he is asserting that what passes for forgiveness in human affairs is never really as pure as the concept that drives it, the one he seeks to parse and analyze in his text and to use as a way of exposing the limits of our moral assumptions. But even if our actual occasions of forgiveness are forms of "apocryphal" or "simili-forgiveness" for Jankélévitch, he does not think them misguided, reckless, or irrelevant. In fact, he argues, it may be that all the practical instances of near-forgiveness we experience in our lives necessarily gesture toward the impossible stakes and unthinkable claims of an ideal we fail to achieve but that nevertheless spurs them. Even if it is the case that "only an apophatic or negative philosophy of forgiveness is truly possible," Jankélévitch still maintains that both impossibly pure and practically impure forgivenesses have this much in common: "they put an end to a . . . chronic hostility that is passionately rooted in rancorous memory" (5). They stop a cycle of retaliatory violence that is rooted in remembrance. In one of his more pragmatic and lucid moments, in fact, Jankélévitch writes that our usual practices of forgiveness, however ersatz or impure they may be, only ask that we "renounce spite, passionate aggression, . . . tit-for-tat considerations" and even the most "legitimate exigencies of justice" (120). This is a restrained, straightforward, and relatively attainable definition. In other words, Jankélévitch understands that his intellectual concerns are narrowly conceptual, because whether pure or impure, forgiveness achieves the same result in human relations: it halts reciprocal violence.

But this is perhaps to undersell the importance of Jankélévitch's critique of the various ways in which wrongdoing is erased; his exhaustive and rigorous policing of forgiveness's claims to purity does serve to uncover what is and is not, finally, at stake in our understanding of the act of forgiving. His argument ends up desperately pragmatic in its own roundabout way. Because it is not just that our simili-forgivenesses can erase the significance of our wrongs. It's also that they can fool us into believing that the facts of a broken past can be rectified by our acts in the present. Whether erasure is due to the physical realities of the mind's decline or to the rationalizations of good excuses, to the memorial indifference that accompanies the passage of time or to the integration of our sufferings into imagined happy endings, we cannot undo the past. Time is absolute and irreversible. Even though some things that have been done can be undone, and a thing once done may be done again, for Jankélévitch "the fact-of-having-done (*fecisse*) is indefeasible" (45). Even if we could completely undo the *effect* of what has been done, we cannot make it so that "the thing that was done never happened" (45). That fact of the deed, and the impact of that fact if not of its effects, shall remain absolute and eternal. And so although we may through various practical strategies (explanation, forgetting, understanding, erasure) be able to address the effects of these facts, the facts themselves demand address as well. And because they cannot be undone or erased, it may be that only forgiveness is poised to meet them. Once again, forgiveness manifestly and emphatically does not overcome wrongdoing. Instead it responds to a wrong that refuses to be overcome. It accepts the past as irrevocable, which means accepting the facts of the past. It is for this reason, then, that Jankélévitch proclaims that "nothing could be more evident: in order to forgive, it is necessary to remember" (56).

Once again, as in the case of justification, this forgiving remembrance resembles an act of love for Jankélévitch. For him, love is irrational, it has no good reason. Love "loves its beloved neither because he is lovable (love would then be esteem)," nor despite the fact that he is "detestable (love, then, would be begrudging and would confirm the love of the lovable)," but "*precisely because* he is detestable!" (133). Likewise, forgiveness cannot undo irreversible wrong, nor can it exist when wrongs have been reversed or their effects undone or amended. It simply "forgives because it forgives, and again it is similar to love in this respect: for love too loves because it loves" (147). What emerges, then, is a loving forgiveness that meets rather than mutes, that addresses rather than overwhelms, wrongdoing.[47] For Jankélévitch, love is strong like death but no stronger, and forgiveness is likewise "strong like wickedness, but it is not stronger than it" (164–65).

Once again, Jankélévitch's intention here is not recklessly to lambaste the normal practices of narrative incorporation with which we are familiar, or to dismiss the typical acts of selective forgetting by which we remember, or to condemn the understandable habits of justification in which we engage. He is only observing that, insofar as our notions of forgiveness conceptually *depend* upon these acts of elimination, marginalization, reduction, explanation, and even expiation of past wrongs, they also serve to reduce the scope and meaning of forgiveness, as well as (perhaps more importantly) the reach and grace of the love that undergirds it, a love in which some of us have placed our deepest faith.

As noted above, these arguments in *Forgiveness* are sometimes painfully abstract. But the difficult lesson of this rigorous attention I think is clear: forgiveness does not overcome wrong; it does not even seek to, lest it overcome itself. It simply responds to wrongs that cannot be overcome. It is as strong as death but no stronger, just like love. Lest we regard Jankélévitch's philosophical attentions as overly romantic or hyperbolic, allow me also to reference his later essay "Should We Pardon Them?," in which he takes a more measured, even hostile, posture toward forgiveness.[48] "Should We Pardon Them?" is a polemical essay that skewers proposed European legislation attempting to impose statutes of limitations for Nazi war crimes. Because he had already written such a long and laudatory meditation on the absolutely unconditioned and gracious gift of forgiveness, his bitter tone in this later essay may be surprising to some readers. Indeed, Jankélévitch acknowledges this, admitting in a preface to the essay that the answer to his titular question might seem to contradict the "purely philosophical" conclusions of his prior book, because in "Should We Pardon Them?," Jankélévitch absolutely and persuasively declares that "pardoning died in the death camps" (553, 567). Furiously, he argues that only victims retain the right of pardon. It "is not in our place to pardon on behalf of the little children whom the brutes tortured to amuse themselves. The little children must pardon them themselves" (569). We cannot offer forgiveness on behalf of the innocent dead. We can only turn "to the brutes, and to the friends of the brutes, and tell them, Ask the little children to pardon you yourselves" (569). Given the horrors of Auschwitz, forgiveness for Jankélévitch is simply impossible.

There are two details to Jankélévitch's polemic, however, that show his fierce argument against forgiveness in "Should We Pardon Them?" to be entirely consistent with the earlier aspirations of *Forgiveness*. The first is that much of Jankélévitch's ire is aimed precisely at the imposition of a statute of limitations, one implication of which would be that after a certain point in time the crimes against humanity in question should no longer demand redress. The deeper and more demanding implication of this imposition, and the one to which Jankélévitch strenuously objects, is that legally proscribing either a redress or its abeyance would suggest that the crimes could be made available to redress at all. On the contrary, before the sheer atrocity of the Shoah, all that is possible is "despair and a feeling of powerlessness before the irreparable" (558). The first moral and practical step, Jankélévitch writes, is to acknowledge that no repair is humanly possible. One "cannot give life back to that immense mountain of miserable ashes. One cannot punish the criminal with a punishment proportional to his crime: for in relation to the infinite all finite magnitudes" dwindle to insignificance (558). Penalty therefore "hardly seems to matter; strictly speaking, what happened is *inexpiable*" (558). The notion that crimes against humanity have some sufficient possible redress not only misunderstands the nature of such crimes, but the suggestion

that the redressive penalties for them might eventually expire simply incorporates the Shoah into a legally systematized mechanism for forgetting and erasure. The passage of time "that dulls all things, the time that uses up sorrow
as it erodes mountains, the time that favors pardon and forgetfulness . . . does
not diminish in the least the colossal slaughter" (556). Paradoxically, the fact
that these crimes present no remotely adequate redress is exactly the reason
that "the penalties against them *cannot* lapse" (556). To suggest that their punishments could expire would corral these crimes into finitude. But the fact of
their having been committed is absolute and eternal. These crimes, Jankélévitch argues, are imprescriptible.

In saying that the crimes are imprescriptible, Jankélévitch is using the
precise legal definition of that word—that the penalty for these crimes cannot
ever lapse. Of course, their atrocity already renders them impossibly inexpiable. While it is true their penalty cannot lapse, they also can never be adequately penalized. Jankélévitch isn't under any illusion that punishment
might replace what has been lost. He is worried that the expiration of punishment's possibility might invite erasure or imply an impermanence to the facts
of the past. And thus Jankélévitch is also pointing toward the second problem
with the proposed legislation: the notion that any written law of pardon, expiation, penalty, or redress could ever be legislated or prescribed. These crimes
are imprescriptible; that is, to respond to them prescriptively, to determine
legally the most apt or just response, to write that apt response into law, is
already to misconstrue their horror as redressable, compensable, and therefore comprehensible. To wrangle these offenses into a system of written justice would only serve to domesticate or diminish them for the sake of that
sense of just resolution. Jankélévitch sees this as a form of forgetting. Better
to leave the unpunishable act forever available to punishment than to declare
that the time for punishment has ended, and thus to impose false finitude on
an unending and infinite loss.

We hear in Jankélévitch echoes of Wistan and Axl; without the possibility
of punishment, even an inadequate punishment, the past may be forgotten
and erased. And so while there is no prescriptible legal response to the inexpiable, to suspend their prescription would be to erase the one resource that
remains: "to remember, to gather one's thoughts" (Jankélévitch, "Should We
Pardon Them?," 572). Though we can do nothing, we can remember and "at
least *feel*, inexhaustibly." The resentment that memory stirs in such imprescriptible cases signifies "the renewed and intensely lived feeling of the inexpiable thing; it protests against a moral amnesty that is nothing but shameful

amnesia" (572). This celebration of resentment is crucially different from the aims of Murphy, Solomon, or Hampton. The possibility of punishment, for them, promises to resolve or satisfy the past. It is the illusion of resolution or satisfaction that Jankélévitch wants to avoid, and that he believes a statute of limitations on war crimes would imply.[49]

Despite their vast difference in tone, *Forgiveness* and "Should We Pardon Them?" argue largely the same thing: that in matters of wrongdoing, there can be no forgetting or expiation; sin cannot be erased either by amnesia or by retaliation. In the former text, forgiveness is posited as the loving response to sin; in the latter, resentment is the only just answer. It may be these are not mutually exclusive, as my argument in Chapter 3 suggests. Yet Jankélévitch remains aware of the potential paradox of this in "Should We Pardon Them?," of the perceived or potential conflict with his other work. In the preface to the article, Jankélévitch presents this paradox unapologetically. For him, forgiveness, if it ever occurs, must arise in this aporetic space: "I have not," he confesses, "attempted to reconcile the irrationality of evil with the omnipotence of love. Forgiveness is as strong as evil, but evil is as strong as forgiveness" (Jankélévitch, "Should We Pardon Them?," 553).

Jacques Derrida also recognizes these aporetic movements in his own reading of Jankélévitch, though I think Derrida is up to something different from Jankélévitch. Derrida takes Jankélévitch's reflections on prescriptibility as a point of departure for a critique of sovereignty. What is most interesting about Derrida's reading of Jankélévitch is how Derrida engages Jankélévitch's notion of the imprescriptible, how he extends and expands on the antilegislative logic of "Should We Pardon Them?" toward an aspirational forgiveness that is truly unconditioned by violence.

Much of Derrida's analysis of forgiveness in Jankélévitch's writing amounts to variations on the theme of Jankélévitch's hyperbole. Like Jankélévitch, Derrida rejects any economic or transactional aspect to forgiveness, and though his logic depends more on the framing of forgiveness as a gift rather than on a worry about the erasure of wrongdoing, Derrida does recognize memory as crucial to his reflections. The "past is past, the event took place, the wrong took place, and this past, the memory of this past, remains irreducible, uncompromising."[50] One cannot adequately consider "forgiveness if one does not take account of this being-past, a being-past that never lets itself be reduced, modified, modalized in a present past or a presentable or re-presentable past."[51] But asserting the irreducible pastness of the past does not exhaust forgiveness's aporias. As Derrida writes, those wrongs that we expect should or must be forgiven do not themselves actually call forth real forgiveness, since forgiveness in such cases is merely what is required. If I *ought* to forgive you, than what I offer you in my forgiveness is not a gift but an obligation. Rather, as he writes in *On Cosmopolitanism and Forgiveness*, "forgiveness forgives only the unforgivable. One cannot, or should not, forgive; there is only forgiveness, if there is any, where there is the unforgivable. That is to say that forgiveness must announce itself as impossibility itself."[52]

What's more, whereas forgiveness must not be given in exchange for any other thing, neither should it be offered in advance of some anticipated benefit. Whenever "forgiveness is at the service of a finality," even when it aims at worthy ends such as atonement or reconciliation, or when it seeks to heal through "a work of mourning" or "by some therapy or ecology of memory," then the 'forgiveness' is not pure" (Derrida, *Cosmopolitanism*, 32). Derrida argues that forgiveness is not and "*should not be*, normal, normative, normalising. It *should* remain exceptional and extraordinary, in the face of the impossible" (32). I should note here that Derrida seems expressly to be denying my own framing of forgiveness, outlined in the Introduction and argued throughout this book, as a practice of mourning. I say more about mourning, and about what Derrida and others think about it, as this chapter advances. In short and for now, however, I observe that the mourning Derrida here avers as impure is one that resolves loss through "some therapy or ecology of memory." In other words, what he worries over is any framing of forgiveness either as the result of a transaction or as the beginning of one. For Derrida a "'finalised' forgiveness is not forgiveness; it is only a political strategy or a psychotherapeutic economy" (50). Forgiveness "does not, it should never amount to, a therapy of reconciliation" (41).

It is when Derrida begins to analyze the writtenness and spokenness of forgiveness, however, when he considers the role language plays in our offers of or obligations to forgive, that he begins to expand on Jankélévitch in important ways. Though he usefully draws a distinction that Jankélévitch perhaps elides in "Should We Pardon Them?"—"One can maintain the imprescriptibility of a crime" and deny the temporal limit to any recompensing penalty "while still forgiving the guilty"—Derrida sees something important in forgiveness's relationship to written law and language, or in other words, to prescriptibility (33). First, in an extension of Jankélévitch's critique of understanding as an ersatz forgiveness, Derrida wonders whether the aporetic paradox of exchange in forgiveness is inscribed in language itself. Because "when the victim and the guilty share no language," when they literally cannot understand what the address or offer of forgiveness means, forgiveness appears to be "deprived of meaning" (49). But as soon as the victim "understands" the criminal, as soon as the victim "exchanges, speaks, agrees with him, the scene of reconciliation has commenced, and with it this ordinary forgiveness which is anything but forgiveness" (49). Even if the victim says "I do not forgive you" to the one who has asked for it, insofar as that one understands the victim's spoken denial, "a process of reconciliation" will have begun; a third will have "intervened" and "this is the end of pure forgiveness" (49). If Jankélévitch's concern is that the incomprehensible be made available to thought, that the infinite be rendered finite, then even his fierce rejection of prescriptibility wanders into complicity with it. Language itself is an ordering of things, it is an economy of exchange. The role that wrongdoing or violence plays in dividing human subjects one from another already begins to be compromised by reconciling gestures and meanings even in a rejected offer of forgiveness, insofar as a base of mutual intelligibility can begin to bridge the divide that sin has breached.

To be clear, Derrida—like Jankélévitch—has no illusions about the usefulness of a critical analysis like this for, say, Belfast in 1981, or Sri Lanka in 1989, or Jerusalem in 2000, or Mindanao in 2017, or indeed in the U.S. courtrooms where we consign a historic proportion of our population to incarceration. What the rigor of his critique is meant to illuminate is how tempted we are to romanticize forgiveness, to regard it as an enchanted salve or unearned resolution. If we confess that it is always in some way impure, we might be able to attend to its impurities with an eye toward justice, rather than to believe its performance or proclamation has magically undone all wrong. This is the point: not that forgiveness fixes everything, but that wrongs remain to be fixed even after any offer of forgiveness. And indeed, it is this foundational impurity that Derrida lights upon, emphasizes, and exposes as a hidden violence. Because Derrida recognizes forgiveness's outwardly antagonistic relationship to law, the impossibility of prescribing it, he regards forgiveness as an act that excepts itself from the strictures of law. Forgiveness is exceptional. It is, as Nietzsche suggests, beyond the law. But like Arthur or like Nietzsche's free sovereign, this does not absolve it of the law's founding violence. On the contrary, it only exposes the exceptionality of forgiveness at the root of law and sovereignty. It is "all-powerful sovereignty (most often of divine right) that places the right to forgive above the law."[53] It is absolute legal authority that declares the abeyance of law. As so often in Derrida's critiques, the "foundation is excluded or exempted from the very structure that it founds. It is this logic of the exception, of forgiveness as absolute exception, as the logic of the infinite exception, that we would have to ponder over and over again."[54] In other words—as I suggested in my reading of Gawain and Arthur—the exception to the law still participates in the structures of power that establish that law, whether or not it follows the law as written. Because the exception's "moment of foundation, the instituting moment, is anterior to the law or legitimacy which it founds. It is thus *outside the law*, and violent by this very fact" (Derrida, *Cosmopolitanism*, 57). In other words, the same fundamental force that establishes sovereignty also permits the sovereign to decide when and if the law applies. Arthur may slaughter innocents in pursuit of peace, or show mercy to Axl in a moment of gratuity. Each act exposes the force of law in his power. Indeed, if forgiveness is beyond the law, it resides there precariously close to a founding violence. Arthur's mercy and his massacre are conceptually and structurally the same. In each case, they are the exceptional decisions of the one who wields power. Each time "forgiveness is effectively exercised, it seems to suppose some sovereign power. . . . [O]ne only forgives where one can judge and punish, . . . [and] the institution of an instance of judgment . . . supposes a power, a force, a sovereignty" (59). The grace of forgiveness depends on the power to punish.

Once again, Derrida's aim—as I read him—is not to jettison all human practices of forgiveness or reconciliation, or to condemn all peacemaking as irredeemably complicit in the founding violences of sovereignty. It is rather to help us recognize how morally complex and complicit even the most honorable practices of forgiveness might be; it is to aid peacemakers in staving off the temptation toward any "therapy of reconciliation" when more challenging political and moral actions might be called for. Though forgiveness might be a worthwhile aspiration, it is *not* a happy ending. Preserving forgiveness's conceptual and impossible purity should assist us in recognizing what is more deeply at stake in our systems of everyday and impure judgment and punishment, even in our orchestrations of sovereignty. What his own critique attempts to stir is a sort of moral longing around the question of forgiveness, a longing that can bear fruit in our politics. "What I dream of," Derrida writes, "would be a forgiveness without power: *unconditional but without sovereignty.* The most difficult task, at once necessary and apparently impossible, would be to dissociate *unconditionality* and *sovereignty*" (59). For Nietzsche the defining quality of the sovereign is this unconditionality. To be sovereign is to be free from the need to answer wrong with wrong. It is to be unconditioned by others, to forgive debts out of indifference. And this is the paradox

Derrida exposes and leaves his reader: the necessary unconditionality of forgiveness links it troublingly to the sovereign exception, and so a forgiveness free of sovereignty, unfettered by law, forever remains impossible for Derrida.

I'm not sure it is so impossible, but even were it so, it might still be morally and conceptually fruitful to try to imagine it. Forgiveness may be forever implicated and rendered impure by language, but where "speaking is impossible . . . so too would be silence or a refusal to share one's sadness."[55] Derrida's ambivalence around speaking and silence here comes from his own wrestling with the memory of his friend Paul de Man, whose anti-Semitism and Nazi sympathy were posthumously exposed. Despite Derrida's previously cited suspicions of mourning, accepting and addressing impossibility with sadness is in fact exactly what is called for when approaching an irrevocable past. And in this, Derrida sounds a bit like Gillian Rose in her description of Arthur and in some of her later philosophical work (however much that work might seek to dismantle the Derridean project). For Rose, the aftermath of violence issues demands to survivors that are simultaneously unanswerable and unignorable. The "last wish of the victims, 'know what has happened, do not forget, and at the same time, never will you know,' does not command a contradiction, but it requires a *work*, a working through."[56] This work is never finally realized or perfected but can only be discovered "by acting, reflecting on the outcome, and then initiating further action."[57]

Unlike mourning as a therapy of reconciliation, an illusion of resolution, for Rose, "the work of mourning is the spiritual-political kingdom—the difficulty sustained, the transcendence of *actual* justice."[58] As an example of this mourning, Rose presents Antigone outside the city walls, violating the lawful decree of the sovereign in grieving for her brother Polynices. Paradoxically, however, Rose states that to "acknowledge and to re-experience the justice and the injustice of the partner's life and death is to accept the law, it is not to transgress it—mourning becomes the law. Mourning draws on transcendent but representable justice, which makes the suffering of immediate experience visible and speakable."[59] That is, much like Derrida, Rose sees gestures of comprehensibility beginning to encroach upon the irrevocable and irreparable once they are put into language and cast into rites—even rites that mourn precisely the pain of their irrevocability and irreparability, ones that mourn the impossibility of any mourning adequately to attend to the extent of our loss. But this encroachment is a necessary one, because (as for Derrida) silence would be just as inadmissible.

And although Derrida would avoid the language of transcendence that Rose prefers, they each regard the law as a work that both acknowledges and engages the impossibility of all our answers and our efforts—that is, they regard it as closely akin to mourning. As Derrida states, law "is the element of calculation, and it is just that there be law, but justice is incalculable, it demands that one calculate with the incalculable."[60] Experiences of unknowing and aporia "are the experiences, as improbable as they are necessary, of justice, that is to say of moments in which the *decision* between just and unjust is never insured by rule."[61] To strive for justice is to strive both under and against the law, to reckon the law's necessarily written limits while unfailingly attempting to rewrite them. Despite Derrida's ambivalence about what he has called "the work of mourning" above, then, he also must recognize the value in a mourning that commits itself to accepting "incomprehension," a mourning that enumerates "coldly, almost like death itself, those modes of language which, in short, deny the whole rhetoricity of the true."[62] A mourning like this would thus embrace its own incompetence to repair the past or even provide redress in the present. Its work would be the work of accepting incomprehension. "I do not know if death teaches us anything at all," Derrida laments in recalling his friend Paul de Man and all of de Man's failures, "but this is what we are given to consider by the experience of mourning."[63]

When mourning seeks to make possible the impossible, when it strives for magic or miracle, Derrida rejects it. But when it accepts incomprehension and the impossible, when it works through it and then works again, it can sometimes summon forth a thing more valuable and usable against the weight of all that incomprehensibility and impossibility. It may be that forgiveness in Jankélévitch's or Derrida's purest sense is always already lost, and so—whatever worries about forgiveness as a work of mourning Derrida has already articulated—forgiveness must preserve some fundamental relationship to grief. But this is the only position from which it or any other politics can begin. Forgiveness must forgive, it must regard the irrevocable without rushing toward resolution or absolution. It must know its own limits and accept what it cannot change:

> History will continue and with it reconciliation, but with the equivocation of a forgiveness mixed up with the work of mourning, with forgetting, an assimilation of the wrong, as if, in short, if I can summarize here this unfinished development in a formula, tomorrow's

forgiveness, the promised forgiveness will have had not only to become the work of mourning (a therapy, a healing away, even an ecology of memory, a manner of better-being with the other and with oneself in order to continue to work and to live and to enjoy) but, more seriously, the work of mourning forgiveness itself, forgiveness mourning forgiveness.[64]

What, then, would a forgiveness that mourns forgiveness, an unconditional forgiveness that is also unconditioned by sovereignty, look like? How might we begin with grief?

BEGINNING AGAIN

Hannah Arendt substantially reconceives sovereignty while modestly recasting forgiveness in the section "Action" from her 1958 volume *The Human Condition*.[65] The aim of the section is not just to offer a philosophical analysis of human action; it is also to construct an alternative and relational conception of subjectivity for human agents. In a series of philosophical reflections that need not extensively preoccupy us here, Arendt distinguishes action from fabrication, agents from makers. Action establishes the agent within a sociality or a plurality; it reveals who the agent is in fundamental ways. As she writes, we enter the human world through our words and our deeds, an entrance that resembles a "second birth, in which we confirm and take upon ourselves the naked fact of our original physical appearance" (Arendt, *Human Condition*, 176). This insertion of ourselves into the human world is conditioned by, and represents a continuation of, our birth, since birth grounds our every opportunity to begin "something new on our own initiative" (177). Word and deed here are actions, and action has etymological roots in beginning "(as in the Greek work *archein*, 'to begin,' 'to lead,' and eventually 'to rule,' indicates)," and setting "in motion (which is the original meaning of the Latin *agere*)" (177). To act on Arendt's account is thus intimately related to human freedom. The capacity to begin, to act, is what distinguishes humans from other animals. Their capacity to begin means that "the unexpected can be expected from" humans, that they can do "what is infinitely improbable" (177). Crucially, these acts are acts of disclosure; through word and deed others come to know us. But it is not as if some internal identity is only uncovered by our action; in fact, acting itself coincides with our identity. In Arendt's version of subjectivity, we become who we are as we enact that identity before others. Identity depends upon human community, upon action

undertaken in the public square. We come into intersubjective being by acting among others in word and deed, by setting forth a new beginning.

Humans never appear or arise in isolation, Arendt argues; to be human is
to act in, with, and among others. To be human is to begin. But the fact that
we do not arise in isolation or under absolutely predictable circumstances
means we can never guarantee the outcomes of our actions. We do not know
how the others among whom we appear will react to our acts; we do not know
what impact our actions will have on a complex and dynamic world. Actions
are necessary; we cannot be human without acting forth. But action also has
its pitfalls, since our acts can have unintended consequences. Here Arendt's
considerations of sovereignty and forgiveness come into play. Actions lead to
unpredictable results. In our actions, we commence a set of responses and reactions over which we have no control. Arthur and Gawain's rationale for
forgetting notwithstanding, not "even oblivion and confusion . . . are able to
undo a deed or prevent its consequences" (232–33). The absolute human im-
potence to undo what has been done—or better, in Jankélévitch's words, the
fact of its having been done—is matched only by the absolute inability of
humans to predict what responses and reactions their beginnings will elicit. In
other words, we are as free to act as we are bound to the unintended outcomes
of our actions. This leads to a dilemma for our sovereignty and our sense of
self-control. Because we place our actions into a public space not entirely—or
even significantly—under our own power, we must ultimately yield those actions and their outcomes to the world to come. This lack of complete control,
Arendt observes, has been a constant worry for Western philosophy. Because
uncertainty haunts all our well-intentioned promises and regret lingers around
all our unintended outcomes, the West has sought conceptual refuge from
unpredictability and uncertainty in its philosophy (232). Western thought has
traditionally displaced action as the singular freedom of the human in the
hope of escaping the unpredictability of sociality, in order to evade that "hap-
hazardness and moral irresponsibility inherent in a plurality of agents" (220).
Indeed, escape from the "frailty of human affairs into the solidity of quiet and
order," a passage from social vulnerability into the perfect freedom of unconditioned self-grounding, becomes a singular priority of Western political philosophy since Plato, Arendt argues (222).

It is in this anxiety over uncertainty and frailty that Arendt recognizes the
manifestation of a misguided sovereignty. If the "solidity of quiet and order"
is the coin of the political realm for the West, if it is the one refuge from uncertainty, this must mean that imperviousness and solitude—unconditioned

exceptionality—should be the mark of the sovereign. Only the person entirely unencumbered by the messiness of intersubjective action, the unpredictability of actions and interactions, will be truly free and truly unconditioned and therefore truly sovereign. Western thought condemns action for "luring men into necessity" because it invariably draws them into complicated sets of unpredictable social relationships, among other independent agents, whose reactions to original acts they will necessarily become embroiled in (234). Think here of Nietzsche's merciful sovereign, who is able to grant mercy only out of indifference, because the crimes of the parasites who impinge on his interests do not even rise to a significance worthy of response. Unlike Nietzsche's sovereign, Arendt's agent becomes immediately entangled in a sociality which that agent cannot control and must relinquish "freedom the very moment he makes use of it" (234). The agent is not unconditioned; his actions enmesh him in a plural world of contingency and condition. The only place freedom is truly possible on the Nietzschean model is alone—entirely self-sufficient, the lord of one's own realm, however tiny or solitary that kingdom may be.

But Arendt sees this desperation for self-sufficiency as revealing a "basic error" that lies "in that identification of sovereignty with freedom which has always been taken for granted by political as well as philosophic thought" (234). Recalling again the sociality and plurality into which any human identity and agency arises, Arendt argues that if sovereignty and freedom were truly the same, then no one "could be free, because sovereignty, the ideal of uncompromising self-sufficiency and mastership, is contradictory to the very condition of plurality" (234). To be free to act among and with others means to be caught up in the consequences of free actions too. There is no human self-sufficiency. If this is what sovereignty amounts to, then there can be no real sovereignty either, apart from the illusions of our rhetoric or our politics. But Arendt insists that there is yet a feasible form of freedom. The fact that humans cannot escape contingency and condition does not mean they are incapable of acting. Whatever the past has been or the future may bring, we can begin, and begin again. This is our freedom, not to be entirely unconditioned, but to initiate a new possibility into the conditions and contingencies out of which we have arisen. To be clear, this is not the newness of an Arthur or a Carl Schmitt, because they both act under the illusion that violence might create a new order free from condition and contingency. On the contrary, this newness accepts the risks of the future without pretending to have broken with the past.

What Arendt is proposing is that the only relevant human freedom is the freedom *to* act, despite the possible, unpredictable consequences, rather than a freedom *from* action and its consequences. Because of this, in an inversion of Nietzsche's indifferent mercy, Arendt links promise fundamentally to forgiveness but in a far less punishing way. For Arendt both promise and forgiveness are acts of human freedom that reveal the human possibility to begin again, to begin anew. The "remedy for unpredictability, for the chaotic uncertainty of the future, is contained in the faculty to make and keep promises," she writes (237). Meanwhile, redemption "from the predicament of irreversibility—of being unable to undo what one has done though one did not, and could not, have known what [one] was doing—is the faculty of forgiving" (237). And it is her meditation on forgiveness that represents her most inspired and inspiring final thoughts on human action and freedom. As Arendt argues, without "being forgiven, released from the consequences of what we have done, our capacity to act would, as it were, be confined to one single deed from which we could never recover; we would remain the victims of consequences forever" (237). This is exactly the unfreedom that solitary sovereignty has traditionally feared. But escape from it is an illusion. The only real freedom is to begin again in the midst of our inescapable consequences, and to risk a new set of unpredictable and irreversible outcomes. Implied here is the danger in the sort of retributive cycle of necessary violence that seems to follow so naturally from wrong, as Arthur and Gawain above assert. Arendt makes this implication explicit in defining forgiveness therefore as "the exact opposite of vengeance" (240). When revenge takes the "form of re-acting against an original trespassing," it binds the involved agents into a predetermined chain reaction of retaliation instead of "putting an end to the consequences of the first misdeed" (240). Revenge, for Arendt, is the "natural, automatic reaction to transgression," so predictable that it ought to be expected and may even be calculated (241). But the "act of forgiving can never be predicted; it is the only reaction that acts in an unexpected way and thus retains, though being a reaction, something of the original character of action. Forgiving, in other words, is the only reaction which does not merely re-act but acts anew and unexpectedly, unconditioned by the act which provoked it and therefore freeing from its consequences both the one who forgives and the one who is forgiven" (241).[66]

Forgiveness is a freedom because, in the midst of endless acts of reciprocal violence, where violent outcomes arise almost by necessity, forgiveness acts unencumbered by the predictive reciprocities of its past and risks a new beginning. Here is the unconditioned forgiveness Derrida longed for, one that escapes the sovereignty of exception. This forgiveness begins not free of historical memory and reality but entirely within it. For Arendt this form of freedom—rather than a particular affective posture or transactional economy—is crucial to the forgiveness Jesus of Nazareth founds. Forgiveness is not a feeling for Arendt, and neither is it a reward for good behavior. It is a beginning. The "freedom contained in Jesus' teachings of forgiveness is the freedom from vengeance, which encloses both doer and sufferer in the relentless automatism of the action process, which by itself will never come to an end" (241).

Allow me once again to revisit *The Buried Giant*. King Arthur seeks freedom from history by erasing it. Wistan seeks freedom from history by avenging it. What then of the haunting character of the British peasant woman in Ishiguro's novel, the one who kills rabbits at the boatman's house, who pulls apart a dying Saxon's flesh with a dull garden tool, and who begs Axl to release her from the relentless scurry of the absconding sprites who torment her? What this woman rails against is death. If the boatman represents the inevitability of separation and loss, then this is what she refuses to accept as she curses his inscrutable and immovable judgment. She is locked in her past; she cannot imagine a way to begin again amidst the losses she has suffered. Her return to his ruined villa is religious; it is a sacrifice against the inevitability and irrevocability of death, an offering made not in adoration but in protest, an attempt to mitigate a loss. It is an effort to undo what cannot be undone, or to forestall what must inevitably come. We can and should read this rejection of death alongside her insatiable desire for vengeance. I have no doubt that this woman's torture of a wounded Saxon war criminal in the middle of a bloody, still embattled field satisfies a deep and urgent longing generated by her pain. But that act and its satisfaction must be morally evaluated on their own merits; they bear no direct economic relationship to past crimes. Whatever pleasures they engender, they do not offer any real compensation for the loss this woman has suffered. Her loss will remain after the torture she performs is complete. "Finish it," Gawain cries, as if any part of her history might be concluded in that act (Ishiguro, *Buried Giant*, 211). Indeed, it seems to me that even to decide that one could attempt compensation for such a loss would radically underestimate the extent of the loss; it would imagine that her pain could be undone or erased, her past restored through violence, which would be subtly to deny the irrevocability of what she has endured. It might even diminish the scale of the crimes she has suffered among those (like

Gawain or Wistan) who authorize revenge. When vengeance is finally paid, they might say, the affair must therefore be ended, the circle neatly closed, the debt to society fully paid. Finish it. But all this would be to presume that the debt to her is somehow payable at all while the dead remain yet dead, our hearts remain yet broken, and the circles remain unclosed and spinning ever outward into growing arcs of retaliation. When the peasant woman invites the Saxon lord into an economy of suffering with the blade of her hoe, she simultaneously expresses and rejects the irrevocability of her pain. She vents and fails to reckon with the immovability of her grief.

Weighed by loss but not paralyzed by it, aware of the past but unconstrained by it, forgiveness acts in freedom. And although I recognize and endorse the rhetorical impossibility Derrida leans upon so heavily in describing forgiveness, it seems that his longing to disassociate unconditionality from sovereignty is realized to some degree by Arendt. If the traditionally free sovereign is the one who refuses to be conditioned by or vulnerable to the plurality of the polis and its laws, Arendt's forgiver is the opposite and discovers a new form of freedom in that opposition. Arendt's forgiver is one willing to commit in vulnerability to a new beginning, one aware of all the risks of acting but ready to risk action nonetheless. Unlike the solitary sovereign, who fetishizes impassibility, the forgiver acts understanding that human beings, though "they must die, are not born in order to die but in order to begin" (Arendt, *Human Condition*, 246). This genius for beginning through forgiving, in spite of risk, unpredictability, and irrevocability, Arendt recognizes as realized in the teachings of Jesus of Nazareth. Because it looses itself from the fetters of a reactionary past, forgiveness "looks like a miracle" (246). Action, and forgiveness as the prototypical action, is "in fact, the one miracle-working faculty of man, as Jesus of Nazareth . . . must have known very well when he likened the power to forgive to the more general power of performing miracles, putting both on the same level and within the reach of man" (246–47).

It's important—if perhaps slightly unnecessary—to make clear that when Arendt mentions miracles here, she isn't interested in any supernatural powers. I note this only because the forgiveness she proposes isn't anything like what Derrida and others have worried might hastily or magically erase past wrongs, as if through miracle. It is letting go of the futile wish that the past might be undone. It is not magical thinking, it is mourning. It does not fix the past. It begins a future. What Arendt describes is a way out of Arthur's (and Gawain's and Wistan's) awful binary in *The Buried Giant*: either retaliate and remember, or forgive and forget. What Arendt instead offers is the miraculous capacity humans have to begin, to initiate action in the midst of history, to escape the necessary reciprocities of retaliation. Arendt's forgiveness recognizes the past and its consequences, and if it is miraculous, it is so only because it arises without calculated rationale, entirely anew, unconditioned by what has come before it, vulnerable to the world into which it intervenes.

FAREWELL MY ONE TRUE LOVE

If forgiveness is about accepting an irrevocable past, then Arendt suggests that beginning again looks more like mourning than magic. Consider again the young Saxon Edwin, Wistan's apprentice, and the promise of hatred he has made to his countryman and teacher. As Edwin sprints away from the carcass of the dead Querig and toward war, Beatrice's plaints echoing in his ears, the reader wonders whether Edwin will be constrained by this promise or loose himself from it in search of a more significant freedom. The reciprocally violent justice Wistan cannot think beyond has bound itself to Edwin in this vow. He realizes as he runs that the mother he has been searching for throughout the novel can no longer be saved. His promise to find her cannot be kept. But the warrior Wistan waits for him still, eager to help him avenge her loss (Ishiguro, *Buried Giant*, 301). As Wistan so often says, the hour is late for rescue but still early for revenge. But vengeance is not necessary here; it is a choice, as is the choice to refuse it. Edwin remains free, free to act in fulfillment or in breach of his hateful promise, free to hate or to love the old couple, even as he hurries off to war. He can still choose to loose himself from the retaliatory binds of vengeance, and this choice would amount to an Arendtian—and on Arendt's definition, a Christian—forgiveness.

This is not the only vow that frames the possibility of forgiveness in the novel. Against the violent political backdrop of the conflict between Britons and Saxons, at its center *The Buried Giant* is the story of a marriage. The forgetting that Querig's breath imposes on Britain is not only public, it is private too. As noted above, Axl and Beatrice have no shared or personal recollections of their life together, and they are worried that without these memories their love for one another is condemned "to fade and die" (45). Indeed, as the novel comes gradually but certainly to suggest that Beatrice's mysterious ailment is a mortal one, Ishiguro literalizes her impending death through the boatmen's test and his offer to ferry companions together across his waters. It becomes clear to the reader in the novel's final pages that the boatman represents death, and his passage is to an island of the afterlife. The rabbit-woman in the villa and the struggle against the absconding pixies in the reedy shallows each foreshadow Axl and Beatrice's long-searched-for passage together into eternal rest and companionship.

I'd like to examine more closely the elements of the boatman's test, as he describes it to Axl and Beatrice when they first happen upon him and the rabbit-woman in the villa. After the woman has been shooed away from her sacrifice, Beatrice presses the off-duty boatman to tell them more about how and why the rabbit-woman failed in her transit with her husband. Beatrice tells him they have heard rumors about a difficult task, and they seek counsel and advantage in advance of their own passage. The boatman confesses to them that, on rare occasions and at a boatman's sole discretion, a couple may be allowed to cross the water together to an island. The two will then remain in that remote land, spared from the usual wandering and loneliness there. But to do so a couple must prove their love true by putting forth to the boatman "their most cherished memories," one at a time and out of one another's earshot (43). If their memories match, then their love will be confirmed as binding the couple so tightly together they cannot be parted in their passage. Memories are thus the basic measure of love for the boatman. But most couples whom the boatmen tests do not bear the love they believe they share. A passage to the island together is highly uncommon, the boatman continues, because where love is professed, memory instead often uncovers emptiness, anger, hatred, or even the simple fear of loneliness standing in for truly held love (44). Abiding love is revealed only very rarely, in which few cases the boatman is happily obliged to ferry the couple together to their rest.

This is why the forgetting fog is of such great personal importance to Axl and Beatrice as they travel together. If they will be allowed to cross together, they believe they must first regain their memories. Only if they can recover their "cherished memories" will they have any chance of persuading a generous boatman of shared passage. It is this fear of separation—even a fear of loneliness, as the boatman says—that leads Axl and Beatrice to aid Wistan in his efforts to kill Querig. For what Axl and Beatrice most fear is losing one another. This is obvious not only in their anxiety before the test they face; it's also clear in their daily words and actions. Beatrice constantly calls to Axl as they walk close in tandem on their journey, "Are you there, Axl?," to which he invariably replies, "Still here, princess." Once they have heard the details of their impending trial, they bravely join Wistan in his dragon-slaying quest in order to recover the memories that have been lost (276). They need their remembrances in order to remain eternally together, and so they must aid Wistan on his mission.

But we learn as they go, and as the fog of forgetting first slowly and then suddenly lifts at the novel's end, that Axl and Beatrice's love is more affectively complex than the one the boatman seeks to credit. What's more, we learn that they have no fear of that complexity—or rather, that if they do, that fear does not diminish their deep love. When a monk at the monastery reveals to the couple that Querig is the cause of their forgetting, he asks Beatrice whether it wouldn't be better for some things to remain shrouded in the mist. She responds that the loss of her happiest memories is a theft of precious possessions. The monk reminds her that bad memories will return along with the good, but she brushes aside his warning, saying that the anger and sadness those memories may occasion will be worth their retrieving, since they will represent parts of a shared life she and Axl now cherish in its whole (157). Even when they show less readiness to remember past pains, they weather this uncertainty together. At one point, as they rest beside an evening fire, an unarticulated remembrance returns to Beatrice, and she asks to walk apart from Axl when they have awakened. When they do eventually rise from sleep, the mist has taken her memory again, and Beatrice's tone with Axl is again warm and intimate. She no longer bears him any resentment. Still, some suppressed echo of its pain causes Beatrice to ask Axl if he fears what might be revealed once the dragon's mist has cleared. Axl replies that what he fears most is not remembering itself, but that after their remembering Beatrice might ask to walk apart from him as she had before they slept. But Beatrice no longer has any memory of this request, and so Axl lets it remain forgotten (249). To be clear, Axl allows Beatrice's lapsed memory in this case. But again, what demands attention here is that his fear is not of fear itself (to borrow a phrase) but that the emotions these memories will stir might cause the two of them to separate. It is not fear but their reaction to fear that worries him. Action, not affect, is what's at stake. And indeed, there are moments in their journey when, as here, Beatrice becomes angry or impatient with Axl, and he with her, but they persist in their quest and remain close at one another's side until at last they reach the stony shore and the small fire of their boatman.

By the time they meet the boatman there, Querig has been killed and all has been remembered. Axl and Beatrice's son does not live in a faraway village. Instead, he is long since dead, and their journey to his home has in fact been a journey to the land of the dead—this boatman's eerie island. When they have at last arrived at their test, Beatrice and Axl each recall the other's faults and failings entirely; they share a history once more. But when the boatman separates them for questioning, it is not nearly as harrowing an inquisition as they have feared. He sets them at a distance and then speaks casually with Beatrice for a few moments before turning back and joining Axl. When Axl shows he remembers the memory Beatrice has first shared—a harmless story about carrying eggs together from the market—the boatman seems satisfied and begins to prepare for their shared journey. But as they stroll again toward Beatrice and the waiting boat, the boatman asks nonchalantly and out of trivial curiosity if there is any painful memory that Axl would like to share. Assured by the boatman that the test is already complete and has been passed, that the answer will carry no repercussion and that he and Beatrice will be allowed to travel to the island together, Axl reveals the pain that has haunted them, unremembered, throughout the novel but that has returned in the clarity of Querig's death.

We learn that Beatrice had once betrayed Axl and that their subsequent quarrels occasioned an estrangement from their son, who ran away as a boy and died shortly thereafter in a neighboring village from plague. We learn also that after the boy's death, Axl forbade Beatrice from visiting their young son's grave, a cruelty that Axl calls "a darker betrayal" than Beatrice's brief infidelity. Axl confesses to the boatman that he did this out of "foolishness and pride" and "a craving to punish" (312). Though he professed his forgiveness to Beatrice, in fact he exacted an awful vengeance upon her by exploiting her grief and hindering her mourning. But in this better recollection and fuller accounting, Axl finds a way through a "transactional and self-serving" forgiveness toward one stirred by both self-recognition and love.[67] Because his love "is not deceived any longer by the mandated forgetting" that has obscured his pain, Axl can remember well enough to love better and step beyond the "darker betrayal" that has secretly framed their marriage for so many years.[68]

But after this confession from Axl, the boatman suddenly changes his mind. Though he blames the waves and tide for this decision rather than Axl's honesty, the boatman informs Axl that he and Beatrice must now each cross alone. Their passage to the island must be solitary, though he suggests—with uncertainty and against his previous counsel—that it might be possible for them to reunite on the other shore. At first Axl is angry, disbelieving the promise of eventual reunion and deeming the boatman to have cheated him. But Beatrice calls Axl close and encourages him to accept the boatman's deal, to make peace with him and allow her to cross alone. Reluctantly Axl agrees, but sensing they may not find reunion across the waters, he lingers by the boat until Beatrice worries the boatman will grow impatient and asks him to let her go. "Very well, princess," he says. "But just let me hold you once more" (317).

The boatman overhears their final words, politely averts his eyes, and waits for several quiet moments while wondering whether they do in fact embrace. He imagines Axl huddled in the keel of the boat around Beatrice's small, swaddled shape. After a long silence,

> . . . their voices return.
> "We'll talk more on the island, princess," [Axl] says.
> "We'll do that, Axl. And with the mist gone, we'll have plenty to talk of. Does the boatman still stand in the water?"
> "He does, princess. I'll go and make my peace with him."
> "Farewell then, Axl."
> "Farewell, my one true love." (317)

As the novel ends, the boatman begins to ferry Beatrice away to the lonely island while Axl turns and walks away from them toward the shore.

The reader might be tempted to think that Axl is right, that he has been tricked, that with this confession to the boatman he has failed his portion of the test. Axl and Beatrice's love and life together have included heartbreak, resentment, anger, and betrayal, and so their love has been found wanting. Indeed, Axl admits as much to the boatman, supposing that some might judge his love faulty since it involves injury and regret. But Axl nonetheless insists that the "slow tread of an old couple's love" will be recognizable to God as truly loving, since God will know their pains and betrayals as part of a loving whole (313). Axl does wonder both to the boatman and to Beatrice whether all the years of forgetting have allowed his heart to heal and be purged of its anger. But it's also clear that, whatever forgetting's role in his healing, their "flawed and broken" love could not have been fully and finally realized without this last and climactic remembering. These final moments of realization are enabled only by a recollection and recognition of their wounds.[69]

In fact, I would suggest that their final separation is a sign precisely of that rich and complicated love Axl claims God recognizes rather than of its absence. Throughout the novel Axl and Beatrice's only concern has been not ever to be separated, either in life or in death. Just as an earlier boatman suspected, their relationship has been one built upon a mutual and consuming fear of loneliness, a mutual terror at the prospect of separation, and little more. But as Beatrice weakens and Axl realizes she is dying, and as their memories return, we see him become more deeply conflicted about their laborious journey together and his desperation to keep her alive. There is that haunting earlier passage, for example, in which another mysterious boat keeper lends Axl and Beatrice two tethered baskets so they may cross a reedy river. While doing so, the dozens of pixies that crawl out of the rabbit-woman's boat attempt to steal Beatrice away. The sprites accuse Axl of perpetuating his beloved's suffering, of knowing that she cannot be cured but nonetheless selfishly refusing to let her die in peace. Axl, meanwhile, remains throughout the difficult journey aged but healthy, and we can imagine Beatrice's reluctance in these final moments to fetter his life to her death as she kindly encourages him to let her go to the island without him. Why should she wish him dead? And why would Axl wish her any further suffering?

In the novel's final moments, Axl and Beatrice love each other. They overcome the fear of loneliness that has followed them throughout their journey, a fear that has functioned in their forgetting only as a placeholder for love. But now, because they have faced their past and recognized that which is beyond all rescue and retrieving, they need no longer fear what they might lose in reclaiming those broken memories. Unlike the rabbit-woman, they have made their peace with the boatman, though it is a grim one. They have accepted what they have lost and finally together grieved their son. They have acknowledged that death must separate them and that they have no sacrifices or bargains to offer the boatman for barter. They have met the fear of losing love and now find they can allow their love to admit loss. They are ready to make a beginning in grief, even if they must do so alone. They have come to love each other enough to let the other go. This is the bitter irony of the boatman's test, its cruel catch-22: in order truly to prove their love, to merit remaining always together, they must show they are willing forever to part and thus set the other free. Axl must set Beatrice free to die, and Beatrice must set Axl free to live. To love each other fully in this final moment is to let go, to mourn what cannot be replaced, to want what cannot be compensated. There is no compensation; there is love and there is loss. In love, Axl and Beatrice must accept what has been lost, what must be lost, and go alone. In love, they must forsake a fearful attachment and move forward. In love, they must allow that their affection can tether them only loosely across infinite distance rather than bind them tightly in intimate bliss. In love, they must bid farewell with breaking hearts. They arrive at a love as tragically powerful and courageous as this, at a love so unremittingly willing to lose, only after they have remembered their suffering well enough to admit its irrevocability, and only after they have offered the forgiveness that accompanies that admission. They are, at novel's end, finally free to set one another free, finally free to forgive.

CHAPTER 2

Repentance

What does it mean to hold wrongdoers accountable, especially if the past is as irrevocable as Arendt has suggested and as irredeemable as Axl and Beatrice have learned? Consider the only extended model of penance that arises in *The Buried Giant*.[1] At the monastery where Beatrice and Axl have gone to seek medical advice, the novel hints at a secret division among the brothers there and suggests that not all is as pacific as it first appears. As the couple are shuttled from hiding place to hiding place in search of the expert but elusive Father Jonus, while also avoiding the abbot, they happen in the dark of a barn upon a hastily fashioned wooden cart that supports a large iron cage. Inside the cage is a wooden post, covered in fetters and wrought bindings, as well as an eyeless iron mask with a small opening for the mouth. The cart and cage alike are covered with feathers and bird droppings. Axl also notes the strange behavior and density of birds roosting around the monastery, and the brothers' oddly angry reactions toward them when they twitter (Ishiguro, *The Buried Giant*, 145).

When Axl and Beatrice are finally taken to Jonus, they find he is gravely ill and that wounds fester all over his body. The Saxon warrior Wistan, who is with them, quickly discerns the cause of the monk's injuries and the purpose of the mysterious iron cage. In a challenge to the convalescing monk, Wistan angrily surmises that the monks employ the cage in a practice of self-mortification, hoping in this way secretly to atone for British crimes that are now shrouded by Querig's mist. The sight of Jonus's wounds repulses Wistan, since he suspects that the severity of the wounds accompanies a self-righteous piety that salves the suffering of the monks (145). Thus commences a brief theological debate between the pagan warrior and the Christian monk over the meaning and character of penitential practice.

For Wistan, a secret penance is no penance at all, and the minor injuries of monks are insignificant against the massacre of masses. The Christian God, he accuses, is easily bribed at the expense of any adequate justice. But Father Jonas insists his God is not one of cheap bribery but instead of boundless mercy. From such a God, he says, it is "no foolishness to seek forgiveness . . . however great the crime." But Wistan protests that mercy is useless, since it gives sinners license to pursue their cruelty knowing that some meager prayers and "a little penance will bring forgiveness" (151). The mercy of this forgiving God, Wistan argues, effectively permits wrongdoing. Wrongdoers cannot be held accountable without reciprocal response, however distasteful Wistan might find that reciprocity in the end. But in fact, the monks are not attempting to evade reciprocity; they are attempting to dictate the terms of the reciprocation. The monks mortify themselves by making their bodies available to hungry birds, and indeed they do so as a deliberate act of penance and atonement. But Wistan reviles them for it, regarding their penitence as weak and inadequate. Recall Wistan's repeated assertions that painful punishment is an effective and necessary mnemonic. These monks are clearly suffering; were the experience of pain alone involved in an economy of simple exchange, this suffering should not spur Wistan's anger. It does so because the satisfaction Wistan seeks is not sadistic, Nietzsche notwithstanding; it is not the mere fact of British suffering that he desires. Instead, it is the secrecy of the monks' piety that angers him here. He desires not only that the Britons suffer; *he wants them held accountable*. Suffering is meant to be a sign; punishment is meaningless unless it is public, functioning as a mark of culpability and confession. Private penitence serves only personal piety, not public accountability. Pain is effective only when it functions as an aid to communal and social memory. It is only when penance is signaled publicly, only when it functions alongside or as a form of confession and repentance, that it serves its rightful purpose.

Father Jonas, it must be noted, is not surprised by Wistan's critique. It may be he already discerns Wistan's insistence that only a public confession can prove penitence. For Jonas, forgiveness is not a thing to be won by suffering. He does not expect his suffering will somehow purchase a secret pardon

that the Britons seek from either God or Saxon. He sees that neither God nor
Wistan finds pleasure in the mere fact of pain and he objects to the monks'
penance remaining secret. The failure publicly to confess, and the penitential
acts that perpetuate this pious failure, are for Jonus exactly the problem. Jonas
tells the Saxon warrior that, despite his own concerns about abusing divine
mercy, his abbot and many of the other monks continue to assert that their
private penance can answer for the past. But the birds, Jonas believes, have
become heralds of a holy anger. Where once small birds with needling beaks
brought only trivial sufferings, now large crows and ravens come to the
monks, furiously tearing at their flesh, leaving deep and lasting wounds (152).
In recent months three of the brothers have died. The abbot wants to continue, believing this private penance pure and useful. But Jonas and a few
others have become convinced that their penitential practice will not win any
forgiveness, that instead they "must uncover what's been hidden and face the
past" (151). For Jonus, forgiveness does not wait on the other end of punishment. Crime is not compensated by pain, and forgiveness is not a prize for
penal purchase. Indeed, this secret and penitential way forward will end only
in death for the monks, not in peace or expiation. If forgiveness is to be found
at all, the past must be faced and its horrors uncovered. For Jonus, then, repentance is essential not as compensation, but for some other reason. Instead
of secretly attempting to atone for crimes through mortification, the monks
should speak plainly about the past's pain, and indeed about the impossibility
of undoing that pain through any act of self-mortification. What's actually
needed here, according to Jonus, is not greater suffering but better remembrance. Memory is stifled at the monastery by more than dragon's breath. The
privately penitent monks eventually attempt to kill Axl, Beatrice, Edwin, and
Wistan rather than have their hidden history exposed, though the band of
travelers narrowly escapes.

If retaliation is one attempt at accountability, Wistan and Jonus suggest
that repentant confession is another. It may be that spoken confession is often
as embroiled in the transactional moral economies of retaliation as the self-
mortifying pieties of these monks. So what is confession and what is it for?
How do and should we hold one another accountable for wrongs, especially
when and if the gravity of our offenses suggests that moral accounts cannot
be balanced? In this chapter I show how practices of repentance can function
either to confirm or to deny the retaliatory urges I critiqued in the previous
chapter. I show that if forgiveness is indeed an act of unflinching and full
memory, then it cannot exercise its memory in isolation. Remembrance must

be public. The repentance that sometimes prefaces forgiveness need not therefore function as the punishing price paid for absolution. It can, under certain circumstances, also or instead serve as the introduction to a better remembering. Instead of functioning as a practice of self-justifying speech, confession can serve as the giving over of our stories to others. It might also allow our story to be told to us by others. It is, therefore, not a transactional element of a forgiving exchange but the intersubjective movement of a common memory. To make this argument, I turn to a crucial example of confessional fiction in contemporary American literature: Marilynne Robinson's *Gilead*.

WHAT ELSE SHOULD I TELL YOU?

The novel *Gilead* was celebrated upon its appearance in 2006,[2] returning Robinson to wide acclaim for her first novel after 1981's critically praised *Housekeeping*. Part of what called attention to the book was its deliberate and self-conscious engagement with religious faith, not always the most attractive topic for literary fiction. In terms of plot, the events of the novel are relatively spare: the year is 1956, and the Reverend John Ames, an aging, white, Congregationalist pastor in a church in the small town of Gilead, Iowa, has married late. He has a weak heart that he's been told will fail him soon, and he is writing to introduce himself to the young son he knows will grow up mostly without him, and as a way to say goodbye to his wife and child. His best friend, Robert Boughton, a white Presbyterian minister, has also taken ill, and Boughton's children all come home, including Boughton's prodigal son, Jack, christened John Ames in the narrator's honor. Ames feels briefly threatened by Jack's friendliness toward his wife, Lila, and has difficulty forgiving Jack for his past sins. Eventually, however, they come to a reconciliation of sorts.

The novel is widely regarded as a meditation upon interpersonal forgiveness, as a modern retelling of the parable of the prodigal son. The gospel reference is not just implied in the novel's plot; it also stands explicit on the page. In one of the few of his own sermons Ames favorably quotes, he considers the parable at length. Ames echoes Jankélévitch in his reflections, asserting that the only sufficient reason to forgive a debt is that it exits. Forgiveness's only condition is sin. Like others, Ames worries over conceiving of forgiveness as an exchange, noting that Luke's prodigal, though he plans to make repentance and amends to his father, never actually acts to be restored to the family or even tells them he is sorry (161). His father has already run to him and embraced him before he can get the words out.

I admire Ames's reading of the parable, and I lean heavily into what the prodigal son should imply for our understanding both of John Ames and of Christian atonement theology later in this chapter and in the next. But first I note that the novel takes an expressly confessional and epistolary form. It is narrated by Ames as a sort of undated diary, a last testament to his young son and offered therefore in the father's absence. As such, it is fundamentally a novel about grief and loss, as well as about what it means to tell one's own story. This is complicated by John Ames's self-conscious sense of himself as a storyteller. Ames knows that the record he keeps of his final days and of his memories will be the version of himself that his son will mostly know, and we can read his grief and anxiety throughout the narrative. Ames opens his letter by imagining his son as a grown man and himself long-since experienced in the habits and manners of the dead, thus signaling the necessary distance between them, a distance that is felt both at the time of the writing (when the boy cannot read what Ames has written) and at the time the boy will eventually read it (when Ames will no longer be alive) (3). Nonetheless, Ames feels compelled to give his son some sense of himself and his history, to write for his son—in his wife Lila's words—the boy's begats, the record of his family, which is also a record of himself. He tells the child his own name and his father's name and his grandfather's name, all John Ames, and then his own mother's and grandmother's names, and he tells his son that he has lived his whole seventy-six years in Iowa. After this, the paragraph breaks and the prose pauses, and Ames asks, "what else should I tell you?" (9).

This uncertainty over how and what part of his story to tell arises again and again. Ames is constantly apologizing for what he should or shouldn't say or have said, constantly tending to a story that will be out of his hands once it is written, even more so when it is finally read. In one moment, after writing somewhat judgmentally of Jack Boughton, he places in parentheses a note to his son that expresses hope that the child will grow into an excellent man, but also an assurance: "I will love you absolutely if you are not" (73). This line is notable for the unconditionality of its love, but also for the awareness of its intended eventual audience. Or, realizing that all his anxieties over Jack will have been resolved one way or another by the time his child reads the story, Ames also confesses to his son his ignorance of the future and asks forgiveness for it, though his inability to foresee also leaves him unsure which of his failings will need forgiveness. It may be the child will need to forgive Ames for warning him about Jack Boughton, or for failing to warn him enough, or perhaps for thinking any of this old man's opinions mattered much at all

(125). All Ames knows is that he will be some way in the wrong, but he cannot know why and how beforehand and so only may but also must ask forgiveness in his ignorance. In this, his confessional worry echoes Arendt's analysis explored in Chapter 1, and indeed on my reading this novel becomes for Ames a confessional practice of emerging from ignorance into repentance and the request for real forgiveness.

Ames's anxiety over language is not confined to this letter to his son, either. In general we can see Ames fretting over the effectiveness of his words, recognizing language as both the bridge and the barrier to others in his life and his loneliness. Consider his account of his proposal to Lila, his wife. Lila wanders through Gilead and into Ames's church late in his life, and he is surprised by her presence and his fondness for her. When they hardly know one another, she says to him "very softly and seriously, 'You ought to marry me,'" and in that moment Ames writes that he realizes he hasn't ever known before what it means to love another person. Speechless, Ames stands startled, before chasing her down the street a minute later and saying, "You're right, I will" (55–56). Thus they are betrothed, though Ames remains afraid to touch her sleeve and Lila keeps on walking. There is a kind of sweetness to this story, mainly in its awkwardness, because John Ames and Lila don't know how to talk to one another. Indeed, in the later novel *Lila*, we learn that Ames's wife recalls this same scene mostly for its awkwardness rather than for its tenderness.[3] Ames doesn't really know what to say. He realizes that all the other words of love he has spoken before now have not been quite right, but even in this revelation he has no words to express exactly what he means. Notably, Ames never does directly ask Lila to marry him here; he only agrees to ask. The difficult thing to say remains, strictly speaking, unspoken; he and Lila just talk about saying it sometime. This failure of language frames nearly all of Ames's most important conversations. When Jack Boughton comes to see him for counsel late in the novel, Ames worries that he won't know what to say. And when he does speak and offer Jack advice, his words cause partly (but not wholly) unintended hurt.

There is an important irony in Ames's inability to speak because he is a beautiful and practiced writer. The cadence and wisdom of his prose in this letter to his son is at times achingly lovely. And no wonder; Ames has spent his life writing. He has volumes of sermons, as many as Augustine (he calculates the pages and compares), all written out in longhand and stored in his attic. But once again, he's unsure of their worth. He tells his son that he sometimes plans to comb through the piles of notebooks to see whether one or two sermons might be worth saving for the boy to read one day. But he worries the writings will all seem boring or stupid to himself in the present, let alone to his someday-grown child, and therefore speculates they might better be burned than read. This too causes Ames anxiety, since he meant each one so sincerely and deeply upon their delivery, and now they mainly present a challenge for proper disposal. So much paper will cause a great fire, he writes. As he approaches death, he has become acutely aware of the limits of his own homiletical earnestness; he understands that these words remain in some way confined to the past in which they were written; and he knows that if he doesn't burn them himself, someone else will have to later. Indeed, as he admits to his son, this fiery fate might eventually be shared by the letter he hopes the boy is holding in his hands and reading, if it too hasn't already been consigned to fire (40).

Fifty years of solitary attention to his interior life has left Ames an eloquent writer and thoughtful pastor, eloquent and thoughtful enough to recognize how meaningful words can be in the moment of their utterance but also how fleeting and transient they can become once uttered. As he writes these words to his son, perhaps the most permanent words he can produce, his worries over their significance, over what they now mean and what they will mean later, over what control he has with any of it, pervade the epistle.

It's not only momentous or singularly strong emotion that occasions this failure of words for Ames, not only a life's work in words or a deep and fierce romantic love. Reflecting on this early in the novel, Ames recalls happening upon two working men in overalls taking a smoke break. They stop joking and laughing when they see Ames approaching. This causes Ames to reflect upon his role as a minister, because people so often and instinctually set him apart with their seriousness and politeness. He confesses to his son that a dying man could use a laugh, but he also knows that revealing his condition to these men wouldn't draw him into their joke; it would replace their laughter with awkward sympathy. Ames's guardedness is matched by another surprising intimacy that he must also acknowledge, because the same people who stop talking when they see him coming, he says, will sometimes reveal to him their deepest secrets of "malice and dread and guilt, and so much loneliness" in places he'd never expect to find it (6). What actually happens in this scene is quite simple: an old man walks by two younger men who are chuckling over a cigarette. But we have witness, through Ames's confessional, first-person narrative, to the rich inner language of Ames, to all those things he wishes he could have said but didn't actually say, to all the ways his words might have failed him had he tried. The malice and dread and guilt and crushing loneliness hiding under the surface of things that Ames names here is ironic, because the surface we are under in this novel is his. And there is, in fact, plenty of malice and dread and guilt and loneliness in Ames's life, where we don't expect to find it and of which Ames himself remains partly ignorant. It will take the whole novel and Ames's full and final confession to draw these things out of himself and into the narrative.

Gilead is a novel of forgiveness, as noted above, a retelling of the prodigal son in a twentieth-century, midwestern American context. But to read this book just as a letter from a father to a son, or as simply a novel of interpersonal forgiveness, would be to miss the deep undercurrents of sin, remorse, regret, and repentance coursing through the narrative. When Ames considers what to tell his son about himself, when he begins to tell his story, he also must tell his "begats": the story of his father and his grandfather, both preachers, and each one bitterly divided from the other over the right use of violence in the cause of abolition in the nineteenth century. Just as *The Buried Giant* is a novel as much about marriage as about war, *Gilead* is as much about American racism as it is about parenthood. When Ames tells his story, the youthful profligacy of Jack Boughton seems trivial and parochial before the national tragedies and traumas Ames's father and grandfather engaged in and argued over.

Ames's grandfather, also called John Ames, fought for abolition with John Brown in Kansas. The eldest Ames preached furiously against the evil of slavery, rightly proclaiming from the pulpit that as long as chattel slavery persisted, there could be no peace, only a war of the powerful against the captive (100–101). Almighty God's call for peace, he told his congregation, was a call to end the war already violently raging on the plantations of the United States. The quickest path to peace, he said, was not to avoid a war but to win the one already being waged and to do so with a force powerful enough to free the enslaved and eradicate the institution of slavery. He preached all this with a "gun in his belt," while his whole congregation, down to the littlest children, shouted and hollered their support (101). The gun was not just for show. At the least, we know that the eldest Ames once shot a soldier who was hunting John Brown. John Ames III recalls his grandfather often returning directly from battles in Kansas to stand in his pulpit and articulate his visions, his shirt still bloody from the wounds of his enemies and his comrades. Indeed, the town of Gilead itself, we're told, was founded as a place for abolitionists fighting in Kansas to retreat to and recover.

Ames's own father, however, though also a Christian minister, interpreted Jesus's teaching to require pacifism. He could not justify any violence and believed peace a principle unachievable through war. This moral and theological dispute between Ames's father and grandfather became a source of deep contention and resentment between the two ministers, and indeed for the whole family. The subject was so fraught they had to avoid it altogether, never speaking of the Kansas wars or the cause of abolition (85–86). The youngest Ames, our narrator, only knew his abolitionist grandfather once the fierce old man had already reached advanced age, after his stories of righteous warfare had come to inspire memories of struggle rather than struggle itself. But the emotion and anger of those years before and during the war linger in tangible ways for the family. Although Ames reflects that the family tolerated and respected the eldest Ames as a sort of a cranky, eccentric old man in his late age, they also knew his eccentricities hid deep feelings of anger and frustration at the family's respectful toleration of his prophetic zeal, and that the "tremors of his old age were in some part the tremors of pent grief" (34). For his own part, Ames's father was angry too at the accusation implied by Ames's grandfather's frustrated fervor. Ames recalls that the two men buried their differences in the spirit of Christian forgiveness, but they "buried them not very deeply . . . more as one would bank a fire than smother it" (34).

As in *The Buried Giant*, private forgiveness is public too. The wounds caused here between father and son are ones of public relevance. But the form of Christian forgiveness they commit to together amounts to a burial of differences rather than to any real reckoning with them—a forgiveness the shortcomings of which we have already encountered in *The Buried Giant*. The eldest Ames's prophetic fire still smolders, as does the elder Ames's resentment of it. Tellingly, crucially, for the purposes of this chapter, the argument between these two ministers, their fight that demands forgiving, is over when violence is justified, when retaliation is warranted. For Ames's grandfather, there is no peace while there is injustice, and so the call to peace is likewise a call to end injustice, with violence employed when and as necessary. For Ames's father, meanwhile, any retaliatory act is a betrayal of the gospel, and violence is never justified. Their dispute comes to an end in estrangement several years after the war, when a small fire is set behind the only African American church in Gilead. In response, Ames's father—now pastor of the Congregationalist church—preaches on Jesus's lines from the Sermon on the Mount that we consider the lilies and worry not for the morrow. Ames's grandfather storms out of church in the midst of the sermon. When he returns Sunday afternoon, the men sit in silent fury across from one another at the kitchen table. Ames's father asks if his sermon caused some offense, to which the old man witheringly replies that the words were too insubstantial to cause any offense. He tells his son that he had withdrawn to the Black church to "hear some *preaching*" (84). There too, though, he was disappointed, as the text for that preacher's sermon was "love your enemies." When Ames's father asks about this displeasure, the old man puts his head in his hands and confesses there are no words "bitter enough" for his disappointment, that he eats and drinks it, wakes and sleeps it (84). Barely suppressing his own emotion, the elder Ames responds that his father has been disappointed only because he wrongly placed his hopes in a war rather than in the peace that is "its own reward." The old man replies, "And that's just what kills my heart, Reverend" (84).

Ames's father and grandfather do not and cannot speak to each other. It's not just the endearing awkwardness we've seen in our narrator that confounds their speech. There are deeper divisions here. They cannot justify themselves one to another, they cannot give to one another an adequate account of the truth that is in each. Shortly after this formal confrontation, Ames's grandfather leaves the family and does not return. Only many years later do his son and grandson journey to Kansas to search for the old man's grave, a pilgrimage I consider later. But the prodigal estrangement and forgiveness readers so eagerly map onto Jack Boughton and John Ames is in fact foundational to the story of Ames's family over three generations. Ames the eldest and Ames the elder are absolutely estranged from each other too, even unto death. Later in the novel we also learn that our narrator's father eventually abandoned Christianity and encouraged his son to do the same, which is its own estrangement as well. The youngest Ames reflects that after the fire at the Black church in Gilead, the breach between eldest and elder widened irreparably. His grandfather's note of farewell was also a note of condemnation and judgment:

> No good has come, no evil is ended.
> That is your peace.
> Without vision the people perish.
> The Lord bless you and keep you. (85)

The ailing John Ames who narrates *Gilead* is a beloved character, a thoughtful and endearing old man. And as I've said several times now, themes of forgiveness resound throughout this book: forgiveness between father and son, between friend and enemy, between warrior and pacifist. But the most crucial forgiveness in the book, I think, is the one John Ames, our narrator, needs. Because when he is reflecting on the disagreement that divided his father and grandfather, he considers that however bad things became in the end, "All best forgotten," as his "father used to say" (76). Like his forebears, Ames believes burying the past is probably the best and the most effective form of forgiveness for his family and his country. In the end Ames decides that his father was right, that peace is its own justification and the past is best reckoned with by being buried. "And that's just as well, because people have forgotten" (76). The day has too many troubles unto itself to think much about Kansas anymore.

We've seen this before in Ishiguro's Britain and should therefore be alert to the risks of this sort of forgiving as they might arise in Gilead, Iowa. Forgetting—especially the forgetting of severe injustice—is not without moral significance, as I have been at pains to explain. Ames's forgetting, on my reading, is thus a profound moral failure, a failure that—as Ames will realize by novel's end—undergirds his whole life and ministry in ways he can neither undo nor escape, however thoughtful and endearing he has been.[4] But although these failures may not be undone, they can be confessed and lamented and mourned; their remembrance can set the ground for a different future. As I read it, this novel is a confession; or better, it is the process by which, in telling his story and having it told to him by others, John Ames finally lets go of forgetting and begins in his last days to remember who he really is and who he ought to have been. All of Ames's anxieties about what it means to give one's story to another, all his deliberations upon the justifications for violence, the moral value of retaliation, and the virtue of peace—all these complex issues merely frame the central drama of this book: John Ames's loss and recovery of memory and the personal, social, and political cost of that sinful forgetting. This book, in the end, is a missive of repentance, and what's more, I believe that the answer to the moral dilemma between Ames's father and grandfather can be most meaningfully considered (if never finally resolved) through the confessional dynamics of memory and responsibility that Ames has so long avoided. In other words, the problem of justifying violence—this dispute between Christian abolitionist uprising and Christian pacifist nonviolence, between retaliation and restraint—can be most meaningfully understood in light of a model of moral accountability that depends on confession and repentance. And so, before returning to Ames and his slow process of coming to memory and grieving his own failures, I turn to Michel Foucault to think a bit further about confession. Following on Foucault, I reflect with Judith Butler on how the structure of our stories can provide a new moral foundation for our ethics, as well as show how this foundation can support a sound forgiveness, even as it scaffolds a necessary grief.

GIVING AN ACCOUNT

Martha Nussbaum argues forcefully in her recent book *Anger and Forgiveness* that a conditional forgiveness, one offered in exchange for apology, contrition, repentance, and atonement, merely replicates the retributive logic of punishment under the cover of a morally sanctified form. Christianity, in what she recognizes as a prominent strand, "juxtaposes an ethic of forgiveness with an ethic of spectacular retribution." For Nussbaum, when forgiveness is offered in trade for penance or penitence, the "forgiveness process itself is violent toward the self. Forgiveness is an elusive and usually quite temporary prize held out at the end of a traumatic and profoundly intrusive process of self-denigration."[5] A forgiveness offered (even obligated) in exchange for contrition and penance is "itself a harsh inquisitorial process," demanding "weeping and wailing, and a sense of one's lowness and essential worthlessness." In a forgiveness such as this, particularly as Nussbaum reads it in its Christian form, the forgiving victim is encouraged "to enjoy the spectacle of this groveling as an intrinsically valuable part of the forgiveness process."[6] This is an important and telling analysis. What Nussbaum argues quite convincingly is that the function of both retribution and repentance is the same: not only to diminish, through social or physical suffering, the status of the offender so that the victim's abuse can be upended, but also to stir enjoyment in the victim, to meet that one's resentment with the pleasure of witnessing the offender's suffering. This is Murphy and Solomon's endorsement of vengeance recapitulated and recast through the manners of penitential practice. In other words, conventional habits of penitence and forgiveness and retaliatory acts of vengeance and retribution follow precisely the same logic; they are, in effect, simply different versions of the same thing. They are payback, to use Nussbaum's word: compensating punishments for irrevocable loss.

But there is another and important dimension to such self-denigrating practices of repentance, one Nussbaum glosses in her text but that Michel Foucault deeply engages in his lectures at the Collège de France from 1980.[7] Foucault demonstrates how practices of Christian confession prioritize authenticity and signal that authenticity through the verbal expression of an interior experience. More than just spectacular self-abasement, repentance and reconciliation first of all demand confession; they require penitents to put their repentance into words, to make their affective experience of penitence legible and audible to an audience, and therefore to submit their interior experience to the governing norms of the confessor or the community. Foucault shows how Christianity, in its origins, imposes on "individuals the obligation to manifest in truth what they are," not simply as a habit of interior self-reflection but also as an outward practice of revelation either to a confessor or to a confessing community. What's more, he continues, this self-revelation is made with "a view to extinguishing a certain debt arising from evil and in this way redeeming the chastisements earned by this evil and promised as punishment."[8] For early Christian thought, apology is itself a form of compensation; it serves to extinguish a debt and obviate the need for punishment. But what is most important about the apology on Foucault's account is that it must be sincere, and its sincerity must be easily recognizable to the community. Moreover, it is the confessing community or the confessor who shall determine what sincerities count as recognizable. Reading Tertullian's De Paenitentiae, Foucault observes how thoroughly an economic metaphor once again operates in determining the legitimacy of a confession, but not one based flatly on transaction. What is at stake in the penitence is its probation, that it be proved. What is required is to "know whether the repentance is good money, not inauthentic, not hypocritical, but indeed true." In this form of the economic metaphor, repentance exposes to "God's sight the truth of the sinner himself, the sincerity of his feelings, the authenticity of his remorse, the reality of his intention not to sin again."[9] This interior state can be only outwardly performed; it cannot be manifestly revealed. Foucault makes clear that the interiority of the subject remains forever hidden. All we have are external signs that have been culturally agreed upon as good currency for our interior experience. The metaphor of currency is crucial here, and Foucault traces out its implications. For Tertullian and other early Christians, repentance "must be a sort of coin, not by which redemption is purchased exactly, but which serves to be put to a test, the one receiving it (in the event, God) thereby being able to verify that the metal, the coin that one offers is indeed authentic."[10]

In truth, sincerity is never knowable; authenticity is conveyed, like any other interiority, through signs and norms of behavior. What counts, what has currency, is that penitents are willing to trade in the accepted penitential symbols, since their interior experience will always remain hidden. The debt metaphor has shifted slightly here, from pain as a form of payment to penitence or remorsefulness as a valid currency, one a confessor or an offended party is obliged to accept. But again, like currency, the coinage we trade is at best a stand-in for value; it is a sign of our agreement that those certain signs will count as currency. As such, a "whole series of acts and procedures" arise in Christianity, through varieties of self-mortification that seek to externalize on the flesh an inwardly spiritual suffering, that are "explicitly intended to invite, exhort, or constrain the person doing penance to show his own truth."[11] In other words, inward turmoil is proved by outward pain. Penance must therefore be "a laborious proof, a laborious probation."[12] The more one is willing to suffer, the more sincere one's repentance probably is. Authentic inward repentance is a secret; our publicly embodied proofs must therefore speak boldly and with conviction.

Foucault is careful to show Tertullian engaging multiple different acts and meanings of repentance. Repentance—from the Greek *metanoia*, literally a turning away or from, and indicating in the Greek something like transformation or change—is only truly brought about for Tertullian by God in baptism. But a number of other ritual activities come under the same Latin name in Tertullian's treatise, and toward various purposes. Truest repentance, this baptismal *metanoia*, for example, must be preceded by a repentance that better resembles the affective experience of what we in the modern West associate with repentance: regret, shame, and the desire to atone. So there is for Tertullian an inward personal repentance that precedes God's gracious and redemptive act. There is also the knotty problem of what sort of penitence should be required if one sins after baptism—that is, after God's full *metanoia* has been accomplished—and it is under these circumstances that Tertullian exhorts his reader outwardly to manifest the inward truth of repentance through public acts of self-mortification, in a set of ritual actions he describes using the Greek term *exomologesis*, literally a speaking out. Crucially, however, these outward acts are not necessary because they deliver information of which God is ignorant. It's not as if our interiorities could be as mysterious to God as they are to other humans. In the case of an omniscient God who sees in secret, confession serves a different purpose. By "confession satisfaction is settled, of confession repentance is born; by repentance God is appeased."[13] Note here how once again compensation is introduced as the foundation for reconciling penitence. But what must be satisfied is not God's knowledge; unlike limited humans, God always already knows a penitent's interior sincerity without the need for outward signs. It is therefore the performance of this confession itself that appeases or satisfies God's desire. God, who knows and sees all, has no need of a probative act. This suffering serves some other need or want. We might ask what desire of God is thus satisfied by these public acts, according to Tertullian. If for the gathered community they are signs of certainty, a currency of probative knowledge, then for an omniscient God they must satisfy some other desire.

When I return to *Gilead* later in the chapter, I posit my own understanding of God's desire. Tertullian, meanwhile, seems to suggest that what God desires is suffering itself, that "temporal mortification" may "stand in the stead of God's anger" and "expunge eternal punishments."[14] A curious transitive logic thus operates in Tertullian: internal human affect is externalized as physical suffering, which in turn addresses and answers God's affective wrath. Thus an interesting distinction also arises for Tertullian, whose model of divine appeasement looks not unlike the framework Nussbaum questions. For the church, mortification is a valid sign; for God, it is a temporal propitiation. But still, it is not quite the case that pain pays directly for sin. In fact, it's not even clear that the penitential acts directly or purely express an internal experience. Perhaps instead or also it is that they occasion and enjoin repentance in the penitent. Acts of fasting, weeping, prayer, and severe treatment, Tertullian says, should be undertaken with the goal of "enjoining a demeanor calculated to move mercy. . . . All this *exomologesis* does, that it may enhance repentance."[15] Painful punishment does not simply undo wrong. What appeases God is the demeanor of penitence in the penitent, which temporal mortification either occasions or expresses. Again, the fuzzy borders of Tertullian's repentance do significant semantic work here. In this passage he clearly means that God's wrath is quelled by humble acts. But, following the slippery sense of repentance running throughout his text—Tertullian's tendency to signify (when he speaks of *penitentia*) not only God's singular act of baptismal redemption but also the human experience of sincere regret—this passage also implies the possibility that in undertaking outward acts of self-discipline the penitent will come inwardly to experience repentance more deeply. In either case, what Foucault shows is tellingly true: suffering functions as a currency in Christian penal acts, not only as compensation for crime, but also as assurance against counterfeit affect. Suffering becomes the means by which we prove we are sincerely penitent, or barring that, it is the rough means by which we try to prompt a real repentance in wrongdoers.[16]

Our interior experience must be made legible to others, and others usually decide which signs we will be allowed to use in proving the good currency of our payment. If penitential pain is a currency, it is not necessarily because pain directly compensates for loss, but because it has been accepted on understood terms, because it arrives as surety of a hidden but mutually agreed upon value. This is what the monks are attempting in Ishiguro's novel. They are hoping that their wounds will demonstrate to God the depth of their remorse. Wistan sees how thin this theological thinking is: if there is a God, God already knows. And these wounds will not bring back the dead. So, since the penance is secret, it in fact conveys nothing to anyone. The legibility of interiority Foucault diagnoses here has far-reaching implications, beyond just the scenario of ecclesial penitence. Foucault's insight that we must translate ourselves into words others are willing or able to recognize can serve as the beginning of a critique of certain modern Western approaches to morals, as well as provide the foundation for an alternative account. How we give an account (the financial metaphors surface inevitably again) of ourselves, and how we respond to others' accounts, can lead us to rethink our understanding of accountability and responsibility. Judith Butler does this, to extensive and persuasive effect, in their 2005 book *Giving an Account of Oneself*.[17]

Butler's starting point is an Arendtian one. They take for granted the intersubjective sociality under which Arendt theorized action. Human subjectivity arises in relationship because we are what we do, and what we do carries meaning because it occurs in the plural, public space of appearance. The meaning of that appearance, therefore, is unstable; those to whom we appear have some say in who we are and what our being means. This is both a constraint and a freedom for Arendt, as I elaborated in my reflections on sovereignty in Chapter 1. Although it is true that no human being can be unrelated to any other, that the space of human appearance always requires relation, the public nature of action also affords humans the opportunity always to begin again, as in the case of Arendt's forgiveness. Butler accepts much of this account, but they are also concerned to expose additional fetters and constraints within Arendt's intersubjective space. While it is true that our appearing and our acting mean that our selves become relatable to and by others, that others can give an account of who we are, Foucault's insights complicate an Arendtian analysis. If part of the aim of *exomologesis* and confession is to render the sincere or authentic self visible and legible to others, then it will also be the case that the account we give of ourselves will always be subject to what others are able to read or willing to recognize. Any story we might tell of ourselves must be told in the form others are either inclined or competent to receive. And in the modern West, we are particularly enamored of simple, straightforward, bounded, fully coherent stories. We like fully self-transparent heroes and indisputably happy endings. Butler wants us to consider how these narrative expectations structure our ethical reasoning, because to "hold a person accountable" for their actions or their life in a "narrative form" may "require a falsification of that life in order" to fit the narrative standards of the story we expect to hear. We may end up privileging a "certain kind of ethics, one that tends to break with relationality" (Butler, *Giving an Account*, 63). In our need for narrative coherence, for heroes and happy endings, it may be that we appreciate only those moral accounts that conform to the stories we expect. In other words, if our ethics presumes a certain sort of individuality, a particularly discrete and bounded subject, then the stories that our morals will accept will need to satisfy those narrative demands. And in doing so, we will be asserting an aesthetic or narrative, rather than a moral, value to our practices of accountability. In requiring that others justify themselves by their stories, we ask them to be "coherent autobiographer[s]" and privilege "the seamlessness of the story to something we might tentatively call the truth of the person." Because the truth of any person, Butler continues, "might well become more clear in moments of interruption, stoppage, open-endedness—in enigmatic articulations that cannot easily be translated into narrative form" (64).

Butler argues that a certain approach to narrative ethics, one rooted in the Aristotelian tradition of virtues and also in Aristotelian dramatic theories of unity and coherence, demands of people a narrative coherence and a subjective transparency that are simply untenable, or at least merely performed.[18] This, in the West, is the standard model of moral accountability, a notion closely related to the sovereignty Arendt has criticized: that bounded, discrete, unimplicated individuality can assume credit and blame singly and without any of the messiness of relation, interdependence, or collectivity. As with sovereignty, as Derrida shows, a founding violence accompanies the imposition of this individuality, since every person must be forced to fit into a dramatic unity we have already been conditioned to recognize and receive as accountable. Indeed, calling an individual morally accountable typically and simply means that they are the sort of expressive subject who can tell a certain story. If they cannot tell that story, or if the truth of them fails to fit the aesthetic or narrative contours we expect, they risk being judged by their hearers as irrational or immoral.

Indeed, this notion of accountability is an expansion of Foucault on repentance: repentance is not internally sincere unless performed and externalized as appreciable self-mortification. Butler grasps the danger in this and argues that "if, in the name of ethics, we (violently) require that another do a certain violence to herself . . . by offering a narrative account or issuing a confession," then perhaps we might also encourage or spur a "certain practice of nonviolence" if we do the opposite and allow interruption and incoherence instead (Butler, *Giving an Account*, 64). If violence is "the act by which a subject seeks to reinstall its mastery and unity, then nonviolence may well follow" if we instead encourage a resistance to the illusions of self-mastery and bounded unity that our narrative frameworks of accountability require (64). Rather than regarding each individual as a single story, the telling of which might require coercion, Butler wants to open a public space whereby stories can be offered, interrupted, contradicted, edited, amended. That Butler has introduced the notion of nonviolence here is crucial, and will merit further examination below, especially in light of the ethical argument among the generations of John Ames. For now I only stress the narrative stakes of Butler's argument. The account we tell of ourselves is always incomplete; not only does it require completion in a death we can never narrate, but others will also always be available to tell our lives differently from the way we have. This makes the self essentially unfinishable and to some degree unknowable to itself. But is "the task" of moral life, Butler asks, fully and finally "to know oneself? Is the final aim to achieve an adequate narrative account of a life? And should it be?" Butler worries that the urge to force a narrative coherence upon our accountability will "cover over . . . the breakage, the rupture, that is constitutive of the 'I'" (69). Indeed, we can recognize how a moral compulsion to narrative cohesion such as this will invite all the problems of sovereignty Derrida has lamented and Arendt describes. It will create the impression among moral subjects that a self-possessed coherence could be "perfectly possible, as if the break could be mended and defensive mastery restored" (69). If a sense of the self is lost on this account, then it will be the loss only of a "certain kind of subject, one that was never possible to begin with," one that depended on "a fantasy of impossible mastery, and so a loss of what one never had." In other words, Butler concludes, it will occasion "a necessary grief" (65). Something is lost, but it is only an illusion, the same illusion of sovereign self-mastery that Arendt has already revealed.

Giving an account of oneself—this alternative sort of narrative confession—is not for Butler a performative act of compensation. It does not balance our moral books. Neither is it the coin that proves our sincerity. Rather, confession in this case exposes our limits, it reveals our intersubjective relations to others. It articulates all the unpredictability and irreversibility of our actions. In other words, the sort of sovereign mastery that Arendt resists Butler also recognizes as potentially at play in our notions of moral accountability. But just as there remains a freedom available to humans once we have been unfettered from a singular sort of sovereignty, there is also a model for morals still standing once accountability has been shaken loose from individuality. There remains a way to give an account that can accommodate the breakages and ruptures of which we are existentially constituted. We can keep telling stories, even if the heroes trip on their capes and the endings aren't always happy. And as Arendt has already suggested, this framework for moral accountability will have to truck much more in acts like promise and forgiveness than in any retributive balancing or compensatory misapprehensions.

Butler understands the stakes here and recognizes that the incoherence of subjects and their opacity to themselves will close some ethical avenues. As they argue, the "way in which we are, from the start, interrupted by alterity" will "render us incapable of offering narrative closure for our lives" (Butler, *Giving an Account*, 64). Because of this, we cannot coherently narrate our own *telos*. But this commitment to articulating our own interruption, to a subjectivity that is neither discrete nor undivided, can reveal to us our basic relationality, how we are "implicated, beholden, derived, sustained by a social world that is beyond us and before us" (64). Giving an account of ourselves is not a moral test by which we package ourselves neatly in the cleanest and most efficient available means. On the contrary, the offering of our account can be a gesture not of mastery but of vulnerability. We can offer ourselves as incomplete, unknown and unknowable, subject to judgment. Giving an account of ourselves in this way will mean telling fragmented stories of breakage and rupture rather than well-crafted tales of fully formed selves (69). And despite our learned moral intuitions, perhaps these ruptured, inconsistent, even incoherent accounts can provide the foundation for better ideas and practices of accountability than the bounded, discrete, and sovereign subjectivity that Arendt has undermined. Because I can "never provide the account of myself that . . . certain forms of morality" demand, because I cannot really "deliver [my]self in coherent narrative forms," a different ethic of accountability arises. The self itself comes to be understood as the founding "moment of failure in every narrative effort to give an account of oneself." However tidily our stories are told, the self remains the ever inexpressible "failure that the very project of self-narration requires. Every effort to give an account of oneself is bound to encounter this failure, and to founder upon it" (79).

Failure is the foundation self-narration requires. Indeed, failure founds selfhood. This cannot be overstated, especially in a book that aims to articulate a useful notion of forgiveness. What Butler demonstrates is that forgiveness is not just an Arendtian instrument used to manage the human problem of irreversible action. Any sense of self is at once relational and also incomplete, incoherent, misguided, and finite; therefore, the manner in which we relate to one another—that is, both how we share our stories with others and how we remain bound to others—will have to accommodate incompletion, incoherence, flaw, and finitude. Accountability begins in failure, so our relations must be forgiving. To be clear, Butler isn't trying to moralize this fundamental failure and finitude as itself an ethical shortcoming. It's simply the state we're ineluctably in, and so our moral relations with one another should reckon with it. This is the crucial point, the one that relates all this critical reframing of accountability to a discussion of forgiveness, and to my thinking about three generations of men named John Ames, their moral lives and arguments, and the sins they have committed, whether they acknowledge them or not. What would it mean to structure accountability not upon the self-mastery that is always already assumed of us, but instead upon the failure that is fundamentally constitutive of who we always are? For Butler, the "very meaning of responsibility" must be reestablished upon these limits. Moral responsibility cannot presume a subject that is "fully transparent to itself." Taking "responsibility for oneself" means avowing "the limits of any self-understanding" and assuming these limits as the basic "predicament of the human community" (83). Once again, this is not to say that every moment of incompletion or lack of self-transparency is an evil corruption or a sinful failing. What Butler is trying to describe are the limits of human finitude in moral relations, and a moral posture that acknowledges and grapples with those limits. These founding limitations and failures do not therefore give the self leave to ignore moral obligations. The fact that we cannot fully account for ourselves does not lessen our obligations to others. On the contrary, since "we are formed" in a web of relations that is always at least partially irretrievable to us, since we come to being "in relations of dependency," we are *more* obligated to others precisely because we are inextricably related to and dependent upon them (20). We are not Nietzsche's solitary sovereign, indifferent to or scornful of others. We are Arendt's interdependent agents. Again, the illusory sovereign needs no one, and his obligations are only to himself. But dependent creatures, like human beings, must begin their accounts from a sense of accountability. The account we give of ourselves, including our narratives of confession or penitence, are incomplete until they are both offered and spoken back to us. We must say who we think we might be while leaving others to tell us who we are. The

moralized language of confession, Foucault's authentic self expressed to con-
fessors or congregation through penance, does not in fact ground us in ourselves or deliver a transparent subject for examination. Rather, it grounds us in
others, and *that* is its primary ethical relevance. It is a grounding to which we
are vulnerable, which—as Foucault and Butler both acknowledge—can be
abused, and it's no wonder, as Arendt observes, that we are inclined to retreat
toward a theorized individual sovereignty as our safe haven. Nonetheless, interdependence is our actual state, and so it is where our ethics have their true
beginning, and where our ethical reflections ought to begin as well. If I "become dispossessed in the telling," then "an ethical claim takes hold" in that
dispossession "since no 'I' belongs to itself" (Butler, *Giving an Account*, 132).
One might therefore sensibly wonder how moral accountability could be rea-
soned from the ineluctable incoherence of our individual accounts. Butler's
argument is that those forms of moral inquiry that assume a self-grounding
subject inevitably lead to narcissism. They ground an "ethical violence that
knows no grace of self-acceptance or forgiveness," and we are thus obliged as
moral agents to turn away from narcissism and toward new forms of sociality
and morality that require and assume new habits of grace and forgiveness
(135–36).

In other words, an ethics of individual sovereignty, of narrative narcissism—
including a transactional economy of confession, repentance, and forgiveness
structured upon such "socially enforced modes of individualism"—would
be unable to realize or even to recognize the "grace of self-acceptance or
forgiveness," since it would deny the vulnerability and limitation that structures
our subjectivity and undermines those narcissistic modes. In giving an account
of ourselves with an awareness that our self-projecting subjects are already
founded on what we cannot say, we can begin to recognize how an act of
forgiveness, which unsettles self-mastery and all its ethical assumptions,
might subject us to untold risk and uncertainty but also free us toward a relationally realized selfhood. To "be undone by another is a primary necessity,"
Butler writes, "an anguish" but also "a chance." It is a chance to be pulled
into relationship with that which is "not me," which is also an opportunity
"to be moved, to be prompted to act," and to escape the illusion of full self-
possession. When we give our account from this position and this place,
Butler concludes, "we will not be irresponsible, or, if we are, we will surely be
forgiven" (136).

These are among the final lines of Butler's book. What strikes me about
this stirring conclusion is its deliberately affective frame. Human being,

human relation, is both an anguish and a chance. To be vulnerable to another is both our undoing and our freedom—if we are lucky enough to be supported in our vulnerability and forgiven when we cause offense. And though they do not explicitly return to the language of forgiveness elsewhere in their body of work, Butler continues theorizing the self's undoing and its dispossession in their writings on nonviolence and grief.

JUSTIFYING VIOLENCE

I began this book asserting that forgiveness is a way to respond to wrongdoing. The Butlerian model of accountability I've just outlined suggests its own response to wrongdoing. Or better, it suggests a way to reflect on our responses to wrongdoing and casts the argument between Ames the abolitionist and Ames the pacifist in a new light. I've suggested so far in this book that I regard forgiveness as a practice of mourning, a reckoning with a world gone wrong and a past that cannot be remade to our will. It is what an accountability that refuses violent retaliation looks like. Butler's extension of their ethical arguments into their theorizations of nonviolence are basic to my own articulation. Although their analysis in *Giving an Account of Oneself* remains in the somewhat rarefied space of theorized subjectivity, the bodily implications are clear and they make them explicit in other writings. As Butler argues in their book *Precarious Life: The Powers of Mourning and Violence*, our political position and identities are founded upon the social vulnerability of our bodies.[19] Because we are both "attached to others" and "at risk of losing those attachments," because we are both exposed to others and "at risk of violence by virtue of that exposure," vulnerability and loss necessarily follow (Butler, *Precarious Life*, 20). Dispossession here is not regarded as both an anguish and a freedom, as above; Butler is starker about the consequences of our various and diverse vulnerabilities and the physical and social consequences of those vulnerabilities we do not choose. However, Butler does not regard this exposure as something only to flee from or to fortify with the well-built Western ramparts of narcissism and sovereignty. Rather, they imagine that our recognition of this vulnerability and relationality might reframe our relationship to community. Their insistence on the frailty and incoherence of the individual should not imply a critique of self-autonomy. On the contrary, they argue that the struggle for autonomy should be grounded in the understanding that we are "by definition, physically dependent on one another, physically vulnerable to one another" (27). What can emerge from this is a new way of imagining community, one in which what we hold in common is the uniqueness of our bodily and personal vulnerabilities. What we share is the fact of this condition and the awareness that it must take a distinctly situated shape in and for each person, so that we have "in common a condition that cannot be thought without difference" (27). The imagination of a community of mutual dependence and vulnerability is articulated by Butler through grief.

It is in mourning, Butler asserts, that the degree to which we are dispossessed of ourselves through others is most fully revealed. This is also true of desire and love, but Butler sees desire and grief as co-constitutive. When I grieve, Butler writes, my attachment to you is part of who I am, and so it is not "as if an 'I' exists independently over here and then simply loses a 'you' over there"; rather, if I lose you I lose a part of myself too. In mourning I become "inscrutable to myself" (22). Echoing my reading of Derrida in Chapter 1, Butler questions the possibility of a rehabilitative or recuperative mourning. A "successful" mourning would be one that reckons with the irrecuperable. One fully "mourns when one accepts that by the loss one undergoes one will be changed, possibly forever. Perhaps mourning has to do with agreeing to undergo a transformation . . . that full result of which one cannot know in advance" (21). Mourning here echoes exactly the ethical incoherence for which Butler has advocated in *Giving an Account of Oneself*; loss is not a problem to be solved in order that the self be restored to some unified Aristotelian wholeness. Rather, it is a dispossession and a transformation the stakes of which we cannot predict, intend, or plan in advance. When "grieving is something to be feared," when it is a threat to our coherent, discrete, undivided, and sovereign self, then our fear spurs us to quash that threat quickly, to "banish it" through actions aimed at restoring our loss or returning the world to its former order, or perhaps to the "fantasy that the world formerly was orderly" (*Precarious Life*, 30). We trust an illusion of compensation to cover a loss we cannot bear. The sovereign self threatened with undoing by grief may act impulsively or violently to set the world right, even if that righted world is a mere fantasy. And because that sovereign insists on being unimplicated and invulnerable to others, those others often become the objects of that sovereign self's impulsive actions.

The political and moral consequences to all this are emerging. If grief is about reckoning with our fundamental self-dispossession, it can never be entirely private, however interior and intense it arises as an affective experience. Though people might believe grieving to be fundamentally interior and

individual, or that the solitary nature of any personal grief will render it therefore apolitical or "depoliticizing," Butler argues that grief can instead furnish
"a sense of political community . . . by bringing to the fore the relational ties"
that bind us to one another in the basic facts of our "fundamental dependency and ethical responsibility" (22). *I* don't just grieve; I grieve for *you*, and
so in that act, relationship and responsibility are both already implied and set
some ground for community. Since grief reveals that "my fate is not originally
or finally separate from yours," it also shows that in denying the relational
nature of the self we also deny "something fundamental about the social
conditions of our very formation" (22–23).

Crucially, these relationalities do not just traverse the dependencies and
responsibilities we want them to. Grief gives rise to a complex form of community that will not only frustrate the bounds of our individuality but also
cross the more obvious lines of our affinity. If we are, from "the start and by
virtue of being a bodily being, already . . . implicated in lives that are not our
own," then the lives we spare cannot only be our own either, nor just the ones
we can most easily imagine ourselves alongside (28). A political practice of
grief would expand solidarities while avoiding any rush to facile resolution. It
would reckon grief—our own undoing by the loss of the other—as constitutive of ourselves as moral agents. Butler insists that there is "something to be
gained from . . . tarrying with grief," that in exposing ourselves to its unbear-
ability and rejecting any fantasy of grief's resolution through violence, we
might arrive at a new ethical posture if not a set of new ethical practices (30).
Meanwhile, to deny our own vulnerability or the intractability of grief is not
only to "make ourselves secure at the expense of every other human consideration," but it is to eliminate an important moral resource "from which we
must take our bearings and find our way" (30). These arguments from Butler
seek to discourage violence. But they also frame how Butler is thinking about
the moral contours of what they here and elsewhere call nonviolence. For
Butler, whatever nonviolence is or ought to be, it must not be arrogated into
the narcissism of virtuous or virtuosic moral individualism. The choice to
refrain from violent retaliation cannot assert, either triumphally or resolutely,
that nonviolence is the way one gains control and achieves moral self-mastery.
On the contrary, if constitutively established on grief, nonviolence will be
"neither a virtue nor a position," nor a "set of principles that are to be applied
universally."[20] Rather, a grief-stricken nonviolence would signify the "conflicted position of a subject who is injured, rageful," and "disposed to violent
retribution" but who nonetheless resists the retributive act.[21] Nonviolence is

therefore affectively complex, not placid and pacific. It is not an expression of self-mastery; it is a thoroughgoing performance of dispossession and loss. It may be and likely is inclined toward a violence against which it simultaneously struggles, and it declines to retaliate—despite itself even—because it recognizes that the social conditions of its own formation depend on the other, even on the enemy. The inclination toward violence is not therefore self-justifying. Thus it is important morally to distinguish between the injured and rageful person who legitimizes retaliatory acts and therefore "transmut[es] aggression into virtue," and the injured and rageful person who "nevertheless seeks to limit the injury that she or he causes . . . through an active struggle with and against aggression."[22] Whether the subject chooses violent retaliation or not, she is injured and rageful. I have more to say about anger and rage in Chapter 3. For now I simply ask what the stakes of this choice are. How does one decide whether to transmute injurious conduct into virtue or to struggle against it?

Gilead is a novel of estrangement between fathers and sons, but its founding estrangement arises out of an argument over whether and when violence is justified, whether aggression or the violent struggle against it is virtuous. Is it morally right to kill in the defense of justice, or morally right to refuse to kill despite the violence of injustice? This is the question that divides John Ames I from John Ames II. Reading *Gilead* with Butler suggests that the Ameses' argument itself misreads the basic nature of human moral accountability because it seeks to ground justification on an isolated subjectivity. It aspires to self-mastery and virtue on both sides, when it ought instead to be attending to dispossession and loss. Recall again these old white men arguing over their Sunday supper, each too convinced of his own righteousness to countenance any criticism. The ethics Butler recommends here resembles neither John Ames I's violent abolitionism nor John Ames II's pacifist quietism. Butler's nonviolence is first of all a critique of individualism as a moral frame for accountability. It does not first recommend a choice between two moral options, that is, whether to do violence to another or not. Instead, it begins from a basic commitment to the interrelatedness of each self to other selves. And this basic commitment limits the moral options for any subject engaged in ethical deliberation over violent action. Even in cases of self-defense, Butler argues, if one begins from an intersubjective position, one cannot conceive of a violence done to our enemy that will not also redound to ourselves. According to Butler, as they write in their recent book *The Force of Nonviolence*, a violence that justifies itself for reasons of self-defense presumes to know "in advance what the 'self' is, who has the right to have one, and where its boundaries lie."²³ But if instead we conceive of the self as relational, then we set ourselves the challenge of determining where the limits of the self are, and who among those surrounding me and partially constituting who I am can be understood as sufficiently other to be made appropriate objects of my violent acts. A self that "cannot be conceived" without others frustrates any facile attempt to demarcate where that "singular self" will "start and end." Butler's argument against violence thus not only implies "a critique of individualism," it also encourages "an elaboration of those social bonds or relations that require nonviolence" (Butler, *Force of Nonviolence*, 15). Thus Butler's nonviolence presumes not only that individuals should not do violence to other individuals, but that individuals are never isolated, that they exist in social relations that necessarily bind them always to others, and so the choice to resist or succumb to aggression is never a solitary one. And since for Butler as for Arendt each self is always implicated in other selves, including the ones against whom violence may be contemplated, "an ethics of nonviolence cannot be predicated on individualism" or on an ethics of individual moral purity and virtuous self-mastery; rather, its foundations are social and it must therefore levy a critique of individualism "as the basis of ethics and politics alike" (9). In other words, two old men arguing in Iowa over whose morals are more theologically pure merely reinforces the religious assumption that either one might prove himself pure in isolation from the other. The Ameses' desire to justify themselves only further isolates them in their moral choices from the primary relations that constitute them. Rather than asserting their respective rectitude to one another, what these two white men need most of all is the courage to begin and end their moral accounts in repentance rather than in righteousness. What they need is to confess where and how they have fallen short, and to let go of the sense of individual self-righteousness that has come to undergird each of them in their pride.

This is all to say that, for Butler, violence is not a dilemma to be solved by nonviolence. Rather, nonviolence is a way of approaching the irresolvable human dilemma of violence. *The Force of Nonviolence* takes as a starting point Walter Benjamin's challenging essay "The Critique of Violence," in which Benjamin argues for a persistence to violence in human relations, stating that "a totally nonviolent resolution of conflicts can never lead to a legal contract."²⁴ However peacefully a truce has been established, it "confers on both parties the right to take recourse to violence in some form against the other, should he break the agreement."²⁵ The echoes of law and sovereignty that arose in Chapter 1 here emerge once again. Violence haunts the law, even a law entirely committed to peace. But Benjamin, and Butler following him, allows for another, less legalistic or programmatic opportunity to arise beyond the law. If law serves as a framework through which we reflect upon particular acts of violence as either justified or not in the pursuit of given ends, then the law will also establish the "justificatory schemes and naming practices" for what counts as violence and when it is justified (Butler, *Force of Nonviolence*, 124). Justification sets the rules for itself, and the rules are mired in violence. Legal, moral, cultural, and religious frameworks decide not just which violent acts are justified, but also which acts even count as violent. So instead of seeking only to determine when violence is justified, Benjamin and Butler want us to complicate that question, or investigate the problem of justification more deeply. Rather than just asking when a moral end should justify some violent means, we ought instead to wonder why we rely upon an instrumentalist means/ends distinction to provide the grounds for our justification (Butler, 18). Because, in fact, "the actualization of violence as a means can inadvertently become its own end, producing new violence, producing violence anew, reiterating the license, and licensing new violence" (Butler, 18). Butler's language here is dense, but they are describing the retaliatory expansion Arendt has already pondered. As Arendt observes, there is a relentless creep of justification where violence is concerned. Violence "does not exhaust itself in the realization of a just end" (Butler, 20). Even if the end is achieved, violence spreads, its tendrils touching others and innocents in a way that can be neither counted nor countenanced. And those other violences, having been done, will give rise to new worthy ends that will call forth violence as their best means. Reciprocity and retaliation never end; the violent license replicates itself and expands. When we reflect upon violence only as either justified or not in the service of some other goal, Butler and Benjamin wonder whether that justificatory framework itself might be determining "the phenomenon of violence in advance" (Butler, 18).

But what if there were no possibility of full justification? What if being accountable meant exposing our limits rather than justifying our actions? What if we allowed ourselves to begin in failure, to reckon with the incommensurability of our lives to law? What if our relationship to the law was not one of corroborating and confirming our own decisions, but of inviting us out of our narrow moral choices into a more demanding and (perhaps) impossible form of responsibility?[26] For his part, Benjamin introduces in his critique the challenging concept of divine violence as a way of condemning

justificatory schemes. Divine violence is a much discussed and difficult concept, opaque in its design and its intention perhaps. But it seems at least in
part that Benjamin's concept of divine violence "operates not by the destruction of bodies but by the destruction of the systems of law or ethics that declare an action right or wrong."[27] Divine violence "does not legitimate new
laws. It does not even legitimate new ethics that could . . . *become* laws.
Rather, it insists on the limits of law. It reveals again the limits of ethics."[28]
Take, for example, the prohibition against killing from the Hebrew Bible.
According to Benjamin, the question "May I kill?" has its straightforward and
irreducible answer in the commandment "Thou shalt not kill." But because
this commandment precedes the deed, it "becomes inapplicable, incommen-
surable once the deed is accomplished."[29] In other words, the existence of the
injunction before the act does not necessarily provide a ground for judgment
of it afterwards. The determinations of divine judgment can be neither derived from the commandment nor known by it in advance. Those who "base
a condemnation of all violent killing" on the existence of the commandment
are therefore, according to Benjamin, mistaken. The commandment "exists
not as a criterion of judgment" but instead as a guide for "persons or communities who have to wrestle with it" and in some cases accept the responsibility of ignoring, betraying, or transgressing it.[30]

We cannot—God does not—simply hold our deed up to a command and
then determine ourselves true to it or not. Judgment is not so straightforward.
What we have is the command and our action and the incommensurability
of one to the other. Like Gillian Rose's Arthur or Arendt's agent, we cannot
right the world or make ourselves self-grounding in our action. We can only
act and hope for forgiveness. Far from providing us a standard by which to
adjudge the actions of others, let alone an opportunity to legitimate our own,
Benjamin's notion of divine violence renews an occasion "for responsibility. It
breaks the binding obligations of an order that lets a person evade responsibility by saying, 'I am just following the law.'"[31] What Benjamin's divine violence
makes possible, even paradoxically coerces, is free action. We cannot morally
hide behind the frameworks of our justification. Like Arendt's agent who
must accept the consequences that her actions initiate, we also must act
knowing that divine violence "demands responsibility."[32] It calls for us to act
on behalf of the good, even where and when we must in some manner fail.
And in holding us in such an ambivalent relation to a law before which we are
never fully justified, it also opens the political space for a new beginning like
the one Arendt imagines is commenced in forgiveness. Though the "effects of

pardon begin with the individual person being pardoned," because they "have to do with what that person owes to others and what is owed to that person, they have a much wider significance."[33] In the same way that violence radiates and expands beyond the bounds of its intention, forgiveness also extends "to the whole network of relations in which the pardoned one exists"; it "interrupts old patterns of relationship—even, or especially, those demanded by ethics—and makes it possible to create new patterns."[34] Much like the challenging movements of divine violence that Butler has read in Benjamin, forgiveness can unsettle what is ethically justified for the sake of new habits and understandings of human relationship. This does not hold justification in abeyance and neither does it upend the law; rather, it illuminates the rough edges of that which we can bring ourselves to justify, and imagines a new possibility for life on and beyond those unforgiving limits.

Judith Butler aligns this version of Benjamin's divine violence with their own account of nonviolence, a nonviolence that seeks not to justify itself but to ask why justification, the moral accounting of an individual conscience, undergirds our rationale for either violence or its restraint in the first place. Nonviolence isn't a right or wrong action; it is an honest and proper posture, a beginning for ethics in the incoherent space of intersubjectivity. For Butler, every authentic nonviolence will seek to "negotiate fundamental ethical and political ambiguities," leaving it to resemble an "ongoing struggle" far more than an "absolute principle" (Butler, *Force of Nonviolence*, 22). It is this Benjaminian commitment to wrestling with responsibility that frees Butler's nonviolence from the justificatory framework they have critiqued. For Butler, nonviolence is neither "a means to a goal nor . . . a goal in itself" but "a technique that exceeds . . . instrumental logic" or indeed any casuistical calibration of proper ends (125). In light of Benjamin's placement of responsibility over and against justification, Butler argues that nonviolence ought to be understood less as an uncompromising and self-grounding moral standard that individuals may choose to hold, and more as a social and political commitment to practices of community that will culminate in "resistance to systemic forces of destruction" (21). For this reason, and in semantic departure from Butler, one might wonder whether nonviolence is the best term for this sort of commitment and restraint. At the least, when those systemic forces engage in their destructive acts against our practices of resistance, violence does occur. As we know, it is visited ruthlessly on resisters. Furthermore, from this position of uncertainty and struggle, a violence for which we commit to remaining responsible may sometimes arise, even from and among the nonviolent. For this reason, following on some of my arguments from Chapter 1, I might prefer to call this posture one of nonretaliation rather than of non-violence. Because what I want morally to reject, and what I believe Benjamin's divine violence troubles, is the tit-for-tat logic of retaliation—the idea that any prior violence can alone justify present violence in response. What I deny is the possibility of any like for like. But whichever language is preferable, the point is not to cling to either violent or nonviolent actions as self-justifying in themselves. The aim is to abandon a form of moral accounting and account-ability that depends in the first place on coherent self-justification, and thus on a coherent self, because to do so instantiates an individual sovereignty and mastery that cannot but culminate in violence. It is better, Butler claims, for the moral subject to accept the ruptures, incoherences, failures, and (perhaps) forgiveness that might follow, or at least to give an account of them.

This is incisive critique, and also surprisingly resonant of the unfinished essays on Christian ethics being prepared by Dietrich Bonhoeffer at the time of his arrest by the National Socialists in 1943, which were subsequently collected and published by his friend Eberhard Bethge after his death. As Bonhoeffer argues throughout this incomplete work, acts we reckon as self-justifying, as morally upright in and of themselves, may often be our own shortcomings pridefully transmuted into virtue. That we might be wholly and morally perspicacious (to use Butler's language), fully knowing goodness and purely enacting it in the world, is the original sin of pride that founds all specious ethical reflection. Bonhoeffer remains suspicious of any ethics that strives for a moral legitimacy based on its own universal or immutable prin-ciples. Instead, ethics should ground itself in the limitations of human fini-tude and the concrete reality of a world with finite possibilities. For this reason, Bonhoeffer undermines the traditional task of what he calls a general ethics, the human urge and anxiety toward self-justification, from the outset. Though, as he writes in *Ethics*, the knowledge of "good and evil appears to be the goal of all ethical reflection," the creation story from Genesis should leave Christians critically skeptical of this goal.[35] In fact, the "task of Christian eth-ics" first and foremost "is to supersede that knowledge" of good and evil, right and wrong. On these terms, Bonhoeffer suggests that it is not sensible "to speak of Christian ethics at all," or if one insists on this language, to speak of them only "as the critique of all ethics" (Bonhoeffer, *Ethics*, 299–300).

We can perhaps hear the perspective of Benjamin's divine violence echo-ing in this critique of justification. For Bonhoeffer, Christians who claim "to know good and evil" understand themselves "as the origin of good and evil, as the origin of an eternal choice and election" (302). I do want to be careful here, perhaps more careful than Bonhoeffer is in this unfinished manuscript. There are of course evils we can and should name, chattel slavery for one, Nazism for another (to cite two examples relevant to this chapter). The list of nameable evils in human affairs is long; they populate the world around us. For me, the force of Bonhoeffer's claim here has less to do with whether we are justified in naming the moral status of the world's obvious sins and more to do with whether we can or should have confidence in the moral status of our *responses* to those sins. The problem arises for Bonhoeffer when we believe that our actions in response to such evils will be self-justifying on their own, self-evidently and assuredly good simply because we believe they are our best, most rational or moral, response. In a way that interestingly intersects with Arendt's reflection on the unpredictability and irreversibility of action, Bonhoeffer simply insists humans cannot hold this knowledge. The pridefulness of claiming that knowledge is the original sin of the first humans' disobedience in Genesis.[36] In fact, the Christian's moral knowledge, writes Bonhoeffer, is severely and significantly limited. We know only two things: first, we know that we are finite creatures of limited knowledge, power, and existence; and second, we know "the reality of being elected and loved by God" in our finite state (302). Our actions, therefore, must be based on *this* knowledge, rather than on any other. Christians risk claiming to know "themselves in the possibility of choosing, of being the origin of good and evil" if they act out of any other conviction than that of their own insufficiency and the endless reach of God's love (302). We never know whether we have done good. We do not know whether we are in the right. We can tell neither by the commandments we have obeyed nor by the outcomes of our actions. We have no knowledge of good or evil. We know always and only that we are loved by God.

What would it mean to act in the knowledge and reality of God's love, rather than in the knowledge and confidence of our own goodness? What would it mean to confess ourselves as fully and finitely human, to conceive of repentance not just as the formal articulation of any particular sin but as a general posture of finitude, dependence, and relationship?[37] In his published reflections on Jesus's Sermon on the Mount and elsewhere, Bonhoeffer states quite directly that a commitment to Christian pacifism is "self-evident" and that the Christian life "is the way of . . . perfect non-violence."[38] And yet, Bonhoeffer's work on *Ethics* was cut short because of his arrest for participation in a failed attempt to assassinate Hitler. The pacifist Bonhoeffer (at least) endorsed and (perhaps) attempted violence. This is not, I believe, because he wavered in his pacifism in this particular instance, but because of how he thought about Christian ethics generally. Again, Bonhoeffer over and again rejects ethics as a system of self-grounding or universal principles. Theologically anticipating and enriching Butler's nonviolence, Bonhoeffer refuses to adopt "nonviolence as an absolute principle in all circumstances."[39] For Bonhoeffer, an action "based on ideology is already justified by its own principle," whereas "responsible action renounces any knowledge about its ultimate justification" (268). Like Benjamin before him and Butler after him, Bonhoeffer wants relentlessly to question our habits of self-justification. These responsible actions, actions taken "after responsibly weighing all personal and factual circumstances," are "completely surrendered to God" as soon as they are enacted. The one who acts responsibly thus remains entirely and willingly ignorant "of one's own goodness or evil" and instead depends absolutely "upon grace." Those who "act responsibly place their action into the hands of God and live by God's grace and judgment" alone (268). In other words, they know only that they are loved, not that they are good, and they offer their actions—actions taken in careful response to the world's manifest sin—up to God's judgment, confident in God's forgiving love.

This means, for Bonhoeffer, that under certain grave circumstances "one must completely let go of any law" (274). There is no "freestanding code, Bonhoeffer insists," that "can decide the exact nature of the spiritual responsibility enjoined upon us in any given situation," and so at times the law must be breached.[40] But the breaking of the law does not become a moral good by virtue of this grave necessity. This responsible action must "include the open acknowledgement that . . . the law is being broken, violated; that the commandment is broken out of dire necessity, thereby affirming the legitimacy of the law in the very act of violating it" (274). The violation does not become justified, let alone valorized, by necessity. It simply remains forgivable. In other words, the necessary action remains a betrayal, an act that can be undertaken only because we have confidence in God's love to forgive us for our waywardness from God's commands. This is not a theology of exception: the necessary act is not excepted from God's law. Jesus's command that we love our enemy was never lifted during Bonhoeffer's life; it loomed over all his actions, even his involvement with assassination. An ethics without principles does not consecrate exceptions. Rather, it declares faith in a love that will forgive our law-breaking.

In this sense, then, once again, confession and repentance are not primarily acts of verbalization that articulate the personal commission of particular sins. Confession and repentance instead signify a posture, a relationship to one's own actions and one's sense of self that embraces the fundamental failure of any full or fully self-grounding justification. The Japanese philosopher Tanabe Hajime taught and wrote, like Bonhoeffer, in the midst of a ruthless, totalitarian fascism. Unlike Bonhoeffer, however, Tanabe failed utterly to resist that fascism and occasionally even endorsed it. But in the months preceding the atomic annihilation of Hiroshima and Nagasaki and in the years afterwards, Tanabe repented, embraced disgrace, and retired to a reclusive life while reframing his fundamental philosophy around repentance, using both the Greek term *metanoia* and the Japanese word *zange* in his writings.[41] For Tanabe, the self is drawn toward self-deceit, but deceit of a particular sort. It's not just that the self interprets all its own actions as basically good or inclined toward goodness. More fundamentally, the self "grows forgetful of its own finiteness and relativity, and comes to mistake itself for absolute existence by absolutizing the finiteness of its existence."[42] In other words, the self cannot abide any awareness of its own finitude, and in its urge to be all in all it arrogates to itself the absolute, an assertion that implies the moral invulnerability of certain of its own actions. In the anxiety to be existentially self-grounding, the human subject regards its acts as morally self-grounding too. Because the self rejects its own fundamental dependency, because it feels it must originate in itself, it presumes that good and evil must also originate in itself, and thus it claims the capacity both to know and to be good on its own. In its desperation to be independent and invulnerable, the self refuses both fallibility and finitude, and these refusals coincide. This is critique Bonhoeffer would recognize, and indeed, Tanabe's turn toward repentance in the years after World War II included a new engagement with both Christian thought and Japanese Shin Buddhism, a branch of Pure Land Buddhism especially concerned with the impossibility of human moral purity. The delusory desire to be all in all is a moral and political danger for Tanabe, because it will reject dependent vulnerability, fetishize sovereign purity, resist critique and reform, and thus tend toward totalitarianism.[43] For Tanabe, and in a way Bonhoeffer would no doubt find familiar, the rejection of finitude and the refusal of repentance each incline troublingly toward fascism.

Tanabe argues, in anticipation of Arendt and Butler, that however desperate our urge to be absolute, we cannot guarantee the goodness of our actions, and intention is no safeguard to uncertainty. Rather, our acts play out in a plural space of unexpected and unintended consequences. We are limited creatures, and our actions and responsibilities invariably exceed those limits.

To repent, to "acknowledge our responsibility for those of our actions that inevitably result in sin," Tanabe argues, is therefore also to admit and embrace our finitude.[44] Again, prefiguring Butler, Tanabe insists that there are subjective and political consequences to our existential demand to be all in all. But to confess and repent is to recognize "the tragic downfall of our own" sense of selves as limitless and absolute (rather than limited and contingent) beings.[45] For Tanabe, accepting responsibility for one's actions is a "forsaking of the self" that implies a relationship to both moral and existential finitude, and thus constitutes a turning "towards one's own death."[46] To accept one's guilt is to embrace the limits of the self, to come into meaningful relationship with inadequacy, deficiency, and death. The human soul, Tanabe writes, in relinquishing a sense of its own acts as justifiable, must also relinquish its unrelenting "demand to exist" without end.[47] But this is no tragic loss, since what the human actually relinquishes here is only that anxious and illusory demand, only that impossible wish. Infinity and invulnerability were never real options to begin with, whatever the unremitting urge of our anxieties, so what is lost in embracing repentance is only the fantasy of the absolute. This willingness to accept one's own limits makes room for others, and Tanabe likens it to love. And in embracing the contingent limits of this love Tanabe also suggests that we might discover new forms of forgiveness and resurrection.[48] I follow up on Tanabe's provocative claim in Chapters 3 and 4, with reference to other novels and other thinkers. But to be clear, the forgiveness Tanabe suggests we will find in embracing repentance as a moral and existential posture is not one that undoes past deeds or returns the self to some recoverable purity or absolute unity. Neither does the resurrection he intimates simply reestablish what has been lost or grant infinity to the finite. On the contrary, Tanabe's thorough undoing of the self through repentance draws the meaning of events like forgiveness and resurrection into new and unsettling relief.

Tanabe obviously makes his cases against self-grounding principles from a very different starting point than Benjamin or Butler or Bonhoeffer. He is important to include in this discussion, however, because he outlines so explicitly how an ethics of repentance, or what he calls a philosophy of metanoetics, must invite an engagement with death that will subsequently frame any redemptive possibilities for love. But what all these thinkers seek in common is a moral framework that can answer the irreducibly concrete demands of a dangerous world, not with virtuously imposed universal principles of either violence or nonviolence, but with honest self-assessment and earnest attempts to limit harm while welcoming constant critique. We may take up acts of violence, but those acts will not be justified even where they are required, not even by the law of talion. We may refuse to defend the defenseless with force, but that refusal will not be consecrated by our fidelity to scripture, not even by the Sermon on the Mount. There is "no *nonviolent* ethics or responsibility" in any pure sense.[49] In our ethical reflection and moral actions "we are instead always already implicated in an economy of violence, and an irreducible element of any ethics is to acknowledge the necessary violence of our own acts of responsible decision."[50] To begin self-consciously from such a position of limitation is to admit our finitude, our fallibility, and our sin. It is to confess that even our best responses carry no guarantee of goodness. This means that to "live, to love, is to be failed, to forgive, to have failed, to be forgiven, for ever and ever."[51] To act out of this admission of failure, this posture of preemptive penitence, means accepting inevitably guilty limits while embracing an endless opportunity for forgiveness.

I have focused in this section on a nonviolence wary of principle not only for how it reframes our notions of accountability but also for how it frames the moral dispute between two generations of Congregational ministers in Marilynne Robinson's fictional Iowa. Though aggression may tempt us to destroy the other through violence, "who we 'are' is precisely a shared precariousness," and "we risk our own nullification" in that destruction, since "we are already constituted through ties that bind and unbind in specific and consequential ways."[52] However sound or shaky their arguments, in their insistence on self-righteousness John Ames I and John Ames II each sunder many of the ties that bind them, especially to one another. It may be that they could benefit from another way of speaking to and with and even for one another, from the giving of a different account. This alternative ethical framework for accountability would insist on beginning and ending our moral lives in failure rather than on a justification of our moral lives. It would acknowledge that our only way forward with one another is through accepting, honoring, and confessing our respective and relative limits. This is not to excuse or overlook our own or others' moral shortcomings; on the contrary, it is to address them so directly and persistently and emphatically that they cannot easily be excused or overlooked.

Another way to describe my concern about the conflict here between father and son would be to say that they make that conflict about righteousness when it should be about repentance. It is altogether obvious that, among three generations of white ministers in Gilead named Ames, only one has committed his life and ministry in any serious way to combatting the signal evil of his time and the founding sin of his country. And John Ames I has the fiery vision and the bloody shirt to prove it. The problem with his bloody shirt is not necessarily that he soiled it through violence; it's that he preaches his violence as righteousness in itself, flaunting the shirt and his weapon before his congregation as signs of God's blessing rather than of God's judgment. There is no sense of his repenting the tragic and sinful necessities of our tragic and sinful world. Were John Ames I rather to have returned from battle and knelt among his congregants in penitence, sincerely grieving for the lives of the enemies he had slain, begging God's forgiveness for those acts he could not but commit, then the tenor and purpose of his argument with his sinfully complacent son and woefully forgetful grandson would alter fundamentally. What all this really amounts to (as Bonhoeffer I think helps us discern) is a lack of faith in God's forgiveness from each side of the Ameses' argument: a secret Pelagian righteousness that insists there must be acts that God judges as invariably good and that will grant honor on their own. John Ames I believes his violence is righteous in itself because it resists sin; John Ames II believes his pacifism is righteous in itself because it too resists sin. But self-justifying righteousness is not the aim of Christian life. It is the obstacle to it. The Ameses misunderstand the plight of our finitude and the immovable demand of God's command. Christian moral argument and reflection, when it matters most, is not about figuring out which act is unimpeachably good. The more necessary and challenging task is to confess to ourselves and to one another that, at times, our only available response to sin will be sinful too, that it will defy God's direct and impossible command too, and that it therefore will best be undertaken in hopes of forgiveness too. This should leave us neither self-righteous in our defiance nor unwilling to act. Instead, it should leave us both active and repentant. Indeed, this is the very nature of Christian moral dilemma: we cannot but act, and we cannot but betray God with our action. There is no reason or religious vision that can carry us out of this bind. Our task in these grave moments is to accept that we will break God's law and fail, whatever we do, and especially—as John Ames II and III show—if we do nothing. Like Bonhoeffer we must acknowledge our sin and our limits, do what we can, and then trust in God's forgiveness. In *Gilead*, neither John Ames I nor John Ames II is willing to sin and be forgiven. They want their acts and rationales to be divinely sanctioned in themselves, and so they ignore the repentance and forgiveness that even their most morally courageous and necessary actions demand.

As Butler describes it, nonviolence doesn't resolve the problem of violence but seeks rather to approach violence as itself irresolvable. Again, I wonder

about the language of nonviolence here, since those who choose against retaliation, against justifying violence with violence, do often suffer violence for
that choice. I propose instead therefore not just a posture of nonretaliation
but of *repentant* nonretaliation, a stance that refuses violence as a means of
moral balancing, regards violence as irredeemable by further violence, but
also admits the ineluctable demand that we must respond substantively to the
violence in our lives through the limited and sometimes sinful means we
have. Crucially, on these terms, wrongdoing would not be a problem to be
solved by forgiveness. And violence would never be vindicated, even when
necessarily pursued in the cause of justice. Instead, forgiveness would be a
way of approaching the irresolvable human problem of wrongdoing, of initiating "the difficult practice of letting rage collapse into grief."[53] It may be we
forgive our enemies. It may also be that we must seek forgiveness from our
enemies and from God for what we cannot but do to protect ourselves and
others. In either case, given the irreparable reality of human wrong, there will
be no moral response that doesn't in some way solicit forgiveness. Much like
confession, forgiveness is a form of admitting and mourning both what we
cannot do and what we cannot undo, and then doing what we can, in deep
grief and penitence for what we have done. To love our enemies might sometimes mean earnestly mourning their loss at our hands and begging their
survivors' forgiveness for our actions. To give an account of oneself is to confess one's own mutuality, it is to begin from one's own finitude and to expose
oneself as dispossessed by the inevitable grief of mutual vulnerability. John
Ames's grandfather and his father confess almost nothing to one another.
They declaim and proclaim, they attest and protest. To be clear: these can be
worthwhile endeavors in our moral and political lives, but they do not begin
or end in themselves. What's needed in Gilead is a confession; what's needed
is the giving of an account that will arise from a grief-stricken place and will
reckon with the irrevocability of loss alongside the implacability of aggression. When our proclamations and our protests accept that loss is not a problem to be solved but a transformation to be endured, perhaps we can arrive
at a proper sort of mourning, for ourselves and for our enemies, and then
establish a meaningful form of forgiveness too.

FAILING FORGIVENESS

John Ames I and John Ames II embroil themselves in a debate of competing righteousness. Their descendent, our narrator, endears himself to his

reader partly for his evident lack of self-righteousness, for his careful and retiring self-reflection. Like Bonhoeffer, he seems to place his faith in God's love rather than in rigid moral principles. With stylistic cautiousness, he notes for example that we are meant to love our enemies not because God wants us to meet some "standard of righteousness," but because "God their father loves them" (Robinson, *Gilead*, 189). This commitment echoes Bonhoeffer yet again, whose own pacifism is rooted in Jesus's teachings about love for enemies from the Sermon on the Mount. Using the language of our last chapter, Jesus tells his disciples to seek neither eye for eye nor tooth for tooth, but instead to love their enemies, bless those who curse them, and do good to those who wish them harm (Matt 5:44). This apparent upending of the *lex talionis* is not an exception to the law but the law's fulfillment. How could loving one's enemy, returning a blessing for a tooth while turning another cheek, fulfill the law of like for like? Perhaps because what is alike in me and in my enemy is neither our teeth nor our eyes but God's infinite love and our absolute fallibility before it. What we share, to borrow a phrase from Judith Butler yet again, is an equality of incalculable value: that God would grieve the loss of either of us.[54] God loves me and my enemy, like for like, and makes the sun to rise on both the just and the unjust (Matt 5:45). To refuse revenge, to resist retaliation, is to accept our losses as irrevocable for the sake and the sign of God's irrevocable love.

As a theological argument for nonretaliation, Ames's principle is sound. But as Bonhoeffer has shown, the distance between theological argument and action, between principle and responsibility, can be long or blocked by sin. Ames wanders into precisely this irresponsibility when he enacts his Christian commitment of love for one's enemies as a practice of forgetting in Gilead. Recall Ames's remarks about the dispute between his father and grandfather above, and the fact that he has concluded his father was right because it's "just as well" that "people have forgotten" (Robinson, *Gilead*, 76). Out of support for his father's principled pacifism, Ames believes the past best buried, its losses and traumas unspoken. This knowing forgetfulness, one that recalls exactly what it forgets but still conceals that memory, is a particularly insidious form of forgetting. The past is obscured rather than erased, shrouded rather than vanished. Ames knows and recollects most of what he thinks better forgotten, and (as Ishiguro shows) moral consequences wait to be reckoned when broken pasts lie buried but unmourned.

As I wrote earlier in this chapter, I read *Gilead* as a long confession, but not a confession of the transactional sort, not one that secures for John Ames justification or redemption. Rather, I recognize in this novel a confession that follows the contours I have described above: in giving an account of himself, John Ames comes properly to mourn, to grieve the sins of his forgetting and his inaction. He discovers not the singular coherence of his own story but its breaks and its ruptures. In other words, he comes clearly to recognize his own failures only in bearing better witness to others and, through them, to himself. Although (in the words of Judith Butler) in the end he may be held irresponsible, his confession does indeed also beckon forgiveness. The dilemma of retaliation that sunders the relationship between his father and grandfather is not one that his recollection entirely resolves; nonretaliation does not emerge as a virtue or a position or a set of universal principles, to recall Butler's phrasing. Repentant nonretaliation, rather, emerges as a penitent restraint set against the falsely sovereign purity of universal principles of virtue, against an unassailable law to which we might give our fealty and pledge our moral purity. When Ames finally and fully recalls the complexities of his own life and lineage, and especially of that paternal dispute over righteous violence that estranged his forebears from one another, he comes at last to recognize the sin of his own complicity in his nation's violent history. He does not resolve their argument or overcome their estrangement. He admits himself as arising from it and forever bound to it, and repents. In the end, he wades into a mired and conflicted space of loss and failure between his father and grandfather, which paradoxically is the only space where an earnest repentance or real forgiveness can ever emerge.

Ames is not unfamiliar with grief; his first wife, Louisa, and their infant daughter, Angelina, both died when he was a young man. Indeed, much of his adult life has been spent in the loneliness of felt loss. But many of the memories he shares of his father and grandfather also speak of how grief has structured his life and ministry. Ames notes how bitterly it grieved his father that his last words to the old man were angry ones, and that the two elder Ameses never reconciled in this life (Robinson, *Gilead*, 10). In an extended recollection, Ames describes a journey he and his father took (like Abraham and Isaac, tellingly) to search for the eldest John Ames's grave in Kansas. He recalls this journey as if it were one of pilgrimage. They nearly starved and were discouraged to find the plot in a small, forgotten cemetery, shrouded in the dust, weeds, and neglect of the poverty surrounding it. At the graveside, Ames recalls his father bowing his head "to pray, remembering his father to the Lord, and also asking the Lord's pardon, and his father's as well" (14). Memory and pardon are married in this prayer of mourning. Ames recalls missing his grandfather and needing some forgiveness too. But "that was a very long prayer" (14). And yet, as they stood on that barren plain, John Ames recalls seeing the rising moon and setting sun each standing on the edge of the broad and opposing horizons of the grasslands. Taut and nearly tangible "skeins of light suspended between them," he says, and he and his father stood there between sun and moon at his grandfather's shabby grave, ethereally illuminated until the sun had gone down and the moon had come up. He and his father departed, humbled and glad to know that the site of their estrangement and bereavement might also be a place of startling beauty (14–15).

This is one of the great gifts and wisdoms of John Ames, why he has such an appeal to readers. It is true that he is clumsy with his spoken words in social situations, but he is also remarkably perceptive in his writing. He is able to recognize the "taut skeins of light" suspended invisibly in our experience. He sees the beauty of two working men sharing a joke and a smoke and wants to share in it. There is nothing so ordinary for Ames as to be unavailable to grace, and so to beauty, and his prose always attempts to answer to that. And this includes all the human ordinariness of grief, loneliness, and sorrow, too. Ames remarks in his letter to his son that he has heard some say "Christians worship sorrow." He insists to his boy that this is not true but also wants to acknowledge that there is a "sacred mystery in it" (137). There is a sacred mystery not just in sorrow but in all of it, in shabby Kansas graves and dying Iowa towns and a life of loneliness and ministry approaching its end. This is Ames's faith, and if he attributes a spiritual failure to what he regards as the moral mistake of his grandfather's zealous belligerence, it is because the old man's idea of prophetic vision was too narrow. His grandfather, Ames decides, was so "dazzled by the great light of experience" that he could not discern the gentle and impressive sunlight shining "on us all," itself no less miraculous than a fiery vision (91). If Ames hopes to teach his own son anything with his long letter, it is that the visionary fire of these ordinary experiences is sometimes only ever revealed to us in memory, in retrospect, with the slow and patient passage of time. This letter to his son becomes the best proof of that good lesson, because a visionary fire strikes John Ames too in his recollection and confession.

What comes to John Ames in memory as he offers this written narrative to his son is a new vision of his namesake, Robert Boughton's son Jack, and through Jack, a vision of Ames's own life too. Ames's vision has been severely limited when it comes to Jack, but this blindness is not the only one that limits his sight. Nevertheless, it will require Jack's private confession to summon Ames to a confession of his own, and also to a broader social and political vision of repentance, a transition I explore at length shortly. A complex matrix of unresolved grief and resentment undergirds Ames's disdain for Jack. After Ames's first wife and daughter died in childbirth, the elder Boughton named his own new son after John Ames, as a gift to his best friend. This came as an unwelcome surprise, as Ames could not recognize in Jack anything other than an unworthy replacement for what he had lost. At the baby's baptism, while Ames christened the child with his own name, he inwardly and silently denied any paternal obligation to the boy (188). It does not help that the young Boughton became largely aimless and rebellious as a youth, though this diminishes Robert Boughton's love for his son not one whit. Jack Boughton's mistakes are not insignificant; he impregnated a young woman from a poor neighboring community and failed in any way to support the child, who eventually died. Ames even shows an awareness of the ways in which his own grief continues to cloud his vision of Jack. Recalling Jack's baptism, Ames confesses that he has wondered whether the infant Jack somehow felt the secret coldness and rejection operating under the surface of that christening, whether the child somehow knew he had never really been blessed by his pastor and godparent. This stirs guilt in Ames toward Jack, but not warmth toward him (188). This self-aware knowledge of his own guilt does not change his posture toward the boy in any meaningful way. Ames devotes a substantial number of pages in this long letter reflecting upon what he does or doesn't owe Jack. The old pastor feels resentment that his wife and child should have died while Jack was content to ignore the mother of his own child and neglect that child unto death. Ames admits that because the death of Jack's child isn't a direct or personal transgression against him, he has no standing to forgive. But he also has no inclination to it either. "I don't forgive him," Ames insists. "I wouldn't know where to begin" (164).

Like Arendt and Butler, Ames recognizes that wrongdoing does not arise in isolation. The notion of transgression itself, he writes, is a "legalism." No transgression exists alone, abstracted from all others. It's not just that wrongdoing replicates and widens into broadening spheres of action. It's also that it comes from somewhere first, it arises from some other wrong into the places where we dwell. Sin is never singular. Rather, there is "a wound in the flesh" of all humanity that "scars when it heals" or seems "never to heal at all" (122). Ames recognizes that there are limits to law, that individual accountability hides a common problem and that a deeper wound ruptures human life. And yet, again, Ames cannot forgive Jack Boughton. The shared wound in their flesh cuts him too deeply. Though Ames has no specific moral standing in the neglect of Jack Boughton's child, his personal grief has made the sin unforgiveable and Ames literally cannot even start to imagine how he might forgive Jack. He cannot, in Arendt's words, find a way to begin.

Jack Boughton left Iowa as a young man, but when he does eventually return to Gilead as his father Robert ails, Ames's resentment toward his namesake seems dramatically misplaced to the reader. Jack is soft-spoken and thoughtful, polite in a way that endears the reader even as it irritates Ames. The young Boughton is not religious, but he is serious and earnest in his religious questions, and his theological conversations with John Ames are reflective and respectful. But Ames can hear only skepticism and cynicism when his namesake speaks. Ames's suspicion is not merely personal; or better, this personal suspicion covers a more public and political shortcoming. An early conversation Robert and John have with Jack suggests how limited Ames's own vision really can be, and how his private blindness is not unrelated to a public one. Ames and the elder Boughton are discussing a magazine article that disparages American Christianity. They see the essay engaging in the same hypocrisy and judgmentalism it wants to skewer, and they parse its failures of biblical logic in its critique of Americans' excessively literal imagination of heaven. Jack joins them on the porch and hears them chuckling over the article. He asks to review the essay, which he glances at quickly and then reveals he has already read by recalling that a central aspect of the author's argument is that America's sinful treatment of Black people is a symptom of religious unseriousness. This quiets the old ministers, and Jack's father warns Jack to be wary of judging too hastily, at which Jack smiles and returns the magazine to Ames (147). Their conversation thus ends. But Jack has obviously discerned the heart of the matter and highlighted what must be the most important and unimpeachable aspect of the essay: that the fundamental failure of American Christianity is and always has been its complicity with white supremacy. Meanwhile, the Reverends Ames and Boughton have been distracted by an ancillary argument about the appearance of heaven. The elder Boughton even dismisses Jack's reading as overly judgmental. There is a subtle hypocrisy revealed here, of course: Boughton's and Ames's own nitpicking complaints attempt to evade the charge of judgmentalism while Jack's recognition of undeniable racism stands to them as judgmental on its face.

Jack's interest here is not academic. Later in the novel, Jack comes to Ames and tells the pastor that he has a wife and a son. His wife, Della, is Black, and so miscegenation laws have prevented them from living together in St. Louis, where they met. Della and the boy, Robert, have returned to live with her family in Tennessee. It is no wonder, then, that Jack recognizes the central concern of the magazine article so quickly and so clearly, and regards white Christianity in America so skeptically. In fact, he has heard the author's argument already and more convincingly from Della, who calls all white men atheists, though only some of them are aware of the fact (220). Della knows, and Jack has seen, that those who proclaim God's justice and mercy but deny it to their neighbors and fellow citizens have no credible faith to speak of.

Jack wants to reunite his family and build a home for them, and he hopes that Gilead, with its radical abolitionist history, might accommodate their collective return. But he wants to know first whether either his father or the town will accept them. In other words, Jack wonders whether this prodigal son might be welcomed back. So Jack goes to Ames for advice, because Ames knows old Boughton so well, and also perhaps because Ames has an abolitionist family history of his own, one that might leave him sympathetic to Jack's plight. Describing his son, Robert, Jack pleads his case to Ames, explaining that his boy is bright and beautiful and being brought up in the church. But Jack also tells Ames that he knows how frail his father is and doesn't want to stress the old man with surprise or disappointment. Jack wants Ames's honest opinion, since Ames is a man of the same age who has known old Boughton so long and so well, and also because he knows Ames's kindness and theology well enough to trust that he will not tell Jack that all his troubles are "divine retribution" for the child he abandoned and lost (229). Unfortunately, Ames is not able to give any assurances to Jack, first because he worries about being wrong, but also because he simply doesn't know "how old Boughton would take all this," a fact he confesses to his own son in writing but not in his spoken conversation with Jack (221). Indeed, in the subsequent novel *Home* we are given good reason to believe that Jack's worries about his father are well-founded.[55] But I think Jack understands all this already, not least because of the corroborating detail we eventually see in *Home*, which is why, after Ames has hedged over speaking for his friend, Jack asks Ames to speak for himself: "If it were you, and not my father" (*Gilead*, 228–29). Sadly, Ames's answer in that moment is not much better than Robert Boughton's might have been. Ames acknowledges that in all their years of ministry and friendship together, the issue of racism simply didn't arise between John Ames III and Robert Boughton (231). Given the scope and depth of their intellectual and spiritual bond, this is a damning omission: in this abolitionist outpost of Iowa, between the two pillar white Protestant ministers of the community, two years after *Brown v. Board of Education*, conversations of race simply never arose—not even after an arson at the town's only Black church. Failing to be reassured, Jack wonders about Gilead, whether he and Della could safely live in the town if they returned to it someday soon and married. He specifically mentions as cause for concern the fire at the Black church that led the eldest Ames to walk out on his son's sermon and leave Gilead forever. Ames refers to it as "a little nuisance fire," but Jack notes that there has not been any Black church in the town since that congregation left (231). At last Jack arrives at what I believe is his actual and basic question in this moment and in this conversation: not whether his own father would protect and accept his family, nor whether the town would, but whether his godfather John Ames will. "You have influence here," Jack coaxes (231). Ames responds that while that may be true, his weak heart leaves him wary of promising very much of his own strength or time. Disheartened, Jack apologizes for troubling the old man and speculates that he is too late anyway: his wife and child are already too far gone to be recovered.

In Luke's famous parable, the prodigal's brother objects to the welcome of the long lost son, but their father insists upon a feast. It is, as Ames himself has preached, a sign and a celebration of reckless, unrelenting love. But what if the father had instead apologized for his lack of strength or influence on his household and turned the prodigal away? The sadness of this scene in *Gilead* and the emotional and physical frailty of the characters perhaps obscures what has patently happened: the prodigal son has not been welcomed home. The intimacy of the moment perhaps occludes how racism perpetuates and extends rejection beyond the estrangement of Jack from his father and father figure, into an additional heartbreaking separation between the young child Robert and his own father Jack. Because one father turns a son away, another son loses his father too. However kind the tone of this conversation, Jack has been told quite clearly that there is no home for him or for his family in Gilead anymore. This is not just a personal matter. Ames's reduction of the political stakes betrays his own relationship to them, not their irrelevance. It may be this fire was just a nuisance to Ames. But it was not just a nuisance to the congregants of that church, who all moved to Chicago in the aftermath; and not to Ames's grandfather, who abandoned the town because of it in search of a preacher who would decry injustice from the pulpit. Eating and drinking his disappointment, old John Ames left his home and church and family to die alone in Kansas rather than remain in the midst of all that failure. We might have some sympathy for the Reverend Ames here: his heart is weak, he will not live long, and there are limits to what he can accomplish in his frail and few remaining days. But it is so telling in this moment that Jack calls Ames "Papa." That paternal reference not only recalls the prodigal parable; it also reveals Ames's failure to live into that parable's lessons in this moment. It witheringly signals the depth and source of Gilead's, and Ames's, sin.

Ames is a character who can recognize grace and beauty in ordinary corners of creation. He shows a moving capacity for love and generosity. When Jack decides to leave Gilead after his conversation with Papa, while old Boughton lies on his deathbed, Ames writes to his own son that he should not judge Jack too harshly if he ever hears this story told by others. In one of the most beautiful expressions of parental love I've read, Ames tells his boy that Jack's departure is sensible and sympathetic, even at this grave time, because it follows the contours of a love Ames also feels and understands. He tells his someday grown son that even if he had somehow lived a different life, if he'd had a wife who had survived and given him ten other children, who each in turn gave him ten grandchildren, he would abandon them all "on Christmas Eve on the coldest night of the world, and walk a thousand miles," just for the sight of his beloved boy's face, and his mother's face (237). And if he never found them, even in all that weather and walking, Ames tells his son he would do it merely for the hope of someday seeing them. That would be enough to rouse him to any effort and sacrifice, just the hope one day to see them both again. Having already lost a wife and child, and now on the verge of losing another family, Ames knows that while all the thriving Boughton brothers and sisters gather at their parents' house to bid their father farewell, the absent, abject Jack would "utterly and bitterly prefer what he lost" to all the wealth and company his siblings enjoyed (237–38). That desperate, reckless love, that love unfazed by loss, moved merely and sufficiently by hope, is the love of these fathers for their sons, of Ames for his boy, of Jack for his son Robert, of Robert for Jack, of father for prodigal, for ever and ever again. But this example does not just convey why Ames's boy must be forgiving of Jack; it also betrays why Ames needs forgiveness himself too.

John Ames has already confessed: "John Ames Boughton is my son" (189). He declares this fact to be as true as anything else he believes. If Jack is the prodigal son, then this is his return, and what Jack Boughton finds awaiting him in Gilead are not robes and rings and a welcome feast of fatted calf. It is a Papa who turns him away. In his moment of crisis, Jack calls Ames his father. He asks if he might come home. The old man's heart is weak; he will not live long; there are limits to his pastoral powers. But could any reader imagine

Ames treating his own biological son, or his long-dead daughter, Angelina, in remotely the same way? Were his six-year-old instead now grown or his daughter somehow risen from the dead, each begging for the chance to be welcomed home, does any reader doubt what John Ames would do, this man who would leave all else behind on the coldest night of the world and walk a thousand miles for the hope of seeing one small face? If given the chance to welcome home a long-lost child, the Reverend John Ames III would gladly cry justice from the pulpit with his last breath and guard the door sleepless every minute of every night and will his failing heart to beat long enough to see his son and that son's family safely home. Ames even says to Jack directly, were the grandchild his own issue, "I would love to know the child" (230). But the child *is* John Ames's issue, in both senses of that word, and the Reverend has nothing to offer his prodigal son here save an awkward blessing of farewell, after which his rejected child and namesake goes away from Gilead forever and for good.

As beloved and sympathetic a character as John Ames may be, I don't think we can read this blessed estrangement as anything other than a profound and damning failure.[56] But again, Ames is a perceptive writer, capable always of discerning both the movement of grace and the need for it. Ames recognizes this error as soon as we do. In writing all this down for his reader, Ames himself comes to see this final blessing as a failure and a sin. In telling his story, a story suddenly reframed by the story of another, Ames suddenly understands how surely failure founds his own narrative. Because after hearing Jack's story, after watching his namesake leave, and then after retelling that story in the context of his own, Ames comes to a new understanding of himself and of his ministry. He becomes accountable to his own account, to his long and labored confession. All at once he recalls everything he hasn't remembered about himself, and about Boughton, and about his town, and about his faith. By "relinquishing his (ir)responsible fidelity to one version of his family narrative and suspending himself between the law of the father and that of the grandfather," Ames manages to learn to tell "the story he fears and needs to tell."[57] As he concludes his letter to his son, he writes that the town of Gilead deserves to sit on the "absolute floor of hell," and that the fault belongs to him as much as to anyone else (234). He laments that over the decades of his ministry he became distracted by his people's daily strife and ordinary troubles, and he stopped paying attention to what all that trouble might mean, and more importantly, what God might want them to do about it. Because they ignored these questions, the questions were taken from them, and so also the chance to know God and God's will in the answers. Gilead was an outpost of abolition, but after the war, in their anxiety to forget the tragedies and dilemmas of that time, the people of the town forgot the good work God had called them to, and in forgetting they rejected it. As he concludes his long letter, Ames finally repents and confesses that he and they have forgotten who they are, and who they have been called to become. In this letter to his child, Ames concedes that even if their children asked them why the town exists at all, none among the townsfolk could well answer (234). In this epistolary novel that is a letter to a child, the confession of that particular ignorance is both telling and damning. These Iowans are not unlike the forlorn, forgetting wanderers in Ishiguro's *Buried Giant*. But at least the Britons knew they were forgetting.

In this realization, in this restoration of Ames's memory and this reminder of all he has forgotten, Ames does indeed come to a new vision, a vision he hopes to bequeath to his son and that the text suggests is at long last fired with prophecy. When Ames allows Jack to tell him the story of his own town and his own ministry in a way he hasn't previously imagined, Ames becomes better able to give an account of himself, that is, of his own sins and shortcomings. And it is through this account that, at the end of his life, he can see the possibility of a new beginning. As with Peter on the beach being interrogated by the resurrected Jesus over breakfast, the "memory of failure is in this context the indispensable basis of a calling forward in hope."[58] All those sermons Ames was humiliated to lose, he now tells the child he plans to have burned. His wife and the deacons will arrange it, he says; there are enough to "make a good fire" (245). Fire serves as a crucial image in this novel. There is the fire at the Black church, of course, but there is another church fire in Gilead too, one caused by lightning, and the town pulls down the charred ruin together while sharing a communion of stale biscuits from ashen hands with the embers still glowing all around. As Ames reflects upon his memories of that fire, he observes that God must hold every moment of our lives in divine memory (115). The infinite love of God cannot bear to forget; or rather, the infinite love of God can bear to remember even all our failures while still reaching out to us in love, like the father of the prodigal in the Gospel of Luke. When we remember who we are before God, which means recalling all our failures and frailties too, we do so in confidence that God will share and bear our memories with love. This sort of confession is therefore not only or even primarily a confession of who we are; it is also "always and fundamentally a 'confession' of God's grace."[59] God remembers to remember what we in our weakness forget, under the sign of this fire. The eldest Ames condemns his son's pacifist preaching because his lips, he says, were never touched with coal by the seraphim (84). It's revealing therefore that this, Ames's own confession, begins in its opening lines with Ames's young son touching the old man's lips, so that the preacher can begin to write this long, and in the above sense fiery, confession. Knowing now that what has been revealed to him in his remembrance is a failure, that the lovely epistle he has been writing his son is in fact a long confession of his sins, all Ames can do is pray that his son will take up his old ruins and begin again, begin anew, coax forth some warmth from all the dying embers of his own life in this small Iowa town and bear witness once again to something of the fiery vision his grandfather once beheld. In his final lines of this long letter of repentance, Ames laments to his son that he has nothing to leave but the "ruins of old courage." He regrets that all that is only an "ember now" but also proclaims faith that God might someday "breathe it into flame again" (246). Most of all, as he readies for death, he imagines going to his final resting place in Gilead's ground as an act of reckless love toward his failed, abolitionist, Iowa town, where—like the embers of old courage he has bequeathed to his boy—he too will "smolder away . . . until the great and general incandescence" (247). At last, Ames concludes his confession, promising to pray that both his child and his country will learn somehow to be courageous. "I'll pray," Ames closes, "then I'll sleep" (247).

The novel ends here, as does Ames's letter, and perhaps (we might reasonably conclude) Ames's life. Ames goes into the ground fully aware of his failure and the impossibility of restoring what has been lost. And yet, having made this long confession, having remembered in full his failures through the witness of others, having invited his reader into the fullness of his memories, Ames prays his son will do better, that he will embrace a bravery Ames himself unwittingly ignored. It's no accident that Arendt's model of forgiveness looks not only to Jesus as the religious genius of forgiving but also to the proclamation of his birth as expressive of the promise of new beginning that forgiveness bears: "A child has been born unto us."[60]

To be entirely clear: Ames's prayer is not sufficient to undo the past. It will not erase a racist arson or restore that church or even make Jack and Della feel at home in Iowa. It is, instead, an old man's prayer for forgiveness, a forgiveness that will take the form of honest memory and mournful hope that his son will find courage to begin and break free from the past's violent ignorance. Repentance and confession in this case are not wages paid to undo a broken history. They are not expressions of sincerity offered in exchange for propitiation. What's done is done; Jack has been banished with no forwarding address, and worse, Gilead's Black church remains abandoned, its congregants fled to Chicago, its arson still uninvestigated. Repentance and confession here simply do not compensate for those sins; they offer no satisfaction in that regard. But in acknowledging rather than overcoming the past's brokenness, they invite both a better memory and the hope for a possible future. Though the "sudden repentance" of transactional forgiveness "wants to collect all the bitterness of sorrow in one draft—and then be off," this swiftness is a delusion.[61] The first draft of our failings is never a full one. Guilt cannot be so easily expunged. Transactional repentance "wants the guilt to be completely forgotten with the passage of time."[62] But there is a deeper, more essential form of repentance and confession that suffers under "a quiet, sleepless sorrow at the thought of what has been wasted; it does not despair, but in its daily grieving it never rests."[63] John Ames has perhaps come to his last rest. But his grief continues on in the written record of his failings that he has bequeathed to his young son and to the town he has loved and lost in more ways than one. What this account summons is neither reparation nor resolution but an endless, sleepless sorrow. It is a humble and necessary confession, written to Ames's son and to his God, a confession that suggests a repentance neither of propitiation nor of transaction but of expanded vision, a confession that prays for the fire of Gilead's abolitionist past to be rekindled by mournful memory in days to come.

PART TWO

Atonement

CHAPTER 3

Remission

John Ames's love for his wife and his biological son is ardent and deep. As we read in the last chapter of *Gilead*, he says he would do nearly anything for them. Even had he raised a house full of children, he writes, he would abandon them all on Christmas Eve and walk the world just in hopes of glimpsing his boy's "sweetly ordinary" face.[1] John Ames writes these lines to explain to his own son why Jack Boughton has to leave Gilead while Jack's father is dying. Ames wants his son to understand that Jack's abandonment is in fact a sign of deep love, a love John Ames recognizes in his own love for his son. Each of these loves echoes the love of the prodigal's father in the Gospel of Luke, who runs away from an obedient child to welcome home the one who has wandered and squandered a fortune. Even were Ames to search forever for those faces, his comfort and Jack's would be in the hope of an eventual discovery, in a loss he would "utterly and bitterly prefer" to any other gain.[2] There's something tragic in the limits of Ames's misrecognition here. All Jack's hope is in his child, Robert, and as Ames approaches death, all his hope is in his own biological son too. Ames doesn't imagine that his hope could also lie with Jack, or with Jack's son as much as with his own. Moreover, the failures of Ames's life and ministry and town and country have all been revealed to him in Jack's love for another faraway child, and he goes into the ground realizing he cannot rectify these failures. But he also dies believing that his own son might live into a new future, even if he can't alter the past, believing that this

father's confession and this account of deep love might ignite in that reading
child a prophetic and purifying fire. Ames dies hoping that there might be
another beginning. Along with Hannah Arendt he believes that human beings, "though they must die, are not born in order to die but to begin."[3] And
his beginning now lies with his son. Thus Arendt ends her argument for the
miracle of forgiveness, as noted above, quoting the Gospel of Matthew, which
itself invokes the prophet Isaiah, whose lips were touched by the seraphim's
coal: "A child has been born unto us."

These are moving lines, from Arendt and Ames both, but they also might
cause us a note of concern. For the depth of Ames's love is matched only by
its narrowness. That he would leave behind all his other children for the
chance to glimpse the face of the child he has lost is good news for the lost
child but disappointing news for all the others. Again, the spirit of Ames's
rhetoric, and of the Gospels too, is that any lost child will merit and receive
this love. What would mark that child for attention would be nothing other
than the fact of his lostness. But still, the fact that Ames says he would leave
behind all the others bears more than a rhetorical significance because Ames
has turned away another child: his namesake, Jack. Ames wants to preserve
the peace of his final days with his own biological son, so he turns his spiritual
son Jack away and sends him off with nothing more than a frustrated blessing. The narrowness of this loyalty is not unrelated to Ames's reaction to the
fire at the Black church in his town. For the sake of some peace and settled-
ness, Ames allowed a whole community of fellow Christians, citizens whom
his town was literally founded to honor and defend, to leave for Chicago with
only an awkward goodbye on offer in their parting. An awkward goodbye is
also all he has to give to Jack. Ames might prefer all he has lost to what others
have gained, but perhaps he reflects too little upon what his own better efforts
might have won. John Ames's love is sympathetic and fervent and identifiable
and deep, and also troublingly limited in its reach, vision, and scope.

Arendt names this problem. In *The Human Condition*, she resists associat-
ing forgiveness with love because she worries that love is too "unworldly," that
it is "not only apolitical but antipolitical, perhaps the most powerful of antipolitical forces."[4] On the one hand, she acknowledges that love might be
uniquely suited to grounding forgiveness. Forgiving, she says, "is always an
eminently personal . . . affair," since it forgives what was done "for the sake
of *who* did it."[5] Love, meanwhile "possesses an unequaled power of self-
revelation and an unequaled clarity of vision for the disclosure of *who*" since
it is "unconcerned to the point of unworldliness with *what*" the beloved has

done, with "his qualities and his shortcomings no less than with his achieve-
ments, failings, and transgressions."[6] Love therefore might seem at first glance
especially well-suited to forgive what has been done for the sake of who has
done it. But this is also love's problem, Arendt says. Love turns its attention
entirely away from the world and toward the beloved. It retreats from, rather
than emerges into, the public square. The only thing that can come between
two lovers, Arendt writes, is a child, which signifies (in her telling) the end
of their love, but perhaps not the end of the narrow limits of their interest,
as Ames shows. Love gives too much attention to the one at the expense
of all others, and so it does not rise into the plurality Arendt argues is
essential to politics. For this reason, Arendt calls for respect rather than love
in public life. What "love is in its own, narrowly circumscribed sphere, respect is in the larger domain of human affairs."[7] In other words, instead of the
narrowness of mutual love, Arendt calls for the expansiveness of common
respect.

I think Arendt's account of love is itself too narrow, as she seems to define
love exclusively as interpersonal, romantic (and in this case, not only romantic, but also culminating in heterosexual, biologically procreative) attraction
and desire. In fact, recent scholarship has emphasized that her sense of public
accountability in the web of relation was also far too narrow and that she was
inclined toward the same racial complacency as John Ames and Robert
Boughton.[8] I believe we might think about love anew and in a way that can
both honor the demands of Arendt's politics while also grounding a notion of
human and divine forgiveness that can expand the reach and scope of our
loyalties rather than close them down. The account of love I give continues to
depend on desire in important ways, but instead of narrowing in on the terms
of that desire's satisfaction, it attends to what Ames has called the utter and
bitter preference for what has been lost and might never be regained. Loss
rather than gain, unsatisfied rather than satisfied desire, is the starting point
and inspiration for this love, even as it seeks to avoid the narrow limits of
Ames's vision. Along the way, I also think in this chapter about the affective
character of human forgiveness and the traditional theological rationale for
divine atonement, while turning to Louise Erdrich's powerful 2016 novel
LaRose.[9]

Gilead is the first of a series of novels revolving around the lives of two
families in rural Iowa. *LaRose* comes as the third in a series that, like the *Gilead* series, explores themes of justice, vengeance, forgiveness, and atonement.
But where Robinson focuses on a few characters from two families, Erdrich

expands her fictional imagination across multiple generations and landscapes of Ojibwe people in North Dakota and Minnesota. Where the first two novels in Erdrich's justice trilogy attend to issues of injustice, retaliation, law, and jurisdiction, the third—*LaRose*—turns to issues of atonement and reconciliation. And although the novel does not use the language of forgiveness explicitly, I believe that the modes of relationship and reparation that it explores are indispensable to my own account of forgiveness.

LaRose begins with a killing. On the second page of the novel, Landreaux Irons, a devout Ojibwe man in North Dakota who follows both traditional and Roman Catholic practices, who offers thanksgiving in English and then puts down tobacco in Ojibwe after completing a hunt, is tracking a buck in between his own and his neighbors' property. Next door live the Raviches, Peter, who is white, and his wife, Nola, who is the indigenous half-sister of Landreaux's wife, Emmaline. Landreaux takes a shot at the buck, but through an unaccountable freak accident, one not fully explained to the characters or by the novel, he kills Peter and Nola's six-year-old son, Dusty, the cousin and play companion of Landreaux and Emmaline's son, LaRose. The families both collapse into anguish, the Raviches' grief marked by rage and desolation, the Ironses' by guilt and despair. Visiting their priest, Father Travis, the Ironses cannot even speak of what has happened. Emmaline claps her hand over her mouth halfway through the meeting, her collar wet with tears, because she has no words to answer for this unspeakable thing. To use the language of our last chapter, there is no account she can reasonably give, and what is unaccountable also feels unlivable. Emmaline doesn't know how she or her husband, or her half-sister Nola, could possibly go on living (6). The Raviches also visit Father Travis, and in that meeting Nola's eyes are "dry with hate" (7–8).

In response to the tragedy, the Ironses decide to pursue an "old form of justice": they give LaRose to the Raviches to raise as their own child (36–37). Without giving LaRose the details of their plan, unclear even themselves what those details are, they pack a suitcase and visit their neighbors' doorstep. LaRose runs in to play with Dusty's toys, not realizing he's staying. The conversation on the doorstep of the Raviches' home is brief. Landreaux and Emmaline place the suitcase down and say simply, "Our son will be your son now," repeating the line to make Peter and Nola understand their meaning as Emmaline breaks down. Peter resists, saying he's never heard of any such thing, but Landreaux says quickly, "It's the old way," forcing out the words, unable to say anything more (16). These events comprise only the first few pages of the novel, and indeed the remainder of the story is concerned mostly with tracing out the ramifications of this fraught decision, the ways in which a history of colonial violence frames the lives of these families and how acts of violence, even ones unintended or accidental, can replicate and radiate through trauma and retaliation outward through time. But what's notable in these first few pages is how both the tragedy these families have known and their reaction to it evade any articulation. Nola cannot speak, Emmaline cannot speak, Peter says only that he doesn't understand, Landreaux forces out just a few words. The tragedy is unspeakable, unaccountable; none can speak of the loss they have witnessed nor of their best but broken response to it. The rationale for this offering of one son as a substitute for another is one that the narrative reveals over time, not only to the reader but to the characters also.

This is the old way, Landreaux says, and by this we understand him to mean that this is the traditional way of the Ojibwe. But Landreaux is a good Catholic, too, and it's hard not to read some version of a theology of atonement in the offering of LaRose, some echo in this sacrifice of a son, this giving of one child for another. The limited scope of the novel—the stakes here are familial and personal, not cosmological—brings the theologies of incarnation and atonement, their logics of child sacrifice, propitiation, and payback, into sharper relief. But even if this offering is a sacrifice, it is not one that accomplishes either payback or propitiation, as I discuss later in this chapter. Why, then, do the Ironses offer their son to the Raviches? Or, better, what good does it do? What is this old form of justice? What does it accomplish, and how? More directly, what does it tell us about the nature of forgiveness, and the political possibility for justice in a love that either asks for or offers it?

AFFECTIVE CONDITIONS

One possibility is that the unspeakable gift of LaRose is an act of atonement, although atonement itself can mean several things. If the penance of the monks in *The Buried Giant* is pious and empty, we might read the Ironses' act as a more productive gesture of amends or reparation. It is the sort of public gift of a wrongdoer that commends, perhaps commands, forgiveness, a kind of transaction. In Chapter 1, I took some time considering the law of retaliation and how it tends toward a fantastical illusion of recovery or recompense. But there's more to be said about the compensatory or transactional model of forgiveness, because the question of forgiveness's conditions tends to factor as one of the central areas of discussion in the scholarly literature, whether philosophical, legal, or theological. When can, should, or must one forgive? Under what conditions is it either felicitous or necessary? These accounts of forgiveness usually also assume that forgiveness is largely an affective experience, that it amounts to the overcoming of rancor or resentment. In other words, forgiveness describes an emotional change or affective transition. I suggest that the preoccupation with forgiveness as an emotional response to wrongdoing not only precludes any deeper reflection on the problems with compensatory justice, but also inevitably leads back toward the problematic forms of sovereignty critiqued by Arendt, Derrida, and Butler. And *LaRose* helps exemplify why and how an affective forgiveness can lead to worrisome politics.

Most contemporary scholars of forgiveness see interpersonal exchange as a fundamental attribute of forgiveness. For them, forgiveness is essentially transactional. In other words, for most major thinkers forgiveness must also definitionally be conditional. A condition or conditions must be met in order for forgiveness to be offered in return. And though thinkers differ in their views of what those conditions might be and the degree to which one might be compelled to forgive once the proper conditions have been met, they all seem to understand forgiveness as dyadic and transactional. Regina Schwartz, for example, observes that forgiveness "is not a unilateral act. It involves two: it is one's response to another's apology."[10] David Konstan, in his thorough examination of the classical sources that might be used to inform a modern interpretation of forgiveness, likewise assumes forgiveness to be a bilateral act that arises only as a response to set and socially established conditions. Konstan follows Charles Griswold, a thinker I engage more closely below, in defining forgiveness as a mutual transformation occasioned by the action of the wronged and prompted by the remorse and apology of the wrongdoer. Each party consequentially undergoes a personal, affective transformation, what Konstan calls a "change of heart."[11]

But it should be briefly noted that Konstan's study, though thorough, learned, and indispensable to any analysis of forgiveness as a moral concept, also somewhat begs his question, because in proving that modern forgiveness has no warrant in ancient sources, he defines a particular modern form of forgiveness as standard. There is little recognition that other possibilities for forgiveness might exist in modernity—he passes over major figures such as Bishop Joseph Butler and William Shakespeare as unhelpfully unrepresentative of modern conceptions of forgiveness, for example, and neglects the possibility that the New Testament ethics of Jesus might be stretching ancient moral expectations or straining ancient moral vocabularies toward new possibilities.

Konstan claims that in Shakespeare's plays forgiveness is illustrated only "in rather a perfunctory way, and perhaps scarcely counts as true forgiveness."[12] By perfunctory, Konstan means that the change of heart required for forgiveness seems inauthentic, rushed, or insincere in the late comedies. But given a figure as crucial to modernity as Shakespeare, one wonders whether a definition of modern forgiveness should minimally be able to account for what Shakespeare dramatically renders. This would lead one to question whether a change of heart should be so fundamental to our understanding of forgiveness. With regard to Bishop Butler, meanwhile, Konstan remarks how little Butler considers repentance and a change of heart as conditions for forgiveness and decides that his concern therefore must not be a full account of forgiveness at all but just a defense of forswearing vengeance.[13] One wonders, again, whether we might take Butler's own word for it and understand forgiveness as more like the forswearing of vengeance than a change of heart. This might lead us in turn to ask whether and why modern forgiveness must always be conditioned in the ways Konstan expects, whether forgiveness might in fact be more about restraining violence than transforming dispositions. Because the modern, transactional, and primarily affective variant of forgiveness is present neither in modern figures like Butler and Shakespeare nor in ancient Latin, Greek, and Hebrew texts, Konstan subtly suggests we jettison the modern preoccupation with forgiveness entirely.[14] Another option is available to us, of course. We could adjust our expectations of what forgiveness ought to mean and then look to ancient, early modern, and contemporary sources to aid us in constructively altering our understandings.

The theologian Maria Mayo interprets New Testament passages dealing with forgiveness in a way that echoes Konstan and likewise regards repentance and confession as prerequisites for forgiveness. In doing so she helpfully teases out the various failures of modern conceptions of forgiveness. But like Konstan, the forgiveness Mayo presumes is one that invariably anticipates reconciliation or affective transformation. Mayo quite rightly worries that the biblical "call for forgiveness" has been transformed at times into "a pop-psychological notion that requires only emotional work on the part of the victim."[15] Indeed she, like Konstan, goes to great lengths to show that the affective dimension of forgiveness is primarily a latter innovation and a contemporary preoccupation. But while she rightly regards affect as artificially attached to forgiveness in modernity, she also uses the ancient sources to argue that forgiveness's affective transformation should come only under firm conditions. She doesn't consider the possibility that there might be another form of forgiveness, ancient or modern, ambivalent about or even indifferent to affect. In other words, if there is a form of forgiveness that involves something other than the emotional labor of victims, then there may yet be a modern moral meaning to be gleaned from both the New Testament and the philosophical tradition we have inherited, a meaning that resists the reduction of forgiveness to affective change and avoids the economy of apology and punishment that tends—Mayo is surely correct in this—to actualize as emotional labor for victims. If so, then perhaps another moral and practical meaning might arise under the name of forgiveness.

Ashraf H. A. Rushdy, meanwhile, asserts the New Testament conditions for forgiveness somewhat differently in his recent book *After Injury*.[16] Or rather, he uncovers what he regards as an additional implication to Christian forgiveness: not only that some conditions are required for human forgiveness rightly to be offered, but also that human forgiveness rightly offered creates new and important conditions of divine forgiveness too. For Rushdy, Jesus's teachings in the New Testament describe human forgiveness as providing the basic conditions for the forgiveness of God: forgive and you will be forgiven (Luke 6:37, Matt 6:14, Mark 11:25). Or, to state the obverse: fail to forgive one another, and you will not be forgiven by God. On Rushdy's reading of Jesus's teachings, we forgive not only because an offender has apologized or atoned or sought reconciliation, but also because we wish for God to grant us divine forgiveness whenever we offer repentance ourselves. Rushdy's book is interesting and insightful as a piece of textual analysis and as a work of moral philosophy, but it has some limitations for a Christian theology of forgiveness. Christian theology, and my theology in particular, interprets both the sayings of Jesus and also the person and actions and story of Jesus—this Jesus who does forgive his murderers without condition and with divine authority while dying on the cross, who wishes his unbelieving betrayers peace in a secret upper room, who shares breakfast with them on a shore before they have had any chance to apologize or to atone, and who invites his disciples, past and present, into ongoing relationship with his unconditioned acts of forgiveness.[17]

One recent and important examination of all these questions comes from the philosopher Martha Nussbaum, whose account I briefly reviewed in Chapter 2 and who critiques forgiveness as essentially (if secretly) retributive in any form. Forgiveness is just another, if hidden and moralized, form of payback according to Nussbaum, and it inherits all the problems of impossible recompense I traced in Chapter 1. It is for this reason that Nussbaum turns away from forgiveness in either its conditional or its "unconditional" (though also sneakily conditional) forms and instead posits unconditional love as a moral alternative to every forgiving. In some respects, Nussbaum takes Konstan's advice: she jettisons the concept of forgiveness altogether because of the retributive conditions it seems necessarily (if secretly) to carry, and she replaces it with a form of peaceable love. Beyond the angry desire for recompense, Nussbaum asserts, waits the moral transformation that accompanies a shift "off the terrain of anger toward more productive forward-looking thoughts, asking what can actually be done to increase either personal or social welfare."[18] Yet for Nussbaum the transformation of affect still remains central; forgiveness must give way to love because pardon always smuggles in an irrational anger, desperate for compensation, under its demanded conditions. Nussbaum also glosses Bishop Butler, curiously paying little attention to his understanding of forgiveness as itself a form of love rather than love's angry antecedent. She appears either to neglect or to ignore that Butler clearly also regards anger as an acceptable affective state for both love and forgiveness. Butler's approach to love, anger, and forgiveness is tricky, and I review it shortly. For now it's worth noting only that Nussbaum terms this movement from secretly retributive forgiveness to forward-looking love the "Transition" or "Transitional" (though she also acknowledges the rare possibility of "Transition-Anger," an emotion she says is rarely purified of the desire for payback).

Nussbaum admits that the line between forgiveness and transition love can be blurry. Several New Testament articulations of love—the parable of the prodigal son, for example—do seem to escort retribution-obsessed forgiveness toward transition-focused love. As Nussbaum states, there seems in the Gospels to be a "version of unconditional forgiveness that lies very close to unconditional love and generosity," one that avoids the dangers of the "superiority or vindictiveness" she has diagnosed in forgiveness generally.[19] Nussbaum cites the forgiveness of some of the survivors and bereaved among the victims of the Charleston shooting, noted in the Introduction, as exemplary of her idea of loving forgiveness, of a forgiveness that transcends its own anger. She remarks that these grieving families successfully avoided expressing any anger, with the exception of Bethane Middleton-Brown, whose statement I addressed in the Introduction and who acknowledged lasting anger while also insisting that love is stronger than hate. Nussbaum notes that this love is not, strictly speaking, "Transitional" since no concrete transition is imagined but that there remains something laudably "Transitional in its spirit, in the idea that love will prevail over hate and that a world can be reconstructed by love."[20] Indeed, Nussbaum uses the example of these families to introduce the concept and practice of unconditional love, and in further support of which she offers a reading of Luke's prodigal son as a parable that transcends the vindictive limits of forgiveness for the sake of a higher love.

Middleton-Brown's offer of forgiveness toward Dylann Roof at that courtroom in 2015 was given unconditionally, it is true. It was unilateral; Roof showed no remorse whatsoever (though Roof did confess, a detail that perhaps introduces the possibility of transaction). This, for Nussbaum, is what elevates it out of the retributive structure of the payback wish toward the loving transcendence of transition. But I find Nussbaum's characterization of this event somewhat perplexing. First of all, I think it reduces the moral complexity of the Charleston victims' reaction to Dylann Roof in important ways. As noted in the Introduction, I do not read Middleton-Brown's acknowledgment of anger as a beam in the eye of her forgiveness; I believe she articulates it instead as a stubborn and central attribute of her grief and therefore also of her grief-stricken forgiveness. She is angry *and* she forgives. Anger doesn't preclude or impair her forgiveness, even if it sits uncomfortably alongside it. (How else should anger sit except uncomfortably?) Middleton-Brown may name herself a work in progress, but to me this says at least as much about the prospect of facing a future full of grief and anger as it does about the purity or character of her pardon. And indeed, unless we are prepared to read Middleton-Brown's forgiveness as somehow fundamentally flawed or incomplete because it still harbors anger, we must be ready to accept her anger as forgiving also. I worry about setting aside this justified anger, not only Middleton-Brown's but also the righteous anger of the several bereaved who refused to offer forgiveness at Roof's arraignment, because I wonder why it is we are so eager to qualify this anger as inadmissible to "true" forgiveness, or as insufficiently forgiving on its own. I suspect the reasons for this have more to do with the politics of race in the United States than with the subtleties of our moral philosophy. I say more about this in the pages that follow, but it seems to me both rationally and morally unnecessary that we ask victims to "surrender feelings" of anger at injustice, feelings that through their witness might "survive as a testimony and living memorial" for the sake of a philosophy of forgiveness that sits uncomfortably with anger.[21]

In any case, as Nussbaum notes, most versions of forgiveness come with conditions, and for her that is their problem. For some, like Konstan or Mayo, it is our failure to enforce the right conditions that irreparably troubles forgiving; for Nussbaum, the fact that these conditions exist at all is what confounds forgiveness. But all these critiques presume not only that real forgiveness is properly conditioned, but also that it is primarily affective. The problematic conditions these frameworks explore are all set around the abatement of anger. Nussbaum regards the transactional forgiveness so common in modernity—the form of affectively transformative forgiveness so deeply engrained in "church practices and, thence, in many aspects of personal and political relations"—as definitionally standard. Indeed, she cites eminent "historians of thought (e.g., David Konstan) and philosophers (e.g., Charles Griswold)" as presenting affectively transformative forgiveness as "the full or complete account of what forgiveness is." But Nussbaum also states quite openly that "the Gospels clearly offer a different model as well."[22] All this makes one wonder why Nussbaum wants so strictly to distinguish forgiveness from love on the assumption that "unconditional forgiveness is still understood as a waiving of angry emotion (as it is in the Jewish texts and in most human instances, though perhaps not in the case of Jesus)."[23] Even were we to assume her reading of the Jewish texts and most human instances accurate, the case of Jesus would seem to be of some relevance, not least for Christians and culturally influential "church practices." One wonders therefore why she should then separate forgiveness from love, the former always transactional and the latter blissfully transitional, in a way that both Joseph Butler and much Christian moral theology—not to mention Jesus himself—might find perplexing. Indeed, it seems to me what Nussbaum brackets is exactly Butler's crucial focus: to mount a limited defense of resentment as consistent with forgiveness, using Jesus's teachings on love as his rationale. Nussbaum first defines forgiveness as the overcoming of anger and then determines that it must therefore necessarily be implicated in the desire for payback because it satisfies its own anger through sanctimonious forms of retaliation. And she does so despite acknowledging that the forgiveness Jesus preaches is perhaps *not* one primarily concerned with affective transformation or even necessarily with demanding recompense. Nussbaum openly recognizes that there are certainly other New Testament responses to wrongdoing that might come under the label of forgiveness, while still marginalizing Bethane Middleton-Brown's Christian anger as inappropriate or morally insufficient.

I have referred to Joseph Butler and to what I take to be incomplete readings of him. I believe that Butler's argument is actually quite clear, and somewhat contrary to the interpretations of him we've seen so far. In fact, in his two sermons of 1729 titled "Upon Resentment" and "Upon Forgiveness of Injuries," Butler sets the foundation for so much subsequent reflection on forgiveness in the modern West through an extended reflection upon Jesus's exhortation from the Sermon on the Mount that we love our enemies (Matt 5:43–44). These are sermons about the nature of love in general, and of enemy love in particular, and what we find in Butler's preaching is that he has few of the affective assumptions or preoccupations we carry today. His conclusion is decidedly *not* that forgiveness simply means to overcome resentment. On the contrary, he argues at length (especially in the first sermon) that "resentment is natural and just" in the wake of wrongdoing.[24] He believes resentment is necessary, because it reminds us of injustice and thus helps us to recognize and resist it. But this necessary resentment does not preclude the possibility of love or forgiveness. His moral purpose is not in railing against resentment as such but in denouncing the fact that "custom and false honor are on the side of retaliation and revenge" when our natural resentments arise.[25] Indeed, Butler's primary concern is to discourage those "abuses" of resentment that become "excessive" and that then flower into "malice or revenge."[26] To overcome resentment does not mean to cease feeling it; it means to cease acting unilaterally with violence as a result of it. For Butler, resentment in itself is not a moral wrong; revenge that takes resentment as its justification is. Whereas Butler rejects the customary marriage of resentment to revenge, he still wants to preserve the moral anger we experience in response to wrongdoing without it giving way to retaliatory acts of vengeance. Crucially, Butler insists that "resentment is *not* inconsistent with good-will," and "we may love our enemy, and yet have resentment against him for his injurious behavior towards us" (emphasis added). According to Butler, then, "to forgive injuries, is the same as to love our enemies."[27] It is not to make enemies friends, or even to become friendly toward them. It is simply to love them, to intend goodness toward them rather than evil.

It is important to emphasize how sharply Butler's view contradicts what has become conventional wisdom: the forgiveness Butler proposes is decidedly not about overcoming anger or any other hostile emotion. It's not even about accepting apologies or restoring relationships and reconciling. Not unlike Arendt's miraculous forgiveness, it is about resisting the acts toward which our anger or despair may tempt us. Despite the usual reading of him, Butler says that neither love nor forgiveness—or more properly, forgiveness as a form of love—is about overcoming resentment at all. Unlike his latter-day interpreters in moral philosophy and theology, negative affect is not a primary preoccupation of Bishop Butler when it comes to forgiveness, at least not on the human scale of interpersonal or even political ethics.

When we read Butler's sermons closely, we discover a pastoral generosity toward victims and their justified anger that is in fact entirely consistent with contemporary critiques of forgiveness as the abatement of anger, since the wronged in Butler's sermons remain absolutely entitled to their anger. Butler's sermons also express a deeper and more pressing theological concern, for both early and postmodernity, beyond the question of moral sentiment. Butler's forgiveness is a form of love, but love is not simply warm or glowing sentiment. Butler is uninterested in love having such narrow affective limits, a narrowness the political consequences of which we see in Arendt's critique above and which I think Butler is trying to avoid. On the contrary, love includes a variety of feelings, such as anger, bitterness, resentment, and sadness. This is why it is a moral possibility with respect to those who remain our enemies. And it's also why the concept of transition, as Nussbaum describes it, might not require the abatement of anger. On Butler's account, anger is essential to forward-looking love. Recall Waltrina Middleton's argument in the Introduction against forgiveness. Anger is the affective response to injustice, and so any adequate response to injustice will include some anger, even if its moral and active response remains loving. Forgiveness for Butler is not simply the overcoming of resentment. If forgiveness overcomes anything, it overcomes the urge to act upon vengeful anger, not the affective experience of that anger in itself. We can decide how we react to our feelings, but there isn't any natural or necessary outward expression of inward affect that must follow from our feelings. Deciding which actions we will undertake rather than what emotions we will allow ourselves to feel seems to me (and I think to some degree to Joseph Butler also) the more pressing moral question in nearly every instance. We can morally police what we do, regardless of what we feel or how well we can discipline those feelings. Especially in the wake of wrongdoing, denoting which emotions victims are morally entitled to feel seems pointless at least and cruel at worst.

But if Butler's sermons are fairly clear, what's also clear is that the modern Western tradition of moral philosophy and theology that followed in his wake tends to read forgiveness as largely, if not exclusively, an affective, experiential, and transactional event. Payback is not just about compensating for loss; it is also about setting a price for the abatement of anger. In her study of forgiveness and revenge, for example, Trudy Govier conceives "of forgiveness as a process of overcoming attitudes of resentment and anger that may persist when one has been injured by wrongdoing."[28] In her own analysis of revenge, retaliation, and retribution, Jean Hampton asserts that "forgiveness should be analyzed as a *process* involving, not only certain psychological preparations (mainly the overcoming of various forms of anger) but, more positively, a change in heart towards the wrongdoer which is something other than a condoning of her action and which is normally accompanied by an offer of reconciliation."[29] For Hampton, the overcoming of inward anger is distinct from "a change in heart towards the wrongdoer," though it's not initially obvious what the distinction between overcoming anger and change of heart signifies. The difference, Hampton explains with great subtlety, comes down to the disparity between our regard for ourselves and our regard for our abusers. Forgiveness, Hampton writes, occurs in two stages. Prior to a change of heart, the victim regains "confidence in [his] own worth despite the immoral action challenging it."[30] This is accomplished in the repudiation of spite, malice, and resentment. But even after this repudiation, Hampton explains, "indignation at the action and some degree of moral hatred towards the wrongdoer may remain."[31] It is only after these lasting emotions are overcome that true change of heart, and thus authentic forgiveness, is achieved. In other words, for Hampton the giving up of anger signifies a "transcendence" of injury that accompanies restored self-worth. Change of heart, meanwhile, involves additionally changing one's regard for one's abuser. Note that along this line of reasoning Hampton must presume anger to accompany hatred; there is no possibility for angry love, or for broken relation. For this reason she also marries the idea of reconciliation to forgiveness, since the offer of forgiveness necessarily signals the crucial change of heart in important ways.[32] In other words, what signifies adequate change of heart is the desire for reconciliation. Thus we see collapsed together into a single, profoundly demanding moral act not only Butler's forgiving restraint, but also the transformation of negative affect, as well as the offer of restored relationship. No wonder critics condemn forgiveness as an outlandish moral and emotional labor beset upon victims, when it requires three such significant tasks in one summative, heroic, and all-encompassing act. I think there is probably some benefit in preventing this conceptual collapse and reflecting on these as separable and separate moral events.

Jeffrie Murphy, meanwhile, whose defense of vengeance and retribution I discussed in Chapter 1, reads Butler's forgiveness as "a moral virtue (a virtue of character) that is *essentially a matter of the heart*, the inner self, and involves a change in inner feeling more than a change in external action." On Murphy's reading, Butler's forgiveness means overcoming "the vindictive passions of resentment, anger, hatred, and the desire for revenge," which nonetheless arise quite naturally when one has been injured.[33] But again, what remains unspecified here is what Murphy means by overcoming. While Butler might admit in a nontechnical sense that resentment is "overcome" by forgiveness, surely what he would mean is that through forgiveness we overcome resentment's violent impulses and active abuses, that its most retributive and retaliatory urges might be contained rather than acted upon. Butler is decidedly *not* interested in condemning the affective experience of anger itself. Indeed, so much of modern and contemporary thought understands forgiveness to be primarily a form of emotional policing or affective discipline that Nussbaum summarily observes how conventional wisdom uses the word "forgiveness" to refer to "whatever attitudes one thinks good in the management of anger."[34] This slippery evasion of specificity, Nussbaum complains, challenges and confuses critical thinking. Forgiving comes to cover a manner of meanings as "an all-purpose term of commendation in the general neighborhood of dealing with wrong-doing."[35]

Note here again, however, that this complaint presumes the management of victims' anger to be constitutive of reckoning with wrong. Forgiveness, in modern moral philosophy, means managing and eradicating anger. In what she terms the "canonical" sense, therefore, Nussbaum too defines forgiveness as "a change of heart on the part of the victim, who gives up anger and resentment in response to the offender's confession and contrition."[36] This particular definition does indeed seem to outline the relationship between affect and condition in a canonical sense. There is a predetermined price for relinquishing resentment, an exchange of anger for amends, the word for which is forgiveness. As Arendt worries, this forgiveness does seem excessively narrow and apolitical. If this is the definition of forgiveness with which Nussbaum operates, it is not surprising that she decries it as transactional and anger as ineluctably obsessed with compensation. Still, it's not obvious to me that anger does or should always expect compensation. If, as Butler suggests, anger signals a persisting wrong, then the deepest anger might be one that recognizes the impossibility of any compensation and so begins to converge with or collapse into mourning and grief.

As with Hampton's slide toward reconciliation, Nussbaum's representative marriage of affective transformation to confession and contrition is significant. The change of heart here occurs only in response to authentic apology. Though Nussbaum does admit that certain forms of love involve "Transition-Anger" and though she concedes that Jesus's ideals of forgiveness might not be primarily grounded in either affective change or the demand for recompense, by and large she frames forgiveness exclusively as an emotional exercise, one inextricable from the conditions of confessional or apologetic exchange, and therefore a moral act that is invariably rooted in the wish for payback and therefore fundamentally wanting. Nussbaum is only the last and among the most distinguished in a long line of scholars who have thus characterized forgiveness. The affective emphasis in modern conceptions of forgiveness is nearly universal, and so too is the insistence that forgiveness is only rightfully offered upon some met or established condition. This link, I think, is not accidental. It, too, can be traced to Joseph Butler's sermons, even if we accept the apologetics of resentment I have tried to reassert in Butler.

LAWFUL CONDITIONS

In perhaps the most exhaustive history and philosophy of forgiveness, *Forgiveness: A Philosophical Exploration*, Charles Griswold observes and defends the same conferral of affect and condition in forgiveness.[37] I focus on Griswold now because—unlike so many others—Griswold recognizes and explores the subtle distinction Butler makes between resentment and revenge, though in the end he still wishes to preserve forgiveness's fundamentally affective character. Griswold rightly notes that Butler is "regularly misquoted" as defining forgiveness "as the 'forswearing of resentment'"; in fact, Griswold clarifies, Butler calls forgiveness "the forswearing of *revenge*" (Griswold, *Forgiveness*, 20). Nonetheless, Griswold insists that forgiveness must in the end "*somehow*" involve overcoming the anger one feels in response to injury" (xiv). Once again, as with my consideration of Jeffrie Murphy above, much depends upon what the word "overcoming" here means. For Griswold, as I show, it means suppressing or eradicating the feeling. Moreover, Griswold states that his fundamental thesis "is that forgiveness comes with conditions attached" (xv). I now explore what overcoming means in Griswold's case, why he sees affect as therefore essential to forgiveness, and why, on his account, certain conditions must be set and attached to the forgiving act. This is crucial, because Griswold's reading of Butler uniquely conveys how and why affect and condition come to be linked in contemporary Western forms of forgiveness, and why a forgiveness thus conceived remains politically limited in a way that Arendt anticipates and Erdrich addresses and corrects.

Griswold clarifies that Butler's distinction between forswearing revenge and forgoing resentment is important at least partly because of how Butler characterizes resentment itself. The conditions that eventually, through Griswold's constructive reading of Butler, come to be attached to forgiveness originate in the way Butler describes resentment and its abuses. Crucially, resentment for Butler and Griswold is "not just a 'raw feel' but embodies a judgment about the fairness of an action or of an intention to do that action" (Griswold, 26). So, for example, the sort of pain or even anger that comes from experiencing a tragedy of natural evil would not properly include resentment, since resentment necessarily assumes some moral judgment of another's actions. These feelings of resentment are, on Butler's account, natural, neither inherently moral nor immoral in themselves, and indeed do serve an important moral purpose in sustaining a healthy self-interest and desire for justice, as Solomon and Murphy argue (see Chapter 1). Without this capacity for affective judgment, Butler reasons, we might too easily relent before harm or accept unjust cruelties. What Butler condemns as immoral, therefore, is not resentment but the "abuse" of it, which most obviously arises in acts of unilateral revenge: "retaliation by an individual as he or she judges to be appropriate" (Griswold, 32).

This unilateral dimension is crucial. What Griswold astutely sees Butler emphasizing here is the independence, the individual isolation, of the judgment. For Butler, revenge's primary flaw is not necessarily that it is violent, but that its violence is undertaken unilaterally, without the tempering reason of social norms and institutions. In responding to one's personal, affective urges rather than to the rational requirements of the social order, resentment gives way to abuse. Moreover, resentment is constantly tempted toward this sort of unilateral action. Because of its judgmental character, resentment is inclined "not just to feel a certain anger, but 'to *do* mischief, to be the author of misery'" (Griswold, 35). It is inclined, that is, toward individual retaliation, toward its own abuse.

Although not yet obvious, this is where I think the modern preoccupation for linking affect and condition arises. According to Griswold's reading of Butler, revenge is not the only possible abuse of resentment, just its most public and obvious one. If the source of resentment's abuse is its unilateral expression, then a resentment that refused retaliation could still become problematic on its own if its emotional expression proved excessively exaggerated or unilateral. In other words, for Butler, one could remain abusively angry in the wake of harm, even if one never actually retaliated. One could be *too* angry, and this would be a moral problem in its own right. But how are we to judge when an emotion has become irrationally or abusively exaggerated? How angry is too angry? Butler suggests that the corrective standard to our excess resentment is a social one. We need a disinterested third party,

Butler argues, or a system of law and justice built upon some imagined impartial observer, to adjudicate the abusiveness of our anger. In other words, social norms will tell us when we have become too angry. We can determine that resentment has wandered too far toward abuse when a disinterested spectator of good character would regard our resentment as excessive, whether or not that anger ever erupted into actual violence. Butler's theory therefore "holds that [forgiveness] includes the *moderating* of resentment" to a level judged appropriate "by a suitably informed and sympathetic third party" (Griswold, 41). Although this could conceivably involve the approval of "a continuing high level of moral anger" (41), Griswold interprets this neutral, third-party judgment in Butler as signifying that some resentments are warranted and others are unwarranted, that some angers—even if entirely divorced from retaliatory action—on their own, simply as angry affective states, should be purged from experience because they exist at all. The problem is determining which anger has warrant. Knotty though that question may be, for this reason Griswold argues that real forgiveness must eventually demand the commitment to pursue an abatement of anger; it must aspire toward a moderation that is socially recognized and conditioned.

This is where Butler and Griswold are led to demand that certain socially and culturally established norms and conditions must be set in exchange for any offer of forgiveness. Were his forgiveness simply the Arendtian exercise of restraint before the temptation toward revenge, it would be a negative sort of obligation: only do no harm, however much you might wish to. In short, do not return evil for evil (1 Pet 3:9). The sin of abuse would merely be the existence of retaliatory violence. So how and why does Butler turn once again to the limitation and expurgation of resentment, if at a somewhat higher threshold, in his relatively resentment-friendly conception of forgiveness?

The slippage here is between individual anger and socially sanctioned acts of retaliation. As I read him, Butler is trying to preserve some space for what he regards as the administration of lawful justice. He is trying to defend a socially authorized system of retributive punishment as rational and moral. In other words, he is defending English criminal law and endorsing the good authority of criminal punishment. Some officially sanctioned vengeance must remain allowable, Butler insists, since the Crown engages in this violence all the time. The very "subsistence of the world," he preaches, demands that "injustice and cruelty should be punished." The problem is that humans are so naturally compassionate that the "execution of justice" proves "exceedingly difficult and uneasy." Indignation and resentment counterbalance the "weakness" of our "pity, and also anything else that would prevent the necessary methods of severity." In other words, we need anger to balance our compassion, so that we will be able to punish others without mercy when and as "the strictest way of moral consideration" demands it.[38] For Butler, the penal requirements of justice demand some level of resentment. To eradicate it entirely would be to lose the nerve to undertake these "necessary methods of severity." Violence cannot be purged entirely from human responses to wrong; it is only individual, unilateral acts of violence that need to be eradicated. Butler seeks at once to undermine retaliation at the individual level while approving it at the social, legal, and juridical one, and he turns to the reasonableness of affect as his primary means of distinguishing between the two. He understands resentment as abuse not whenever it manifests as violence, but only when that violence is founded on the irrational urge of an individual rather than on the common and rational sense of a social order. Butler's concern to protect some social interest in retributive criminal justice thus opens the way for affect and resentment to return to our idea of forgiveness and fundamentally govern it. Griswold's forgiveness does therefore allow for some lingering anger, but in his case the forgiver must commit to diminishing her resentment out of existence over time. In addition to forswearing revenge, Griswold writes, forgiveness should connote an "ethical commitment" to come into a new relationship with the wrongdoer, a commitment that signals the forgiver is already working to expunge resentment even if some rancor presently and temporarily remains (Griswold, 42). Griswold admits that forgiveness must account for Butler's argument that resentment is natural and for the everyday human experience that anger often lingers following an offer of forgiveness. For this practical and pastoral wisdom his thorough analysis is to be commended. But he also problematically believes that our notion of forgiveness should still preserve "the intuition that fully achieved forgiveness would let go of resentment altogether" even though "resentment doesn't respond immediately and wholly to cognitive emendations or to one's will" (42–43). All this because Butler wants to defend the Crown's right to administer pain as recompense for crime.

I worry about this, and not just because of the concern over recompense and retaliation I outlined in my first two chapters. Butler does not want to sanction human inclinations toward vengeance because of their propensity to give rise to violence, and because of violence's propensity to invite violent response. He's worried about the escalating reactions of retaliation Arendt has already described. But we also know that social and cultural norms are just as (if not more) prone to violence as individual passions, especially when they run along the familiar lines of structural oppression we see in white supremacy, patriarchy, colonialism, etc. Once we become concerned like Butler to preserve some socially sanctioned forms of violent retaliation, the sort of violence that a "sympathetic and suitably informed third party" might judge kindly and endorse, affect invariably reenters the equation. Griswold wanders back toward this preoccupation with affect when he astutely notes that Butler too, even for all his sympathy toward the experience of resentment, believes that some states of anger are in and of themselves morally problematic, and what makes them abusive is the fact that others might regard them as excessive. But who are these others, what moral authority do they hold, and what interest might they have in eradicating righteous anger—especially an anger already disinclined to violence? Or to put it more succinctly: Who gets to decide which angers are justified and which are not? Because resentment is so naturally inclined toward abuse, Griswold and Butler worry, it can easily exceed rational bounds—the sort of bounds that, say, an impartial but interested third party might recognize—and when it does this, it becomes excessive and unwarranted in itself, its potentially peaceable restraint notwithstanding. The trouble is, the social order that Butler and Griswold have entrusted to adjudicate excessive affect is anything but impartial. We know this because that same social order has historically been responsible for the unfair administration of our criminal punishments. The people most likely to bear the brunt of criminal punishment are also the ones whose anger we find least socially acceptable. In other words, these affective and lawful conditions smuggle white supremacy, sexism, coloniality, and other forms of structural violence into forgiveness.

Consider again the Charleston families. Recall the speck Nussbaum sees in the angry eye of Bethane Middleton-Brown. Nussbaum is our disinterested third party judging the appropriateness of a victim's anger here. This should bother us. It bothers me. It benefits white supremacy to regard forgiveness as an affective erasure of anger, because when anger dissipates (as Joseph Butler has argued), we can convince ourselves that our problems have been resolved. This is why Butler so stubbornly defends resentment; it reminds us of persistent injustice. Were we to feel better, we might believe our broken world prematurely redeemed and coax ourselves into complacency. Thus emerges the temptation to dislodge justified anger from proper forgiveness. When forgiveness is governed by the affective permissions of social norms, when the amount of acceptable anger is determined by a system that is racist, then we get only the forgiveness whiteness wants. In other words, if America's forgiveness is one that demands anger's abatement, then we should not be surprised to see the contours of that demand in white Christianity's squeamishness before the justified righteousness of Black anger in this country. We should not be surprised to find white philosophers unable to read Middleton-Brown's anger as forgiving. We should not be surprised that we were so quick as a nation "to embrace this gracious act of forgiveness as our own."[39] It is because white people, even after they have been forgiven, do not want to feel discomfort over or accountability for their wrongdoing. Rather than address the uncomfortable social and historical causes of that justified, righteous anger, they demand their forgivers relinquish it. If the anger has passed, so must have the problem, and the injustice need no longer demand redress. But this is a delusion.

In the words of Waltrina Middleton, DePayne Middleton-Doctor's cousin, it is because "we live in God" that we "can live into forgiveness." But the manner in which many received the Charleston families' forgiveness, Middleton continues, "took away our narrative to be rightfully hurt. . . . We're not allowed to be angry? We . . . have to tell the truth: the racism is real."[40] It is a much more morally rich and demanding forgiveness that refuses to retaliate after violence but that *also* refuses to relinquish righteous anger. It is a far more challenging and essential forgiveness that indignantly insists on the impossibility of compensation. If white, Western morality cannot recognize a rage like this as forgiving, this has more to do with the moral insecurities of whiteness than with the righteous judgments of real forgiveness. In other words, if Bethane Middleton-Brown and Waltrina Middleton are angry, it is because they have a right and a reason to be. And if academic philosophy cannot recognize their forgiveness as operating in and alongside that anger, it may be that the beam in its own eye has obscured its moral vision. Even more insidiously, it seems that the urge to discipline affect is conceptually married to the practice of disciplining bodies in Western moral thought. The system of justice that Butler's argument preserves leaves no room for Black anger, while also providing the moral rationale for the disproportionate punishment of Black people.

The affective frame that defines forgiveness under this model, a frame perfectly willing to sanction state violence while diminishing white anxiety, has dramatic consequences, particularly for the forgiving victim. When forgiveness signifies the abatement of anger as a promise of reconciliation, forgiveness itself becomes a moral problem. The primary moral challenge a potential forgiver faces is no longer simply, Should I commit an act of retaliatory violence? Instead, with social norms looking over her shoulder, the forgiving victim must ask, Is my anger uncomfortable to others? Are my emotions the real sin? Am I obligated to abate my rage for the sake of my abuser's feelings? The collapse of anger abatement and reconciliation into a single, passive forgiveness shifts away from a question of how a victim should respond to real harm and instead invites the regulation of the victim's emotional state. This forgiveness sets an unreasonably favorable price on the mollification of anger. Moreover, the price is always already set beforehand, usually by cultural systems of meaning that are sympathetic to structures of violation, and so the deck is always stacked in advance and in favor of forgetting, change of heart, and reconciliation on the part of the victim. Forgiveness on this model might "not attempt to get rid of warranted resentment," but it does seek to recognize when "resentment is no longer warranted," and its focus thus shifts from the victim's complaints toward which conditions the offender "should meet to qualify for forgiveness" (Griswold, *Forgiveness*, 43). In other words: when the offender pays the right penitential price, one is morally obliged to abandon one's anger. Moral accountability has thus moved from abuser to victim. Forgiveness on this account is an exchange in which abusers coerce the purchase of their own freedom from anger, memory, and estrangement. It is because of Butler's concern to preserve the legal right of punishing offenders in a socially administered system of justice that victims lose their affective freedom, their rageful remembrance becomes stigmatized, and their forgiveness loses its moral relevance as an act of unrelenting and nonretaliatory judgment.

I find Griswold's argument troubling, even if it does follow from a careful reading of Butler, whose sermons on forgiveness and defenses of resentment remain crucial for altering our contemporary understanding of this moral act. But we should not misunderstand the stakes of this reasoning. At first Butler seems to have no moral problem with resentment in itself; a "just anger or continuing sorrow" may be a necessary element of the loss forgiveness answers and the sin it judges.[41] For Butler, as for another Anglican bishop, Desmond Tutu, forgiveness simply amounts to "abandoning a right to revenge or payback," since "one can't let go of pain by an act of will."[42] There is moral potential for this form of forgiveness, one unbeholden to either affect or condition. But Butler's anxiety to defend lawful punishment leads him away from this simple definition toward the complexities of lawful conditions. What Butler first casts as a challenging practice of love for enemies, what functions in his Christian sermons as a habit of a nonviolent judgment that at once affirms victims' anger without theologically condoning their acts of vengeance, ultimately opens the way for an erasure of that anger and for the commodification of forgiveness as a form of exchange in which equanimity is paid for in pain. Responsibility has shifted in crucial ways in the concern to restrain not just revenge but also "unwarranted" anger. Restraint from retaliation is a demanding moral task in and of itself, but it is a negative one. To do no harm may at times demand immense moral strength, but even when it does, it is resolve and restraint rather than a positive obligation. But on the model Griswold has given, once an abuser satisfies the right conditions for proper anger abatement—the sort of conditions an "impartial" third party might recognize as reasonable—suddenly a new moral burden falls to the victim: to eliminate righteous anger, to begin the process of reconciliation, or at least to promise to do so as quickly as possible, since the abuser's acts have rendered resentment unwarranted, unjustified, and therefore immoral.

It must be acknowledged that Griswold, for his part, doesn't see a lot of merit in vengeful penal practices. What's done is done. In his account, "forgiveness accepts that the past is unchangeable, but asserts that our responses to it are not (and these include our decisions about the future). It denies that the alternatives to vengeful violence are either condonation or resigned and submissive acceptance" (Griswold, *Forgiveness*, 29). With this I wholeheartedly concur. But Griswold's sympathy with the idea that an external norm should govern and adjudicate individual affective responses leads him to identify forgiveness primarily with anger abatement and to err on the side of obliging forgiveness when certain conditions—the normative ones—are met. Griswold's policing of the victim's affect thus assumes the same role that the state's law plays in Butler. It becomes the metric by which the victim's anger can be measured, managed, and marginalized. Nussbaum meanwhile recognizes these conditions as the victim's secret maneuvers of retribution, but because she too clings to a notion of forgiveness as a primarily affective response, she regards forgiveness as itself a moralized form of payback. For her, "forgiveness remains backward-looking," incapable of imagining a new future. Though it "may remove an impediment to the future, . . . it does not point there in and of itself."[43]

I write more about forgiveness's relation to the future in Chapter 4, but for now let me say simply that I think Nussbaum may be more right than she realizes. Forgiveness may retain clear memories of the past, especially when it remains angry and wounded in the wake of loss. But this is its gift, not its burden. Forgiveness understands the past's brokenness, and that is precisely why it offers the only real promise for a just future. To reduce forgiveness to backward-looking rage is at once to undersell the promise of nonretaliation and to rush forgiveness too quickly toward reconciliation. It is simply reductive to assert that the removal of an impediment to the future does not point to any future at all. As Judith Butler has argued, when the threat the future promises is reciprocal violence, choosing restraint can be an incredibly constructive action and will preface whatever peaceful future might follow. Any adequate vision of the future must surely be willing to reckon with what has been lost. It does no good to imagine a future arm in arm with a brother who is dead and murdered. But I can perhaps envision a possible future in which I learn to grieve his loss and then try to live meaningfully in the wake of that death.

What I have been striving to argue is that forgiveness is more than just one among a set of options that victims can undertake in the aftermath of wrongdoing. It is not strictly speaking an alternative to vengeance or to retribution or to punishment or to penance or to confession. Rather, forgiveness upsets the entire compensatory economy of loss, whereby acts such as vengeance, retribution, punishment, penance, apology, or confession are conscripted into futile attempts at recompense. In other words, forgiveness operates outside the transactional assumptions and retaliatory economies of our systems of justice. And there are, in fact, deep retributive and transactional assumptions to our sense of justice—so deep they are often regarded as natural. Trudy Govier notes that there "is a conviction in many circles, often a very powerful one, that when wrongdoers are punished, justice is done." When revenge becomes "linked to punishment through concepts of retribution, and punishment, retributively construed, is essential for Justice," then *it is the wrongdoing of the offender, making him deserving of punishment, that morally legitimates and requires his suffering.*[44] According to our basic moral intuitions, punishment and retribution, these formalized articulations of revenge, are simply how justice is served. Indeed, punishment becomes its own end. It is not just how justice is administered; it is the form justice takes. But it is also, of course, conceptually and practically possible to decouple punishment from the attribution of guilt, since judgment doesn't, in fact, itself include the imposition of punishment. To judge and to render judgment is to assign blame, whereas the determination of sentencing, or administration of pardon, is a separable and separate act. As Margaret Holmgren elaborates, "once an accurate judgment has been formulated, the task of judging has been completed. Any further step we take beyond mere judgment must be in service of some further end, and requires additional justification." This would be especially the case, she continues, when those additional ends are meant to inflict "serious harm on the recipient."[45] But if our conception of justice instead sought to secure for each individual "the most fundamental benefits in life compatible with like benefits for all, [with] no individual . . . required to sacrifice a significant interest so that others can benefit in less important ways"; if, in other words, the expression of our judgment were based not first on what any particular individual was owed, let alone what unrecoverable debts might be (impossibly) paid, then our judgments might find expression outside the transactional frameworks of retributive justice Nussbaum critiques.[46] Again, this would be neither to silence anger nor to coerce reconciliation. On the contrary, it would be to allow our own anger, rather than a wrongdoer's penal suffering, to serve as our primary reminder of the broken past, and to put off reconciliation until it will demand no unreasonable sacrifice from victims. Forgiveness on this model is therefore "emphatically not about failing to have a moral, emotional, and possibly heartrendingly painful response to being hurt or seeing others hurt"; rather, forgiveness is about "having and experiencing this response and finding a better way forward than rage, revenge, bitterness, or grudge."[47]

Despite the implication that might accompany the work of scholars like Mayo or Konstan around the particular issues of forgiveness, or of thinkers like Nussbaum on the relevance of Jesus's teaching, the New Testament proposes exactly this different framework for justice, one where, as Christopher Marshall writes, "the basic principle of moral order is not the perfect balance of deed and desert but redeeming, merciful love."[48] Whereas a justice based uncritically on an oversimple illusion of compensation seeks only to "check and punish evil; the justice commended in the New Testament," he continues, "seeks to overcome evil with good, to repair the damage done by sin, and to restore peace to human relationships."[49] Our retributive intuitions notwithstanding, there is "one dimension of God's action" that the New Testament suggests Christians "are expressly *forbidden* to imitate—namely, God's role as avenger and judge."[50] As such, a concern "to imitate and extend Christ's transformative, healing justice to those in need should shape and guide Christian involvement in and evaluation of the criminal justice system."[51]

To be clear, I don't mean to assert that there is no moral viability to any form of punishment, only to insist that punitive practices must be "redemptive or restorative in design" to be "capable of demonstrating or affirming

what actually is, what the world, from God's perspective, is really like."⁵² In
other words, they would be motivated neither by retaliation nor by retribution, but by protection and healing. Nor do I intend entirely to impugn
rights-based considerations of justice and the common good. To invoke Theodor Adorno again, I'm simply exploring that conceptual space where moral
questions arise, precisely at those places where our moral grammars fail. Our
retributive and retaliatory response to irrevocable loss is one place our language seems particularly impoverished and inadequate.⁵³

FORGIVING ANGER

There is something about equating justice with punishment that allows
power to have it both ways. It reserves the right both to respond to violence
with violence and to condemn the anger of victims. I return now to *LaRose*
and this other justice the novel troublingly models. When Landreaux acci-
dently kills his neighbor's boy, Dusty, he and his wife, Emmaline, offer their
son, LaRose, to Peter and Nola Ravich in place of the child who has died. It's
the old way, they say, what the local priest calls an "old form of justice,"
though at the beginning of the novel no one has any words to describe either
what has befallen them or what the justice to which they are aspiring might
promise or entail. In what remains of this chapter, I explore the contours of
this justice as it is ultimately revealed in the novel. I argue that the offering of
LaRose, quite apart from modeling a simple like for like compensation in
which a child is given for a child (as if an eye for an eye), instead reveals one
version of a different justice, a possibility for what atonement might be, an
atonement that acknowledges the impossibility of compensation, builds and
expands social bonds beyond the narrowest limits of love, and seeks to promote peace rather than to undo violence. This is not to suggest that the exchange of children between victims and wrongdoers should become a
normative practice for peace-building. But the old form of justice we read in
this novel will give us a sense of what is at stake theologically and politically
in our acts of forgiveness; it will give us a framework for thinking through
how and why we say that God has offered God's son for our sake; and it will
suggest how we might turn to the death of Jesus as a spiritual and moral foundation for the possibility of this different justice, rather than as the rationale
for a redemptive suffering.

First it is crucial not to abstract the startling offer of this child in *LaRose*
out of the colonial and racist history in which it appears. This story does not

start with this story; indeed, part of the significance of the novel standing third chronologically in a series is to show its place in a continuing history. The text itself, and the community it narrates, is quite aware of this history and self-consciously tells and retells the story out of which it arises. To use the language of Chapter 2, it gives a rich and complicated account of itself.[54] The novel does not stand alone. As noted in the Introduction, *LaRose* is the third in a trilogy of novels, each one distinctly incisive about the complexities of justice and redemption across several generations of linked families in an Ojibwe community in North Dakota. And these families do not stand alone; they stand among countless others in time and space. What's more, LaRose himself does not stand alone. He is the fifth LaRose in six generations, the first four of whom were women. These women's stories, and specifically their stories as metonyms for the history of the Ojibwe encounter with white colonialism, frame the novel. This framing exposes the ways in which violence radiates and replicates in uncontrollable ways. Emmaline's mother, the fourth LaRose Peace, lives happily in the Elders Lodge (a sort of tribal assisted living facility), telling dirty jokes to scandalize young visitors, playing pranks on staff, and staying ahead of her chronic pain with the regular use of time-released fentanyl patches. Once while self-administering fentanyl, the shade of her mother, the third LaRose, walks up from the graveyard near the lodge and stops by to visit Mrs. Peace. Mrs. Peace pulls out some press clippings from the Aberdeen *Saturday Pioneer* and shares them with her mother, clippings in which Frank Baum, the author of the *Wizard of Oz*, advocates the utter annihilation of the indigenous American peoples. "Having wronged them for centuries," he writes, "we had better, in order to protect our civilization, follow it up with one more wrong and wipe these untamed and untamable creatures from the face of the earth."[55] This editorial is real; elsewhere, unquoted in the novel, Baum commends the dead Sitting Bull for his "white man's spirit of hatred and revenge." What wonder, Baum continues, "that [Sitting Bull] should obtain every opportunity for obtaining vengeance" given that the whites with whom he dealt "were marked in their dealings with his people by selfishness, falsehood and treachery."[56] Vengeance and retribution, Baum says, is the white man's justice. Mrs. Peace's mother then recalls being taken from her family and forcibly sent to Fort Totten boarding school where the children's braids were cut off and their traditional dress destroyed so these children could be "sacrificed for" others, so they could show white folks, in her mother's words, that the Ojibwe people could "become human" (Erdrich, *LaRose*, 70). Their casual conversation reveals a systemic and entirely unveiled attempt at genocide, one that manifests itself across generations. Mrs. Peace's grandmother was also sent to boarding school. And LaRose's father, Landreaux, Mrs. Peace's son-in-law, was sent away to boarding school. The first LaRose was given by her vicious mother to a white man as payment, and this man, Mackinnon, sexually assaulted her until she escaped with (and eventually married) his white assistant, Wolfred. In this multivoiced, multivalent history we learn that children have been removed from indigenous families for generations, systematically and by white people, in a deliberate attempt to ruin those families and indigenous culture. The giving away of a child, then, is not unfamiliar to the characters in this book. What's different is that the offering in this case is meant to heal the community rather than to destroy it. It is not Frank Baum's justice of vengeance and hatred. Though it takes a similar form, its aims are not destructive, not retributive. It represents an older form of justice, one set upon and rising toward different values.

In *LaRose*, violence does not easily end. It reverberates across time. When the first LaRose is given by her abusive mother to the cruel fur trader Mackinnon, LaRose then conspires with the assistant Wolfred to poison Mackinnon with mushrooms in his stew so Wolfred and LaRose can make their escape. Mackinnon is not quite dead as they run, and he stumbles through the forest after them, crying out, "Wait, my children . . . do not abandon me!" (127). There is a troubling irony in Mackinnon's calling them his children and their escape an abandonment. It exposes the colonial encounter as one that assumes white supremacist paternalism even in the midst of its violence. This flight is a real escape; the first LaRose is abused and becomes free. But the violence of the murder follows them, and the hauntings and echoes of it prove more difficult to leave behind. Days later in the forest, long after they've escaped Mackinnon, they see a specter of his head roiling with agony through the snowy woods, its hair flickering with flame, using its tongue and ears to prod itself along and "sobbing in frustration" (132). Mackinnon's struggling, weeping head visits LaRose for the rest of her life, through all her travels with Wolfred and the family they eventually raise, even up to the day she contracts tuberculosis and is taken away by a researcher to be studied for her rare bacterial resilience. When she dies somewhere east, her remains are never returned to her family.

This violence echoes in the history of indigenous boarding schools represented by the many generations of LaRoses who were forced to attend them. But even in narrower instances, wrongs that arise from these forced boardings replicate and repeat themselves. Landreaux's forced boarding at a school away from home leads him to run away from the school with his friend Romeo in an attempt to get back to the reservation. They hide in the undercarriage of a bus as it speeds down the highway for hours, then escape at a rest stop and make their way to Minneapolis. After living for a time on the streets, they fall from the high railroad pilings where they spend their nights, and Landreaux lands on Romeo, badly breaking Romeo's leg and causing a permanent limp. Romeo undergoes multiple surgeries and becomes addicted to painkillers as a result. He bears a grudge against Landreaux for years that has significant consequences in the novel.

In *Gilead*, John Ames claims that there is no single transgression, just a deep wound in all of humanity. What might better be said is that there are both single transgressions and a deep universal wound; otherwise, the former would sink into the latter and abolish individual responsibility. What the example of boarding schools demonstrates in *LaRose* is that the offering of LaRose Irons to the Raviches after Dusty dies is not an isolated act. It is a loss that also has a history, and it can be understood only within that history and that history's harmful repercussions and resonances. Reflecting on the boarding schools further, Mrs. Peace's mother recalls one kind teacher at Fort Totten but also rues the insufficiency of kindness in the face of all that history. Though at the school there were good teachers and bad teachers, she remembers, nothing could "solve that loneliness," a loneliness that sets "deep in a person" and goes "down the generations" (71). It may be, she wonders, that an original violence might "finally [work] itself out with the boy" and be resolved, though the echoes of harm are long, and it's too early to see whether "he's finally okay" (72). The old women of the Elders Lodge know well how violence echoes across generations. In another conversation, when two other women, Malvern and Ignatia, are chatting with LaRose, they tell him a traditional Anishinaabe version of the rolling head story, and Ignatia explains that while the "Catholics think we are chased by devils," in fact we are chased by things "done to us in this life," by trauma (294). Recalling the haunting logic of retaliation, Ignatia tells LaRose that what we do to others and what they do to us each in turn pursues us, leaving us always "looking behind" or "worried about what comes next"; meanwhile, we ignore the present moment as it passes: "Oops, it's gone!" (294). This traditional telling places Mackinnon's gruesome flaming head, rolling and stumbling after the first LaRose and Wolfred for the rest of their lives, into a meaningful cultural context, not because he is a devil come to haunt them, but because the trauma of that first LaRose's abuse and her violent response to it chases them far beyond the reach of Mackinnon's own mortal life. As Beth Piatote has argued, the "rolling head story does not recognize motive. It recognizes effect; it registers violence as a fact." Ignatia's reflection on the tale's meaning suggests that the "rolling head is the manifestation of wrongs, whether committed by or against us."[57] LaRose and Wolfred's murder of Mackinnon is not, to be clear, the singular sin that calls forth all the rolling, haranguing devils. Rather, the trauma out of which that act arose already promised to chase them forever, however and if ever she escaped. Violence is not easily contained; it echoes across lives and times and ages. But in the traditional Anishinaabe tale, the children are able to stop the monstrous rolling head through "their own ingenuity, special gifts, and the assistance of others." Thus also emerges the possibility, one offered meaningfully by Malvern and Ignatia to LaRose in this retelling, that trauma and its retaliatory repercussions can be contained.

I suggested that the offering of LaRose to the Ravich family, unlike every other offering of children in the memory of this community, is intended to sustain rather than to destroy the community. But this still raises the question of how the offering operates to effect healing, and what healing might look like once it has been effected. This isn't simple arithmetic. There is no like for like in human lives. LaRose is first of all not a simple replacement for Dusty. If LaRose compensates for the death of Dusty, it is not in any directly economic sense. As Jankélévitch and others have said again and again, a loss such as the death of Dusty cannot be recovered. That fact of his death remains irrevocable, and the characters' desolation revolves precisely around its irrevocability. Following the familiar patterns of grief, Landreaux attempts to will time backward. When visions of Dusty visit him, he tries to force the image back into heaven while praying with all his might to will himself backward in time and cause his own preemptive death in the moments before the accident. He wishes to give his own intentional death in advance of the accidental one he caused: an impossible like for like. But for all his efforts, each time he closes his eyes and tries to undo his actions, Dusty remains "ruined in the leaves" (Erdrich, *LaRose*, 9). What's done is done, and the offering of LaRose doesn't restore Dusty or repair the Ravich family. If anything, it follows one loss with another, because Landreaux and Emmaline are devastated by the loss of their son to the Raviches. Though they reflect on this difficult choice thoughtfully both before and after their offering, Landreaux feels progressively worse as time passes. He feels acutely the absence of LaRose's regular embrace, the guilt of knowing the boy is his "secret, favorite child" (54).

But Landreaux and Peter each carry an intuition that this offering some-how does respond to the death of Dusty in a roughly compensatory way. Af-ter several difficult weeks of LaRose living with the Raviches—weeks perhaps more difficult for LaRose than for anyone else—Landreaux and Peter sit to-gether and talk. Peter acknowledges that a retaliatory action would not actu-ally restore the loss he has suffered. He tells Landreaux quite directly that although he might have chosen to murder him, it "wouldn't do the thing" he wants—it wouldn't restore Dusty. Though Peter has grown to love LaRose, he still dreams of Dusty every night. This gift of new love is real but has not compensated for his loss. Landreaux tells Peter in response that he would give his life to restore Dusty to the Raviches if he were able. He tells his neighbor, "LaRose is my life. I did the best that I could do" (68).

Peter knows he has the opportunity to exact vengeance, but he also recog-nizes that his dreams of Dusty will not stop should he pursue revenge. And Landreaux knows the same; he would offer his life if it could actually restore what has been lost. But since it can't, since a death can't be given to restore a life, Landreaux offers a son to replace a son. Peter loves this new son, but his lingering grief clashes with this new love to produce a new guilt that accom-panies his standing grief. Just as Jack Boughton's baptism reminds John Ames of his dead daughter, Peter knows LaRose is not his child. The new child may be an object of love, but he is also a reminder of loss. Again, there is no like for like. LaRose does not simply right a wrong or transform a loss into gain. This old justice is one steeped in grief. It follows loss with loss.

And Peter's guilt is well-founded; LaRose suffers most of all. Despite Peter's vengeful anger toward Landreaux, during their conversation Peter can't bear to tell Landreaux about LaRose's deep daily distress, his weeping and striking his head with his hands. And Landreaux acknowledges that giving his son to re-place Peter's son, especially when the gift is given because his own death cannot restore a life, is a terrible and unfair substitution. He admits as much to Peter, confessing that at times he feels as if he has used LaRose to bear the weight of his own guilt. "Traditional ways. Fuck. This isn't the old days" (75). Once again, it seems as if one loss is simply following another. The impossibility of compen-sation has led Landreaux to imagine an impossible adequacy in an intolerable compensation. And yet, Peter says, LaRose's presence does somehow make a difference to his and Nola's grief, even if it doesn't erase it. When Peter and Nola are with LaRose, he says, "we're thinking about him, and we love him" (75).

So first of all, the gift of LaRose operates as a substitute for an impossible payment. But what's also clear is that the offering of LaRose does nothing to replace Dusty and little to abate Nola's anger and hatred toward Landreaux and Emmaline. After Dusty is killed, she wants desperately for Peter to murder Landreaux, to beat him to death. Though she has never done violent harm to anyone before, she graphically envisions Landreaux's death in her mind's eye, reveling in the brutality of that vision (4–5). This desire does not pass with the arrival of LaRose. It just becomes more complicated. Nola loves LaRose and does her best to welcome him into her home as a son, but Peter wonders whether she actually accepts this gift on its own terms, or whether she does so only because she knows how deeply it must wound Landreaux. It may be, Peter reflects, that her warm reception of LaRose also satisfies a deep retributive desire for malice and vengeance (17). Nola suffers immensely throughout the novel. She spends a great deal of the book pondering suicide, going so far as to make plans that LaRose and the Raviches' surviving daughter, Maggie, secretly discover and then repeatedly confound.

At times, we see resonances in the novel of the urge we have traced in moral philosophy to abate anger. The terrible gift of this child might be seen as an act of appeasement, a way to mollify or manage the Raviches' anger— what Nussbaum might call therefore a form of forgiveness on those terms. This discomfort with anger, this urge to overcome it even in the wake of devastating loss and irrevocable wrong, is also present in the Ravich family. LaRose is miserable at first, missing his own home and siblings, suffering cruel teasing by Maggie. Nola makes cakes for him nearly every day, trying to replace his hurt with sweetness, to assuage both his anguish and her rage with confection. But the family can't actually stomach all that sweetness, and later in the novel Nola discovers dozens of her uneaten cakes (along with a mouse infestation) hidden in the garage. If the gift of LaRose is likewise meant to abate anger with sweetness, it fails spectacularly on these grounds. Much like Wistan in *The Buried Giant* disdaining the monks' self-mortification, Nola refuses to receive the Ironses' gift as a pure offering. Nola recognizes that it is also partly a piety and a self-absolution that she cannot accept. Talking with Peter about her relationship with her half-sister Emmaline, Nola skeptically names all the cynical benefits this awful gift will reciprocally bestow upon its givers. Like Ignatia, Nola knows that this act too will echo for generations; she knows the long memory of her people will repeatedly exclaim, "How generous you are, Emmaline, what a big-time traditional person to give your son away to a white man and almost white sister who is just so pitiful, so stark raving" (234). Nola's racialized and colonial framing for this gift is crucial. Again, there is no single transgression; whatever the moral character of this act, it occurs within the traumatic generational echoes Ignatia has named and under the racist weight of a colonial history. And yet, she can't deny its power, even if she resents some of its consequences. Nola still harbors fantasies of murdering Landreaux, fantasies she knows her husband shares, and she declares that she would take an axe to Landreaux's head herself if it weren't for the pain it would cause their new son LaRose. So, she concedes, "their damn unbelievable plan worked" (234). This passage occurs late in the novel, once Nola has moved beyond her most dangerous suicidal impulses. What is clear, though, is that she still wants vengeance. She still is angry. LaRose has not erased or transformed her resentment in any significant way. So, if LaRose has not appeased or erased her anger, what has changed? What has the gift of LaRose accomplished?

What's changed are those actions available to Nola's anger, what behaviors her anger can now countenance. Her rageful fantasies of vengeance have not disappeared, nor has she committed in Griswoldian fashion to eradicate them eventually. She simply cannot realize those fantasies without causing grave harm to another child she loves, without irreparably wounding LaRose. Whatever this gift is, it is not an appeasement, and it is not entirely innocent either. Notably, the racist history out of which this community has arisen still looms, and the idea of sending an Ojibwe child to a family with deeper ties to whiteness, like the Raviches, is part of the complicated significance of this offering. This gift thus not only reveals Landreaux and Emmaline as virtuous; it also positions Nola as white, though she too is Ojibwe and is also distantly related to the original LaRose. Landreaux and Emmaline thus make themselves "big-time traditional" people, more authentically Ojibwe, in the giving of this gift, however awful an experience it is for them. Nola cannot abide the self-congratulation it implies, the benefit it accrues. But there's also the fact that, in spite of her self-conscious anger and cynicism, Nola loves this child. She cannot but refer to LaRose as "our son" and says she refuses to exact vengeance only for her son's sake, which in this case means LaRose rather than Dusty (234).

In the end Nola's anger isn't necessarily the problem. The problem is that Dusty is dead. Peter understands that his wife is full of rage, and he understands why. Emmaline and Landreaux understand. Father Travis understands too. In fact, no one holds her hatred and anger against her. When Peter questions whether or not Nola is any better, it's not because she's still angry; it's because she's been trying to cover her anger with sweetness, literally to frost it with buttercream and to perform an empty cheeriness because she doesn't know how else to inhabit her despair. It's during this desperate period of cake-baking that Nola contemplates and several times nearly commits suicide. In fact, Peter recognizes Nola is actually and finally starting to get better only when she gets into a fight at a volleyball game with some parents on the opposing team. Erdrich narrates from within Peter's perspective during the fight, and Peter sees a Nola he finally recognizes, one more like his belligerent betrothed than the cake-baking "supersmiley" one who has haunted the house since Dusty's death (308).[58] Peter is relieved to relinquish the false "happy family with . . . no anger" or stress, where no pain is allowed (234).

LaRose is obviously not a replacement for Dusty. LaRose's suffering is neither a compensation nor a substitute for Landreaux's. And LaRose's presence does not abate the Raviches' vengeful rage. So what does LaRose do? How does he heal these families, or better, what is the healing that he introduces to them? I suggest that Peter has given us the answer to this question, though it's a deceptively simple one: they love this child who is not their own, not as a crude replacement for their own, but as their own nonetheless. And here we see the narrow limits of love, about which Hannah Arendt worried, expanding. When Landreaux is in the smoke lodge with the elder Randall, baring his soul and his grief and seeking healing in the traditional ways, Landreaux calls Nola his wife's half-sister. Randall immediately corrects Landreaux, saying that sisters do not come in halves (53). Arendt is suspicious of love; she worries that it turns human beings inward and away from the world, that it is inherently and necessarily antipolitical. But in this novel LaRose shows how love can in fact accomplish the opposite, for in the community in which this gift is given, there are no half-sisters. Nuclear families are not separate and competing enclaves; they are socially bound by a shared history of stolen children and also by a shared witness of survival and a shared hope in a common future. LaRose, in other words, does not simply belong to Landreaux and to Emmaline. He is not given because he is theirs to give; he is given because he is not theirs to keep. He is not a possession to be held. From his birth he has been a gift to be shared. LaRose expands rather than constrains the nuclear limits of these families' love. I have more to say about how he does this, and about the relevance of that miraculous healing to Christian theology, but first I take another excursus, this time into atonement theology.

ADDRESSING ATONEMENT

In the Christian tradition, there has long been an association between divine and human forgiveness: forgive and you will be forgiven (Luke 6:37); when you stand praying, forgive, that your Father in heaven may also forgive you (Mark 11:25); forgive us our trespasses as we forgive those who trespass against us (Matt 6:12). And though, as I've already explored, the translation of these ancient Greek terms into contemporary moral concepts can be a tricky thing, it is clear that divine and human forgiveness stand in some relation to Christian ethics, at least according to the New Testament.[59] What we make of humans' forgiveness of one another will depend somehow on what we make of God's forgiveness of us. And of course, much of the tradition's reflection on God's forgiveness of us passes through the cross of Jesus Christ. Atonement theology is an obviously vast area of Christian thought, and I do not intend to recount or explicate all of that theology here. But I do hope constructively to intervene in it: to invite a reconsideration and reconstrual of its language and frameworks, if not to recount wholesale a history of its conceptual development.

The dominant theories of the atonement in Christian theology have come under the name of satisfaction. Sometimes it is God's honor, or God's wrath, or God's judgment that demands satisfaction before human sin, but really these are each proxies for an idea of justice; they are theories about the practical mechanisms by which God's justice is met. Whatever the means, it is the justice of God that demands satisfaction. And this is an interesting framework for understanding divine justice, since the language of satisfaction itself implies both desire and want. Satisfaction takes lack as its fundamental condition; it presumes the possibility of compensation; when met, it fulfills a longing desire. So all these proxies for justice that the theological tradition has posited—honor, wrath, judgment, punishment—are really just theological interpretations or speculative suggestions about what God desires, what compensation God wants. They are theories about the nature and character of divine love. They suggest, sometimes by explication and other times outright, what God's love looks like.

But there's a problem, of course, in calling the abandonment and torture of Jesus of Nazareth a sign of God's love. Recall Mackinnon's flaming head, chasing Wolfred and LaRose throughout their lives, giving visage to the white supremacist paternalism of Western colonialism. If suffering like Jesus's is potentially, let alone prototypically, redemptive, doesn't this valorize suffering in a way that can be and indeed has been weaponized by power? Doesn't the familial language used when describing Jesus's death, the language of a son abandoned and given over to torture by a father, of a son given indeed to satisfy that father's demands, find especially disturbing expression in many traditional theological articulations of Jesus's death? The prevailing interpretation of this event is of course by no means universal. Theologians from feminist and womanist traditions especially have rightly critiqued traditional atonement models and have denied suffering any redeeming value.[60] But the idea that Jesus's suffering stands as substitute for our punishment, that his death somehow compensates for human sin and that it satisfies divine justice, continues to dominate both doctrine and devotion throughout the Christian West.

I'm convinced by those critics of satisfaction and substitution models of the atonement who condemn it for its valorizations of suffering, but I also remain committed to the meaningfulness of the cross. Like some indigenous American and other theologians, I believe the meaningfulness of the crucifixion can be severed from the valorizing abuses of a purely transactional, sacrificial atonement.[61] I think the cross still signifies something crucial about the nature of God's love and forgiveness toward us and that therefore it also indicates something indispensable about the nature of our love and forgiveness toward one another. Inspired by *LaRose*, I want to think again about how and why we might reflect upon Jesus's death other than as a compensation or a satisfaction, and I hope as a result then to rethink what we could mean when we consider Jesus as a substitute or his offering as substitutionary.

I spent a great deal of my first chapter criticizing the idea that sin or wrongdoing can be undone in any absolute way. The past—Jankélévitch's fact-of-having-been-done—cannot be altered, whether by sacrifice, vengeance, or justice. I stand by these arguments, but they become somewhat more complicated when we try to think about them with respect to God. John Milbank gives a rationale for this claim in his book *Being Reconciled*.[62] According to Milbank, the modern arithmetic of forgiveness is basically wrong because it misconceives the nature of sin. While it is true, Milbank acknowledges, that past wrong cannot strictly speaking be undone, he regards the anxiety to undo past wrongs as itself a misguided modern concern, grounded in a heterodox arithmetic of evil. This is because, for Milbank as for classical Christian ontology, sin is a privation in being. Evil is nonbeing. Since it is nothing at all, there is simply nothing for forgiveness to undo. There is not an evil that exists and demands undoing; there is rather a nonexistence that manifests as evil and demands fulfillment, completion, or repletion in being. And God is replete being, so the infinite gift of God's grace necessarily overcomes the privations of sin in the movements of salvation. Real "Christological forgiveness," for Milbank, is "not reactive, since it is only the sustained giving of the original gift, despite [that gift's] refusal." For this reason, "forgiveness as response to fault is not a reaction superior to an original action, since it is *only* this continued action, neither more nor less."[63] In other words, the superabundance of God's original gift of being is itself always already forgiveness as well. Forgiveness is a continuation of the original gift of being that in its beginning and at every turn overwhelmingly overcomes nothingness. Though we recognize evil in creation, its nonbeing does not demand our efforts to undo it, and certainly does not require God's efforts either. God's original and eternally superabundant gift simply fills in the gaps of, rather than decreating the sinful realities of, creation.

It's not, for Milbank, that any evil needs erasure by forgiveness. Rather, the nothingness of evil plus the unending gift of being equals the positive and eternal grace of forgiveness. Milbank lays several contemporary conceptual problems around forgiveness at the feet of what he thus regards as our bad theological arithmetic. It is only when forgiveness is read as a cancellation or decreation, he says, as the negation of a wrongheadedly positive evil, that it must appear as an exception to the order of creation. Conceptual forgiveness appears to fall under the despotic sovereignty about which Derrida worries only when it breaks the proper rules of being, when it needs to undo what cannot be undone. But since, for Milbank, forgiveness is nothing other than the continuation of an original, infinite gift, forgiveness stands not as the sovereign exception to, but as the persistent expression of, God's rule—in both senses of the term "rule," that is, as both lordship and order.[64] What Christ's death signifies on this account therefore is not the sort of sacrifice that might undo or erase sin. Rather, the "divine answer to the original human refusal" of God's fullness and goodness "is not to demand sacrifice—of which [God] has no need—but to go on giving" despite our refusals until "these refusals are overcome." Christ's "abandonment offers no compensation to God."[65] What is compelling in Milbank is his insistence that Christ's death is not at all compensatory, along with his utter confidence in the willingness of God to love us beyond our refusals of that love. What is less compelling is his understanding of the nature of that love. Although Milbank accepts that Jankélévitch is "right to insist on a certain stubborn resistance of 'pastness,'" he also determines that Jankélévitch must nonetheless be "wrong to ignore the fact that the 'passing away' of time reveals a complicity of time with the nothingness of finitude itself—a complicity which nonetheless furnishes the ground for the possibility of redemption."[66] In other words, the nothingness of sin is also the ultimate nothingness of finite creation. The passage of time signifies finitude's complicity with nothingness, with evil and sin, which God's being entirely overcomes. Redemption for Milbank thus is a kind of erasure, since all that we love in creation—and all that God loves too—will fade with the nothingness of finitude before the overwhelming and inexorable and totalitarian infinity of the divine.

I think, as Jankélévitch argues, there is something compelling and powerful in a love that seeks neither to overlook nor overcome brokenness and limitation, but to love the beloved as broken and limited. There may be ways of describing God's love as infinite that better capture God's endless willingness to love us in our finitude (a willingness Milbank does recognize), without implying that our failures and our very being must be entirely and eventually outstripped by God's perfectly replete being before that love may be consummated (as Milbank seems to suggest). Finite creation doesn't first exist and then receive God's love; it exists at all because it is loved. It is made finite by that love. Even as finite, it is loved. God's love does not scorn our finitude or strain to love us in spite of our created limits, as it patiently waits to overwhelm us with infinity and undo our sinful finitude. Rather, God's love creates us in that finitude and loves us in and for exactly those created limits. To be, to be beloved, is to be finite. Though the love Jankélévitch describes has no metaphysical aspirations, its willingness to love the sinner as a sinner models God's love of finitude as finite better, I think, than the replete erasure of Milbank's overcoming infinity. The human anxiety to be all in all that Bonhoeffer and Tanabe criticized (Chapter 2) surfaces here as a totalizing metaphysics of atonement. Mindful of Bonhoeffer and Tanabe's moral concern, then, I'm reluctant to follow Milbank in celebrating the ultimate erasure of finite beings beneath the repletion of God's relentlessly overwhelming infinity.

Be that as it may, Milbank and I can agree that divine forgiveness is not a compensation. But my reading of his work does suggest that we might need a better theology of God's love, as well as further reflection upon the category of sacrifice that Milbank has introduced. Much of this chapter has reflected on the emotional character of forgiveness. To forgive, in the standard modern model, means for the offended to have a change of heart, to overcome anger, and to invite reconciliation with an offender. In many ways, this is and remains common in Christian approaches to sacrifice, atonement, and the forgiveness of God. God bears just anger and righteous wrath toward human sin, and this wrath must be answered and assuaged. For centuries in Christian theology, the assuaging answer has been given through punishment. As Holmgren has noted, justice is reductively collapsed into or conceptually equated with punishment, and so God's wrath comes to be understood as appeased by penal suffering. This theological reading has deeply structured Western approaches to crime and punishment, as other studies have ably documented.[67] There is some scriptural warrant for the theological appeal of an appeasement of divine anger through human suffering. Paul Fiddes notes how Paul's letter to the Romans does in fact describe Jesus's death using the Greek word *hilasterion*, that is, a propitiating sacrifice—in other words, a sacrifice that appeases or placates a god.[68] But Fiddes also persuasively insists that "our understanding of its meaning in the New Testament cannot be decided by mere appeal to a dictionary" since the "New Testament writers are challenging established ideas of religion in the world around them, and they do so by drawing upon the Old Testament."[69] According to Fiddes this understanding of sacrifice as an appeasement, however much it may accord with common Greek usage of its time, conflicts with the fundamental sacrificial framework arising out of the Hebrew scriptures and also with the nature of God understood and assumed by early Christians. In the "Israelite and earliest Christian conceptions," sacrifice is not "something human beings do to God (propitiation) but something which God does for humankind (expiation)." For Fiddes, the point is "not just that theories of propitiation misunderstand the biblical view of sacrifice, but that in doing so they miss the value" of expiatory sacrifice as a religious image and experience. In other words, for the Hebrew scriptures as well as for Christian theology, God "is always the subject of the process and never the object" of sacrifice.[70] Fiddes isn't strictly bound to a notion of divine impassibility (though this too would provide sufficient reason to resist any notion that God's affective posture toward creation might be altered). As he notes, several "early Christian Fathers were rightly uneasy about the notion that sacrifice *propitiated* God," but their reasoning was wrongly rooted in a "philosophical prejudice against the idea that God could suffer change in any way"; nonetheless, Fiddes affirms that the Fathers were "surely right to find unworthy the idea that God's hostile attitude to us could be mollified by being offered a sacrifice."[71] He therefore finds it both scripturally and theologically nonsensical to support an idea that anything humans do, up to and including the sacrificial murder of God's son, could alter God. The concept of propitiation then, the idea of a ritual offering that appeases anger, "however sensitively it is stated, is all about dealing with the reaction of God against sin, not about the taint of sin in human life itself."[72]

To put things more directly and somewhat more starkly, the idea of appeasing God's anger through sacrifice suggests that the obstacle to full and final reconciliation with God is a problem God has with God's own feelings, rather than a problem we humans have with our own sin. As Fiddes explains, the theory of substitutionary atonement is "unworthy of the character of God as love" as well "an infringement of the freedom of God in subjecting divine mercy to some eternal principle such as law."[73] Most importantly for Fiddes, as for *LaRose*, so flat a framework for substitution is "largely useless for understanding the possibilities of human renewal."[74] In lieu of propitiation, then, Fiddes posits what he calls expiation, which in English is just a synonym for atonement but which he more specifically wants to define, drawing on the Hebrew scriptures, as the removal of sin. Following Hebrew imagery, sin is a stain or blemish; expiation wipes the sin away. The New Testament imagery of Jesus's blood washing away sins, which can unsettle readers today, given the tradition of valorized suffering in which it is read, should in fact be seen in light of this imagery of sin as a stain. What is crucial, Fiddes argues, is the image of washing rather than the suffering that antecedes the spilling of blood. Thus in the Israelite ritual "for the Day of Atonement sin could be dealt with not only by cleansing it away in sacrifice, but also by chasing it away, that is, by loading it on the scapegoat and sending it out into the wilderness."[75] For Fiddes, "the sacrificial death of Christ" does not therefore propitiate God, it "expiates sin; it expiates sin by changing sinners."[76] As I was with Milbank, and with Jankélévitch still in mind, I'm a bit uncomfortable with the idea of removing sin entirely here, though the stakes for Fiddes are largely rhetorical rather than ontological. In other words, when Fiddes speaks of the expiation of sin, his concerns are primarily to do with the possibilities for human futures to arise from broken pasts, and largely not to do with the metaphysical nature of diving being. In the end, Fiddes mitigates the rhetoric of erasure, and his idea that humans are changed by their relationship to Jesus differs markedly from Milbank's claim that they will be entirely overcome by God's infinity.

LOVE AND LONGING

So, we have two critiques on offer that, while incomplete in my view, might still frame our considerations helpfully. From Milbank, I want to emphasize the relentless persistence of God's love, even if we are worried about that love's tendency to overcome the independent otherness of finite creatures. Like Fiddes, I want to abandon the sense that sacrifice appeases God's angry justice, even if I still wonder how the Son manages to transform the sinner without erasing the fact of sin. Having said that, I want to start over with this story of atonement. Milbank is helpful in showing the persistence of God's love, but his model of divine forgiveness remains insistently economic. Even if he attempts to disrupt the economics of transaction with an infinite gift economy, I think he remains to some degree beholden to the transactional models of the economic metaphor. Or, at least, the model he proposes regards being as the superabundant gift of God that grounds all other gifts (or their refusals), rather than recognizing being as the finite outgrowth of God's infinite gift of love. There are not first finite beings, the ontological largesse of God's replete being, who then receive God's love. Rather, because God loves, there are finite beings to be loved. Their finitude is conditioned rather than overcome by that love. And where Milbank starts from being or economy, Fiddes starts with sacrifice. He, too, does well to overcome the difficulties of a sacrificial rhetoric, but if the central aspect of sacrifice is the way that it allows human beings to be transformed in and through their relation to Jesus Christ, why not start with a theology of that relation? Why not begin with love? I want to begin with love, and so allow me to start again with a few words from Julian of Norwich.

Julian of Norwich is a complex theological thinker, and I do the rigor, intensity, and importance of her work no justice in only briefly mentioning it here. I do so only because her insights are so important to any reframing of atonement theology, even when her thought is called into service only for the sake of that reframing. In her collected visions, she is able to upend all of the worst assumptions of Western atonement theology and also perhaps the expectations of human forgiveness. Indeed, it might seem curious to begin an account of divine forgiveness with Julian since, as Milbank has noted, she asserts that God "never needs to forgive" since God "is never offended."[77] Milbank is being a little disingenuous with Julian's claim here though; his implication is that God, in God's replete superabundant being, can never be compromised by sin or by nonbeing and therefore needs never to forgive. But Julian simply means God has never been angry toward us and never could be. Her arguments are affective, not ontological. As with the modern philosophers, Julian presumes an affective character to forgiveness. For Julian, it is "against the nature of [God's] power to be angry, and against the nature of his wisdom, and against the nature of his goodness." Our soul is united to God in God's "unchangeable goodness"; therefore, "between God and our soul is neither anger nor forgiveness."[78] For Julian, a deep love binds us to God, and the notion that that love might somehow be sullied by wrath, let alone need repair through pardon, simply misunderstands the nature of that love.

But this is only one line from *Revelations of Divine Love*. Forgiveness is not only an affective response for Julian. It is also itself an expression of God's unending and unchanging love, indeed a response to the anger that we imagine must intervene between us and God but that in fact never does. As Julian writes, when we recognize the depth of our own sin, we come to see ourselves as "so loathsome, we think God is angry with us because of our sins," and we are moved by the Holy Spirit to contrite acts of prayer and earnest "longing with all our might to amend our life, so as to abate God's anger." We believe God is angry and we act to appease that wrath. And after our penance, we find peace, trusting in the "hope that God has forgiven our sins; and it is true." But this "true forgiveness" is not a gift earned by our contrition and prayer. On the contrary, we learn that God was never angry or needed our propitiating penitence in the first place. When Christ reveals himself to us in our hopeful peace, he speaks sweet and steadfast assurance: "My darling, I am glad you have come to me. In all your misery I have been with you, and now you see how I love you, and we are united in bliss."[79] Much as with Fiddes's conception of expiatory atonement, for Julian forgiveness transforms the sinner rather than God. God has not changed; Christ and the sinner have never been estranged from one another. What has changed is the sinner's vision of God, her understanding of the persistence and intimacy of God's love. Divine forgiveness, on these terms, is not the reacquisition of God's favor but the recognition that God was neither angry nor distant in the first place. Forgiveness for Julian does not signify God's change of heart; rather, it signifies the unchanging willingness of God to love God's enemies. As Milbank might concur, forgiveness is the continuance of an original love. God is always present in and as love to the sinner; it is the sinner who comes to realize this love in time as forgiveness.

This is why I find Julian crucial to any reconsideration or reconstruction of atonement theology, even if only briefly to reframe the starting point for any discussion of Christian atonement or Christian forgiveness. The idea that God demands some satisfaction, as I noted above, implies a desire. What desire can forgiveness ever satisfy? It cannot undo the past. It brackets our urge for vengeance and cannot compensate for loss. It does not appease our anger. It does not erase our guilt. To ask this question in a more theologically pointed way: What does God most desire? What is the divine longing that God's forgiveness satisfies? In her ninth revelation of Divine Love, Julian answers. She is given a vision of the First Heaven, where she sees the workings of the Father. The Father, she says, is "pleased" and "full of bliss" to reward the

Son for the Son's redemptive work. God the Father's only desire is to give the Son what he desires, to reward the Son, to compensate him gloriously for his trials. But if this gift is the Father's reward, what is the Son's compensation? Julian wonders what blissful gift the Son must await from the Father for his tortuous work on earth, what royal and majestic delight of God the Son must now possess as fair reward. Then she realizes, in "an especial marvel" and "a most delectable vision," that "*we* are his bliss, *we* are his reward, *we* are his glory, *we* are his crown" (emphasis added).[80] What God most desires is neither punishment nor honor nor penitence nor apology nor any other proxy compensation. God is love. What God most desires is *us*.

This cannot be overstated in any discussion of Christian atonement and its satisfaction. We are the only compensation God desires. What God has lost is us. What God regains is us. Justice or honor or punishment are not part of this equation. When one begins thinking about atonement from this different starting point, the questions and their answers flip quickly upside down. Consider Jesus's question to Julian in the ninth revelation of her vision. "Are you well pleased that I suffered for you?" The Middle English carries the relevant sense more arrestingly: "*Art thou wele payd that I suffrid for thee?*" Christ asks.[81] As Rowan Williams has noted, the verb "payd" here carries a notion of satisfaction rather than of pleasure. This is not about relishing another's redemptive suffering; rather, it is about upending the assumptions of our theology. As Williams continues, theology has "typically agonized over what it would take to satisfy God, to 'pay the price for sin.'"[82] Williams worries that thinking about the problem of sin in such compensatory or transactional terms may "leave us with the familiar anxiety that God is faced with squaring a circle in which God has to 'do justice' to his own justice, his own mercy and our guilt." We become entangled in a theological conundrum where "God must—so to speak—pay himself a fair price." Julian's articulation of atonement, meanwhile, turns this problem "entirely on its head" and reveals that the "anxiety and the circle-squaring" lie "not with God but with us: can *we* be satisfied?"[83] Rather than presenting a dilemma in which divine justice is satisfied and salvation is won for us by proxy through a meritorious punishment on the cross, in Julian's version, Jesus simply asks us if we are satisfied—if we are convinced, that is, at the depth and reach and power of his love for us. And if not, then he will simply love us more. It is an "endless delight," Christ tells Julian, "that I ever suffered my Passion for you, and if I could suffer more, I would suffer more."[84] For Williams, these cannot be propitiatory sufferings. Jesus's offer to suffer more would be nonsensical in a purely compensatory scheme, where once sin is paid, the debt to God is cleared and no more suffering is required. Jesus offers to suffer more because the only need he seeks to meet is a human one—the need we have to be convinced that we remain lovable even despite our sin. The challenge for humans is not, then, to overcome an impossible and infinite debt to God or to have their finitude entirely overcome by God's replete being. The only significant meaning of satisfaction for Julian is "radically simple."[85] Rather than God being "faced with a challenge to which the ingenious stratagem of a suffering that has infinite merit is the answer, in Anselmian mode; the challenge is posed to us. Are we content to believe that we are loved?"[86] Because if we are not, God in Christ remains ever at the ready to love us more and "meet our need."[87] These loving consolations from Julian continue throughout her revelations. God, Julian says, "regards sin as sorrow and suffering for those who love him, to whom he attributes no blame, out of love."[88] Thus we will be rewarded and comforted for our sinful suffering in God's heavenly company rather than eternally punished for it. Sin does not incur an obligation to suffer; for Julian the sin *is* the suffering. "Christ has compassion on us because of sin."[89]

In the *Revelations*, love is the reward for love. I don't want to paint too rosy a picture of Julian's visions here, either. Though she famously describes Jesus's assurance that "all shall be well, and all shall be well, and all manner of thing shall be well," the future tense of that promise is quite obvious.[90] The Jesus who speaks these consolations to her is tortured and bloodied. She lies on what she believes is her deathbed when she receives them, and after Christ disappears the devil returns "with his heat and his stench" to torment her.[91] As Nicholas Watson has noted, if we are indeed Christ's crown, we should recall the injury that crown has caused to Christ, especially in Julian's own visions, when sheets of blood pour down Christ's face from the wounds of the thorns.[92] But what both Christ and Julian express here is a willingness to be present to the beloved despite the suffering that beloved one endures. At one point in her revelations, while gazing at the bloodied and desiccated visage of the crucified Christ, Julian hears her reason cajoling her to look away from Jesus's mutilated face and instead gaze upward toward the blissful picture of his Father in heaven. She knows that, if she does, all her distress and anguish will dissipate into that beatific vision. But instead of casting her eyes upward, Julian answers "inwardly with all [her] soul's strength," and says to Jesus, "'No, I cannot, for you are my heaven.'" In her deep love, Julian prefers to remain "in that pain until Judgement Day" rather than "come to heaven in any other way than by" Jesus.[93] There is nothing between the cross and heaven for

Julian; she has free access to paradise. Yet she will not look away from her beloved. As with Christ, love is its own reward, even if it is accompanied by anguish and grief. Love does not win Julian ecstasy, nor even much relief. Indeed, she turns away from paradise for its sake. But since her beloved already is her reward, paradise is a poor compensation by comparison. In Julian's *Revelations*, the company of God and the bliss of eternity are not rewards we receive for loving. Julian does not need to look up for escape into heaven. The object of her love is the one suffering before her, and loving him is already her reward. And it may be that this reward of love always introduces longing and loss. Because at the beginning of her revelations, Julian says that the last thing she prayed for to God, in her youth, "was the wound of purposeful longing for God." She asked for this gift "without any condition," we are told.[94] Julian does not pray to have her longing satisfied; she does not pray to overcome her longing in consummated contemplation; she does not pray to be united to God. She prays to long for God, to love God and be loved by God even if at an earthly distance. She prays to gaze at him in pain upon the cross, rather than overcome that vision with the infinite bliss of heaven.

This sense of longing as constitutive of love, of a separation necessary for relation, not only stays the consuming totalitarianism of Milbank's overflowing gift, but it also recurs in interesting pockets of twentieth-century theology.[95] Adrienne von Speyr, the Swiss mystic who inspired the theological work of renowned Roman Catholic theologian Hans Urs von Balthasar, gives an account of love that echoes Julian's longing. Von Speyr regards abandonment and estrangement as internal to the very being of God in the eternal separation and movement between Father and Son. Before God is other to creation, in other words, God is other to God's very self as Father and Son. The alienation of the Son from the Father precedes the alienation of creation from God, so this alienation need not be read entirely negatively. Von Speyr's theological metaphors appropriately assume figures from family life. On von Speyr's account, the incarnation of God in Christ signifies an essential separation within the Godhead. The Father is "enriched by the Son, even by [their] separation, although it contain[s] their mutual sacrifice." The Father thus "draws the Son to him through the suffering." Like "two lovers who have lived long in a happy marriage" and who are preparing for a long separation, the Father and Son "consider their love and reaffirm it for the future beyond their coming separation, throwing out an anchor into the future or into eternity to secure it there." However "bitter the time of loneliness may be, something remains that draws them together over and above all separation."[96] It is difficult reading these lines from von Speyr not to recall Axl and Beatrice on that final shore, anticipating a time of unending loneliness but also consenting to it and content to be bound together only by love in their endless separation. There is thus in von Speyr the paradoxical insistence that the joy of mutual love depends on a separation between lovers.

As Julian knows, love and longing mean want and desire, they mean otherness, estrangement, and separation. Though a love ever binds them, the loving space between lovers also allows for the possibility of a painful distance. Thus the "period of the mutual abandonment of Father and Son is the period in which the most secret mystery of their love is fulfilled. Their estrangement is a form of their supreme intimacy."[97] Estrangement and abandonment, for von Speyr, are forms of the deepest intimacy. To be loved demands a separation, a separation that (in the unique case of God) is also an existential alienation and abandonment from the source of all being and goodness itself. It is not that God's repletion overcomes all sunderings; it is that God's love sunders the unity of being itself. It is because God withdraws from Godself that a space is made for humans to be, to be free to love and be loved, to be abandoned to freedom and estrangement in love.

As I said, von Speyr's visions inspired von Balthasar's theology, and his account of the atonement in the *Theo-Drama* maps this model of loving estrangement directly and dramatically onto the cross. This theology of the cross also subsequently orders his account of the Trinity. As von Balthasar writes, following von Speyr, the "divine act that brings forth the Son . . . involves the positing of an absolute, infinite 'distance' that can contain and embrace all other distances that are possible within the world of finitude, including the distance of sin."[98] This is a remarkable statement, that the love within God admits space for the distance of sin. Within the "Father's love is an absolute renunciation: he will not be God for himself alone." The Father therefore must turn away from himself toward the Son. Meanwhile, the "Son's answer to the gift of the Godhead can only be eternal thanksgiving to the Father—a thanksgiving as selfless and unreserved as the Father's original self-surrender." And proceeding from and passing between them "there breathes the Spirit who is common to both: as the essence of love, he maintains the infinite distance between them, seals it and, since he is the one Spirit of them both, bridges it."[99] The distance love opens is one only love can span. This is a startling claim, in fact, one that—following the upending question posed by Julian in the fourteenth century, "Art thou wele payd?"—also upends the conventional assumptions of Christian atonement theology today. The positing of a distance between the Father and the Son here manages to contain all distances from God, including the distance of sin, including nonbeing itself. Much as with Julian, for von Balthasar, sin is behovely: sin is fitting.[100] Loss is not a bug but a feature of God's love. There is a renunciation, a sending away that accompanies the loving separation that grounds the internal, immanent life of the Trinity. As Gillian Rose writes, if "the Lover retires too far, the light of love is extinguished and the Beloved dies."[101] But if the "Lover approaches too near the Beloved, she is effaced by the love and ceases to have an independent existence." Beloved and Lover, Lover and Beloved must therefore "leave a distance, a boundary, for love."[102] They approach one another and "retire, so that love may suspire."[103] This "economics of eros" is also "the infinite passion of faith: *Dieu se révèle en se retirer*."[104] It is therefore conceptually crucial that the metaphor for sin in von Balthasar's atonement theology is not one of debt or obligation or crime or even of stain but of distance. Sin is separation from God, and separation is the condition for love.

Even more startlingly then, von Balthasar continues, the Son "is infinitely Other, but he is also the infinitely Other of the Father." This means that Christ both "grounds and surpasses all we mean by separation, pain, and alienation in the world" as well as everything we might imagine "in terms of loving self-giving, interpersonal relationship, and blessedness."[105] In other words, the otherness internal to God is both blessedness and estrangement, both love and loss, at once. This suggests "such an incomprehensible and unique separation of God from himself that it includes and grounds every other separation—be it never so dark and bitter." Astonishingly, von Balthasar concludes, "hell is only possible given the absolute and real separation of Father and Son," that is, given the nature of God's love.[106] Every alienation from God, including sin, death, and even hell itself, is a possibility only because of the absolute and real separation of Father and Son, a separation which is also the original estrangement that gives rise to love. Von Balthasar uses a classical theological distinction between the immanent and economic Trinity here, between God as God exists to Godself and God as God exists in history, to resolve his dilemma. In the immanent Trinity, the action of the Son in obeying the Father corresponds to an infinite nearness and infinity, because of the Son's obedience, whereas in the economic Trinity, the renunciation of the Son by the Father corresponds to an infinite distance that lands an obedient Jesus of Nazareth in hell. This is a clever way to read intimacy and estrangement as one, to put von Speyr's claim in the terms of academic theology. But what is crucial here is that love is a separation, that it sends the beloved away. And what's excruciating is that sin is a separation too. To be perfectly clear: the logic of this atonement is not that Christ pays the debt for human sin. Rather, Christ crosses the distance of sin, a distance Christ also opens in that crossing. We humans, in our waywardness, may wander an infinite distance from God. But the reach of God's love, in the person of Christ, can cover every distance, even all the distance of sin and death. However far we wander, Christ stands always one step farther away, eternally estranged from God in sin, but also extending the span of God's love so that we might always remain within reach of the divine embrace.

The economic metaphors of sin, forgiveness, and atonement have been replaced by spatial ones. Christ reaches rather than redeems us. Or, as Simone Weil observed about forty years before von Balthasar wrote the *Theo-Drama*, among the persons of God "there is more than nearness; there is infinite nearness or identity. But, resulting from the Creation, the Incarnation, and the Passion, there is also infinite distance." Between "God and God," the "totality of space and time" interpose "their immensity" and "put an infinite distance between God and God."[107] The problem of atonement is not a problem to be solved; it is the lived paradox of God's sundering love. The infinite "distance between God and God, this supreme tearing apart, this agony beyond all others, this marvel of love, is the crucifixion."[108]

Love means separation. This is common sense; if we identify too entirely with the other, we consume or overcome that other. We erase the other and destroy the one we wish to love. The true freedom of the beloved therefore requires a distance, it demands a separation. But for "those who love, separation, although painful, is a good, because it is love."[109] This separation, this deliberate setting of distance remains itself, writes Howard Thurman, the merciful rationale for any and every nonretaliation. When "a man inflicts injury upon me, I must establish voluntary distance with him, between what I would do to him, and what I do to him."[110] Though reciprocal justice might justify my retaliation, in exercising will and power over another "I render him a thing in my hands."[111] But when I "relax my power, and establish voluntary distance within myself in this regard," I not only confirm the humanity of my enemy, however much I resent that enemy and however far a distance I require from him, I also imitate a distant and absconding God who "hath not dealt with us after our sins, nor rewarded us according to our iniquities" (Ps 103:10).[112] Divine forgiveness, then, is not the righting of a wrong or the resolution of a dilemma. It is not a divine change of heart or the appeasement of just wrath. It does not fix or overcome alienation and estrangement. It simply binds the estranged and alienated together in love, from a distance. Forgiveness "does not come as a return for some achievement: it comes because any such achievement was impossible."[113] I can't help but note once again (see the Introduction) that the words from the New Testament that are most often translated into English as forgiveness—*aphiemi, luo*—carry a sense of sending away or of letting go rather than of giving or of paying back. *Aphiemi* in the Latin is *remittere*, from which the English "remission" is derived, and remission has been used metaphorically to refer to debt repayment; but literally it means simply to send away, to set a distance. *Luo* means to set loose. Even when Christ's life is described as a ransom (*lutron*) given for many, the *lutron* is the price required to set a slave free. Manumission is the operative metaphor, not compensation. What is at stake for Jesus with regard to atonement and forgiveness in the Gospels is the manner by which we might love across the distance sin has breached in our lives, rather than the price we must pay for the debt sin has accrued to our being.

ALL LOST THINGS

On the first New Year's Eve after Dusty's death, Peter Ravich stays up late. It's 1999, the turn of the millennium, and he's curious to see whether the world will fall apart because of the Y2K problem. But overnight there is "no panic." He wakes in the morning and finds the new year "sad, calm, and brimming with debt" (Erdrich, *LaRose*, 62). In this, of course, the year 2000 matches every previous year for this Ojibwe community: sad, calm, brimming with debt. As the Ojibwe elder Randall knows, for his people there is always "loss, dislocation, disease, addiction, and just feeling like the tattered remnants of a people with a complex history" (51). This history presents both a mysterious absence due to the violence of colonial erasures and a burdensome presence due to the trauma of that violence. For Randall and his people, there is always "so much fucked-upness" wherever they turn (51). And, as the Ojibwe also know, fucked-upness tends to multiply. This happens throughout the novel, in ways large and small, some of which I've already noted. There is the head of Mackinnon that follows the first LaRose and Wolfred for years, and there are the generations of children sent off to boarding schools as a form of cultural reeducation and genocide. But even trivial conflicts spin out of control through mutual retaliation. A boy named Dougie Veddar bullies LaRose in first grade, stabbing his pencil into LaRose's hand and breaking off the graphite under the skin. In retaliation, Maggie Ravich, LaRose's new sister, kicks Dougie in the crotch and stuffs a candy bar in his mouth to silence him. But Dougie chokes on the candy bar and nearly dies. Maggie is nonchalant. "So now you know what revenge looks like," Maggie tells LaRose (125). Only he doesn't quite, or doesn't yet, because the conflict keeps widening and escalating. Dougie's older brother and some friends sexually assault Maggie in retaliation, then in reciprocal vengeance LaRose learns taekwondo and attacks them in turn. A sister of one of the boys who attacked Maggie plays on a rival volleyball team and Maggie spikes a ball into her face. The girls' parents get into a fistfight in the stands at the game. Maggie's boyfriend Waylon and some friends try to attack the girl's brother, but he's addicted to heroin and has been thrown out of his house. A situation of growing and life-threatening tragedy arises from a small puncture wound in a child's hand.

Or consider Romeo Puyat, the friend of Landreaux's whose leg was badly broken in a fall from a high railroad piling in Minneapolis. Romeo has serious substance abuse issues, and his son Hollis is therefore given to Landreaux and Emmaline to be raised. But Romeo bears Landreaux deep resentment. He blames Landreaux for his limp and also for losing his only son, and Romeo was in love with Emmaline before she married Landreaux. Romeo wants to ruin Landreaux's life the way he sees his own life as ruined, and at the end of the novel Romeo convinces himself, and more importantly convinces Peter Ravich, that Landreaux was drunk the day Dusty was shot. Romeo knows this will cause Peter to kill Landreaux, but he believes it to be justice, and he feels satisfied that it is a justice he has helped in his own limited way to catalyze.

The circle of mayhem and pain continually widens. Violence "goes out in the world and begets and begets" (105). Ending this begetting "takes great effort, which is why LaRose [is] sent" (105). So, what does LaRose do? How does he effect forgiveness? At the beginning of the novel the Ironses show understandable worry over their choice to give their son away. Emmaline goes to Father Travis because she wants to undo what she has done, to rescind the offer she's made. Emmaline's afraid that LaRose will believe she rejected him, left him abandoned and estranged in another family's house. Father Travis notes to himself how much Emmaline resembles the Virgin Mary in her sky blue parka as he assures her that her good intentions will bear fruit in the end and that LaRose will one day return to them. Emmaline asks him if he is sure and he affirms his certainty, then can't help but quote Paul in Romans 8: "Neither life, nor angels, nor principalities nor things present, nor things to come, nor powers, nor height, nor depth, nor any other creature will separate you" (Rom 8:38–39). That elaborate verse concludes, of course, "from the love of God which is in Christ Jesus our Lord," and the line in its entirety is actually a pretty good paraphrase of Julian, von Speyr, von Balthasar, and Weil. What Father Travis offers Emmaline, however awkwardly, is the faith that her love can span the separation between herself and her son, even if it cannot close it. Landreaux goes to Randall for similar counsel, only he worries that all the members of his family will forever resent him for sending LaRose away. But after some time, Randall assures Landreaux he did right and that others will come to know it too. Randall traces the history of violence in LaRose's family, a violence bound up generation after generation in the genocidal maneuvers of colonial white supremacy, LaRose after LaRose, with evil always trying "to catch them all" (51). But every LaRose "fought demons, outwitted them, flew" (51–52). Landreaux's son would do it too. Just like Mrs. Peace and the ghost of her mother, Randall sees generations of his people responding to violence but containing it, managing its relentless spread. Landreaux knows that the past cannot be changed. The story of his sin and of his son LaRose's role in its atonement will remain with Landreaux all his life and shape that life immovably. But even as he recognizes the irrevocability of the past, Landreaux also knows that "LaRose ha[s] already changed the story" (28).

LaRose changes the story, but not by skewing the facts or altering the history. The Raviches just love him. That's all. They love him too much to see him hurt. As desperately as they each wish to retaliate against Landreaux in vengeance, they recognize that it would crush LaRose to see his father murdered, and so they restrain themselves and relent. When Peter and Landreaux talk early in the novel, a conversation I cited above, suddenly a "sinuous contempt" grips Peter and he considers what brief but rapturous pleasure he would feel were he to split Landreaux's skull with an axe (76). Peter is consoled by the imagination of this rapture; he spends his days chopping wood, imagining his neighbor's head on the stump as he brings the ax down again and again for hours. But Peter always relents. "If not for LaRose," he says, "if not for LaRose" (76). When he thinks of LaRose, an image of this beloved child envelopes his imagination and he cannot act on his rage.

During the days when Nola is most seriously contemplating suicide, she wonders why her death must be the one to grant her release from the weight of her grief. She considers that she would get all the emotional release she needed if she simply killed Landreaux instead of herself. The prospect of prison is little counterweight to her deep desire for vengeance, and she imagines that everyone, her family especially, would understand her act of retaliation, perhaps even approve of it. Everyone, of course, except LaRose. She pictures his face, "devastated, crumpling," then in his face she sees Dusty's face too, "devastated, crumpling" (112). And in that moment of restrained reflection, Nola realizes that the old traditional ways have worked, because she cannot bring herself to harm the father of the child she now loves. And so she holds LaRose close and rocks him to sleep, his slow breath "steaming a passage to the crater of her heart" (112). When Joseph Butler preached his sermons on forgiveness, the text he chose from the Gospel of Matthew was the command to love your enemy. But loving your enemy is a difficult task; forswearing vengeance can be an almost impossibly burdensome labor. Peter's and Nola's broken hearts desperately want revenge. They fantasize about killing Landreaux. Peter doesn't even necessarily dislike him, but the urge for retributive vengeance is so strong that he spends hours imagining the murder. Peter and Nola might succumb to this urge, were it not for their love of LaRose. But because they love LaRose, because he is their son now too and their son loves Landreaux and Emmaline, they do not act on their hate.

In traditional Christian atonement theology, Jesus Christ is often called a substitute. He stands in for God's wrath and stands under the retributive justice intended for us. He is a propitiatory substitute for our punishment. But perhaps this is the wrong way to think about how and for whom Jesus Christ acts as substitute. Perhaps Jesus does not stand in for us before God's judgment. Rather, perhaps God asks Jesus to stand in between us and the enemy we hate. Because we cannot bring ourselves to love our enemy, we love the one who loves our enemy—Jesus—and for Jesus's sake relent from enacting our retributive urge. As John Ames confessed in *Gilead*, the reason we are called to love our enemies is not because they are lovable or even because we should love them. It is because God loves them. Because Peter and Nola love LaRose and LaRose loves Landreaux, they must leave Landreaux in peace. We don't forswear vengeance because we lack desire for it or even necessarily because we believe our enemy no longer deserves it. We forswear vengeance because someone we love loves our enemy, and we can't bear to break that beloved one's heart. We relent from revenge because the one we love, Jesus Christ, loves our enemy, and we can imagine Christ's face, devastated, crumpling, as in the vision of Julian, were we to act on our anger and hatred. To love our enemy in this sense, then, is to love only as much as our broken human hearts might allow us to: full of anger and resentment, wary of reconciliation, but committed to allowing the one we hate to live in peace, for the sake of another one whom we love. I cannot love my enemy, but I know Christ does, and so for Christ's sake I do no harm.

And indeed, some of the most pragmatic models of forgiveness and of peace-building take exactly this stance. The Christian ethicist Timothy Jackson defines forgiveness as neither affective transformation nor compensatory transaction, neither restored relation nor achieved reconciliation. He calls forgiveness simply, if somewhat awkwardly, "the cessation of againstness."[114] Forgiveness means simply "the courage to do good to those who spitefully use us, to refuse to return evil for evil."[115] This means that forgiveness will take any number of forms, since what acting on behalf of my enemy looks like will differ from situation to situation. Love always "offers forgiveness, meaning it steadfastly wills the good for the other," but the nature of the good in any specific situation will vary considerably. Willing my enemy's good should never mean pandering "to evil by ignoring or tempting it"; in many cases it will mean engaging in "confrontation and reprimand as means of encouraging contrition and satisfaction."[116] When confrontation and reprimand intend toward the well-being of my enemy, they are forms of forgiveness on Jackson's account. They are "cessations of againstness" even if they appear to be oppositional or antagonistic. Though Jackson insists that even adversarial goodwill must be unconditional— that it ought not depend upon successfully inspiring contrition in or attaining satisfaction from my adversary—that unconditionality doesn't equate to equanimity or passivity. Peter Ravich remains vengefully angry at Landreaux when he offers to let LaRose spend regular time at home. Peter doesn't necessarily wish Landreaux well; he just does him some good for LaRose's sake, because LaRose misses home. The good for my enemy may sometimes demand confrontation, admonition, judgment, resistance, and anger. And the good for myself might require suspicion, mistrust, distance, estrangement, even reconciliation delayed until the eschaton. These things are not contrary to forgiveness; in fact, they are potentially constitutive of it, depending on the circumstances. In resolving to "will the good for others rather than to despise them," my hostility and theirs notwithstanding, Jackson declares that "forgiveness *may* make another feel accepted and acceptable, and thereby bolster her self-esteem; forgiveness *may* help induce repentance and thus contribute to another's moral reform; forgiveness *may* even make enemies into friends. But it need not do any of these. I might *hope* that forgiveness is appropriated by a guilty party as a means to 'at-one-ment'; harmony-as-restored-relation is *often* an ideal fruition of mercy. But, again, forgiveness is not offered with reconciliation as either a precondition or a necessary effect."[117]

The experienced peace-builder John Paul Lederach confirms these pragmatic cautions even while naming restraint from reciprocal vengeance as a morally courageous and significant act in and of itself. As he describes it, peace-building demands, among other things, "the capacity to imagine ourselves in a web of relationships that includes our enemies . . . and the acceptance of the inherent risk of stepping into the unknown that lies beyond the far too familiar landscape of violence."[118] Lederach counsels patience in peace-building, affirming that deeply engaging violent histories will mean that distrust, caution, and pessimism might and even ought to persist. For Lederach, "the birth of constructive change develops in the womb of engaging complex historical relationships, not avoiding them."[119] Reconciliation is not a quick or magic resolution to conflict. And forswearing vengeance isn't identical with reconciliation. Reconciliation requires patience and a willingness to engage a fraught and violent history at depth and at length, and then to tell the story of our sufferings again and again, in a way that progressively comes to include and imagine the possibility of my enemy's future well-being. In other words, peace-building means the process of envisioning a future that is deeply rooted "in the reality of what has existed while seeking new ways to move beyond the grips of those patterns."[120] And for Lederach, Christ affords the possibility of this patience. "Through Christ," he writes, "through a person who reaches out across lines of hostility, through his very flesh and person, enemies meet and are held together. Thus they form a new humanity, a new relationship."[121] Christ is the mediator, the one who stands in the space between and in place of the enemy I hate, as the object of my love. Atonement, writes Lederach, is not about how Christ can cleanse the sins of individuals before God. It's about how Christ can act as a conduit between groups of people. Atonement in Christ is marked by "his *persistent movement toward* people, their pain, and the formation of new relationship."[122] And there is significant and necessary theological humility in Lederach's assertions here. Jesus Christ, the Son of God, is the one who, in his paradoxically estranging and binding movement, holds together those things that have been torn apart by sin. Our immediate human task is only to stop tugging at the tears with our vengeance. We are not necessarily and never hastily obligated to cross the awful distance sin has breached. Christ is not the one who stands as the substitute for my enemy (or me) in punishment. He stands as the substitute for my enemy (and me) in love. The enemy I do not love and would do harm, I do not harm for the sake of him whom I love: Jesus.

This is what happens with LaRose in Erdrich's novel. Through and only through the person of LaRose enemies are held together. It's troubling in the novel that LaRose is not given any choice about his place in binding these two families. But it's also clear that, once he has been thus bound, LaRose fully embraces this role, asking to return to the Raviches whenever he's been returned to his original home and feeling responsibility toward both families. Only at the very end of the novel is there anything resembling a cautious reconciliation, and even this resolution has its problems, which I explore in the next chapter. And I want to be clear here: I don't mean to name LaRose as an unqualified Christ figure, lest I reproduce exactly the colonial erasure I regard this novel as resisting. LaRose is neither Jesus nor a simple cipher for Jesus, but because of LaRose I can read the meaning of Jesus and the ambit of Christian atonement quite differently. Because of LaRose, Peter and Nola can somehow manage in all their rage and hatred to imagine Landreaux alive rather than dead. Because of LaRose, these families are held together instead of torn apart. Because of LaRose, Nola decides not to die. Because of LaRose, Maggie gains a new brother, and his siblings become her siblings too. Because of LaRose, peace is kept and the chaos and ill luck that begets and begets is painfully contained. Forgiveness here is costly: the Raviches are not allowed to salve their rage with violence; the Ironses must let their son go. LaRose has an almost magical capacity for bearing this suffering and assuming responsibility for it. But he cruelly suffers too and is made unfairly responsible for the stability and future of two families. The gift of LaRose isn't a painless fix. In fact, it isn't a fix at all; Dusty remains dead. The process of these families' healing is long and unending. But when the Ironses let their son go, and when the Raviches let him go back in return, we see confirmed everything we have read from Julian and von Speyr and von Balthasar and Weil about the nature of love: that it is, indeed, a letting go. It is an openness to estrangement.

This is what Arendt, I think, gets wrong. The love she accuses of insularity is not the love we see between Axl and Beatrice at the end of *The Buried Giant*, nor the love between John Ames and his son at the end of *Gilead*. In each case, love sets the other apart, and also sets the other free to begin again, to begin anew. This is what Arendt gets right—this beginning that becomes possible only through the freedom to be and to set the other free. When love does set the other free, it relinquishes possessiveness and necessarily begins to break the boundaries, limits, and borders we set around ourselves. Indeed, as Judith Butler argues (see Chapter 2), these limiting individual boundaries are the conceptual condition under which the retributive forms of forgiveness Nussbaum has worried over arise. But a sense of intersubjective sociality would set the ground for a more fundamental form of forgiveness, one that understands selfhood, wrongdoing, love, and forgiveness as essentially and relationally communal at the outset. And these are understandings already implied in many indigenous American communities, philosophies, and theologies. Where sin has been privatized in Western theology, its propitiation and atonement will be understood as private too. But for "Indian people [sin] is a matter of responsibility to a community," and rescue from the wages of sin is "defined as the ability of an individual or a community to return to a state of communitas that has been disrupted."[123] The indigenous American philosopher Brian Burkhart explains that when we regard the world as composed of relations rather than of objects, we escape the privatizing tendencies of possessiveness and property while discovering new possibilities for moral kinship, moral reflection, and moral action.[124] Again, LaRose is not a possession to be kept but a gift to be shared, a human bound in multiple and overlapping relationships. And when he is free to be in those relationships, when his humanity is courageously shared, love exceeds the privatizing bounds Arendt has feared and establishes the conditions for a difficult but just forgiveness. And when forgiveness works on this model, new relationships form, and a new and broader network of kinship, commitment, and loyalty is progressively established. There are no half-sisters.

To be clear, this attention to relation is not an exhortation toward hasty or unearned reconciliation as an ersatz for forgiveness. Rather, it is an invitation to begin our reflections about the nature of both wrong and our response to wrong at a more fundamental level. And it's also why there is a little bit of Arendt's sense of miracle in the conclusion of *LaRose*. As soon as LaRose realizes Nola wants to kill herself, he begins removing from the house tools she might use to do so. He throws out coils of rope, flushes pills, pours out poisonous household cleaners, and unloads all the ammunition from Peter's rifles. Then, when Romeo misleads Peter into believing Landreaux was drunk the day he shot Dusty, Peter finally relents to his rage under the influence of this lie. He goes home, takes his rifle, and then picks up Landreaux in his truck. They drive together to a deer blind Peter knows, and Peter tells Landreaux to walk slowly through the grass until Peter has a clear shot and can execute him. Still racked by guilt and sorrowfully unsurprised, Landreaux agrees and submits to Peter's intention. But when Landreaux comes into Peter's sight and Peter pulls the trigger, the chamber is empty. The failure to fire gives Peter enough pause to see "LaRose in Landreaux's solid, hip-slung walk" (Erdrich, *LaRose*, 342). The slow gait of the beloved son becomes, in this miraculous moment of pause, visible in the image of the despised father.

And in that moment Peter also understands all LaRose has done to save his family. He sees the "phosphorus of grief consuming those he loves," and before his mind's eye pass pictures of "all lost things," the ruins of his son and his family and his hopes. But these abstract losses soon concretize in his mind into "the actual lost things" from his home: pills, weapons, rope, chemicals, all "deadly in Nola's hands" and disposed of by LaRose. And the cartridges LaRose has thrown out too, "deadly in his own hands" (342).

Every character in this terribly sad book is a lost thing; grief consumes all those Peter can see to love. But he can also suddenly see LaRose, whom he loves, in Landreaux's despondent march toward death, and the missing ammunition gives Peter a chance to witness LaRose for an instant as a beloved substitute for Landreaux. LaRose has saved Peter from committing murder, miraculously. But even this miracle is tempered by the unresolvable reality of human vengeance and violence. Realizing LaRose has saved him and Nola from themselves, Peter throws his rifle into the lake and "feels one moment of lightness." Sensing that he has been freed from the cycle of violence, Peter "lifts his arms" and waits for some "energy of absolution," but nothing comes (342). Nothing descends upon Peter from the pleasant blue of that warm spring sky other than the knowledge that he pulled the trigger and tried to murder his neighbor. Landreaux still lives, but Peter is still guilty. What he has done may be unknown, but it cannot be undone. It may, however, be forgiven.

CHAPTER 4

Resurrection

What does forgiveness do? So far in this book I've focused on what forgiveness is and is not. I've suggested that it's not retaliation, that it's not transaction, that it's neither an affective appeasement nor a simple restoration of relation. I've argued instead that it is a self-reflexive and nonretaliatory ethical posture that begins and ends in failure, that it is a practice of mourning that reckons rather than redeems past wrong. But what should it mean to reckon with wrong in this sense? What does forgiveness do, and how might such a reckoning affect our relationship both to the broken past and to a waiting future? Consider the ending of Louise Erdrich's *LaRose*. At the conclusion of the novel's long series of tragedies and acts of violence, after all the scenes and memories of retributive vengeance and blind rage and abject terror and persistent grief, the novel ends with a large, festive gathering, a send-off for Romeo's son, Hollis, who has been raised by the Ironses. There are all the trappings of a happy ending here. Because of LaRose's unwitting intervention, Peter's rifle is empty when he tries to murder Landreaux, and so the circle of violence seems miraculously to close. Romeo, who falsely betrayed Landreaux to Peter, dives suicidally down the steps of the church but recovers from his injuries, having somehow lost both his lifelong limp and his addiction to painkillers in that fall. He announces to the group that he has saved three thousand dollars and he gives it all to Hollis. The Raviches join the Ironses for the feast, extending notions of love and kinship beyond narrowly private bounds. The community continues to grieve for Dusty, but they have found a way forward with an extended family and with the establishment of loving relationships that did not exist when Dusty was alive. The first LaRose's bones may even be coming home. The family might finally have the chance to bury her remains and mourn that original loss. In fact, the spirit of the original LaRose walks out of the woods and promises as much to her namesake, the boy LaRose. Along with her walk Dusty and Ignatia and two other generations of LaRoses, perhaps with many others. In two languages these spirits sing consolation and comfort to LaRose:

> We love you, don't cry.
> Sorrow eats time.
> Be patient.
> Time eats sorrow.[1]

Romeo gives Hollis the three thousand dollars to set him off for college, and before they cut the cake, Randall—the elder who had accompanied Landreaux into the sweat lodge after Dusty's death—joins Landreaux in singing about the sweetness of the cake and the sweetness of the future and the sweetness of the love all those gathered have for Hollis, as well as the sweetness of the love Hollis has for all his people. Hollis is uncomfortable with all the attention but also brims with awkward happiness at the tenderness of the moment and the song (Erdrich, *LaRose*, 372).

At first glance this seems an indubitably happy ending. If we compare the harrowing first ten pages of this novel against the comforting final ten, that tragic killing against this festive gathering, we might agree with the elders that time rewards the patient by consuming sorrow at last. But LaRose's sister Josette, who is in love with Hollis, realizes that this happiness is fleeting and that nothing really has ended. Believing that the three thousand dollars means Hollis doesn't have to join the North Dakota National Guard, she starts to serve cake until Hollis tells her it's too late to change his mind, he has already signed his enlistment papers. "Oh, Hollis," Josette says, standing beside him, staring into the future, and her voice suddenly having become the "voice of a woman" (372).

LaRose is a novel where bonds of loving kinship reach beyond dyadic relationships, and these bonds often move through children who bridge nuclear families through mutual love. The obvious example here is the boy LaRose, but Maggie also becomes a sister to LaRose's biological sisters Josette and Snow, and Hollis is of course Romeo's child, raised by the Ironses. Part of the joy of this final scene comes from the fact that these two sons, LaRose and Hollis, having been offered to other families because of tragic circumstances, now serve to link these fraught relations and to repair old wounds. But in a novel where children are offered to and for others and where this giving is framed by a colonial history of children stolen from their families and estranged from their culture, the fact that this narrative concludes with Hollis enlisting in the National Guard has some unsettling implications at least. Hollis is assigned, we're told, to a Guard unit that specializes in the detection and removal of IEDs. He will deploy to Iraq. Father Travis's injuries from the Marine barracks in Lebanon, along with Landreaux's service in Desert Storm, remind us that the old wounds of Western colonialism, ones that linger so painfully in the lives of these characters, will continue to cause injury as these same characters are deployed as fighters to other parts of the world. Even the cake, the sweetness of which is sung as a representative celebration of the family's love for Hollis, has its own troubled history. Recall Nola baking cakes for LaRose each day when he first moved to her home, in an attempt to sweeten the sadness of his sacrifice. But the family couldn't eat all that sweetness, and Peter ended up hiding all the cakes in the garage, leading to a massive infestation of mice. Cake can't sweeten this scene. Hollis is being offered up again, an offering framed by colonial violence, and Josette knows there is no guarantee that Hollis's offering will show the miraculous results of LaRose's.

Hannah Arendt insists that what marks forgiveness as a moral and political practice is that it is a beginning, that it starts something new in the midst of revenge's retaliatory necessities. But the implication is that forgiveness also ends something, that it brings a close to violence. Forgiveness, we're meant to understand, begins something by ending something else. In this chapter, I complicate and undermine these assumptions by arguing that forgiveness does not provide a happy ending. It is not a simple resolution to conflict because the legacies of harm are long-standing and not easily eradicable. They can be survived and struggled against but not simply erased. To do this I consider some reflections upon memory and our relationship to it as well as some theories of narrative and writing, while also attending closely to Toni Morrison's novel *Beloved*. I argue that forgiveness does not end a story of violence and replace it with a new story of peace so much as inherit a terrible history of violence and then imagine what peace might look like given the ineradicable persistence of that history. And for the Christian in particular, this insistence that histories of violence cannot be easily undone, that there are more important things than to insist on happy endings, has profound implications for the way we understand and practice forgiveness, and for the way that we interpret and inhabit the story of Jesus. It affects the way we read and write resurrection.

HAPPY MEMORIES AND HAPPY FORGETTING

The issue of memory has been at stake throughout this book. Ishiguro's Britain is clouded under a fog of forgetting; John Ames comes to remember his past clearly in *Gilead* only through acts of confession both given and received; the story of the first LaRose intervenes into and frames the tragedy of the Ravich and Irons families. But now I look more directly at memory, especially in its relationship to happiness. If in the previous chapter I was concerned to defend the continuing possibility of anger in forgiveness, here I question the necessity of happiness for it. In contemporary moral philosophy and theology, there is a common claim that forgiveness should involve some sort of forgetting, an alteration of our relationship to the past such that our recollections of that past need no longer surface to impinge on or impair our presents and futures. For some versions of forgiveness, this is especially important insofar as "excessive" memory prevents the restoration of relationship with worthy wrongdoers. In other accounts it prevents proper individual healing. Of course, I would argue that restored relationship isn't constitutive of forgiveness, but the issue of healing is crucial. If forgiveness is about addressing past wrong, then it must engage discussions of traumatic memory, of how our traumatic pasts persist into our presents, and the degree and manner by which those traumas can or should be managed or expunged.

But the advocates of forgetting also acknowledge that to forget the past entirely would be to demand a problematic erasure. Indeed, in our age of mass violence, a "most appalling goal of genocide, massacre, systematic rape, and torture has been the destruction of the remembrance of individuals."[2] To remember as if some past wrong or trauma never happened at all would not only be psychologically improbable and impractical, it would undermine justice. For theological reasons, as Jankélévitch argues, it might also hinder love. How then do we avoid either "wallowing in the past or forgetting it"?[3] What lies "between too much memory and too much forgetting," and where does forgiveness fall along this route?[4] How much forgetting does forgiveness demand? What is the proper role of memory? For many contemporary philosophical and theological discussions of forgiveness, forgetting is necessary and perhaps even inevitable. But how much forgetting our forgiveness requires remains an open question, with somewhat inchoate answers.

In Dante's vision of Purgatory, the forgiveness of sin (perhaps more properly the purgation of sin) contains two aspects, poetically rendered by Dante as drinks of water from two streams flowing down the slopes of Mount Purgatory. At the top of the mountain, we are told, the waters of forgiveness divide into two rivers: "down the near slope pour the waters of Lethe, or of forgetting; down the farther side rush the waters of Eunoë, or of positive remembrance."[5] According to Dante, these waters must be tasted in the proper order for sin to be purged: first, forgetting must be drunk, and only then may the waters of remembering be tasted. Thus, forgiveness is, as John Milbank argues, "poised vertiginously between obliteration and a recollection that amounts to restoration. It is either, or both, a negative gesture and a positive deed."[6] Whatever concerns I may have expressed about Milbank's arithmetic of forgiveness in Chapter 3, his assertion here about the position of forgiveness in the Christian West as situated between forgetting and remembering is surely correct, and it familiarly grounds much contemporary reflection on forgiveness. Forgetting must play some role in the moral act of forgiving those wrongs we remember, we are often told. Forgive and forget, so the saying goes. But how and how much forgetting is required?

The American philosopher Jeffrey Blustein gives a practical answer: enough forgetting to forestall what he calls rumination—the sort of rumination on past wrongs that perpetuates bitterness or prevents reconciliation with a worthily penitent offender. Blustein argues that when memories burden either the victim's well-being or the community's chance at reconciliation, those memories should be forgotten. Remembering, for Blustein, "can actually impede forgiveness if it is such that the wronged party dwells on or ruminates on the wrongs that he suffered."[7]

Of course, forgetting—as Blustein acknowledges—should not amount to a wholesale obliteration. Memory will always be "foundational for forgiveness, since forgiveness is a means of confronting past wrongdoing that one holds before the mind, and it overcomes the emotions it engenders without relinquishing the judgment that one was wronged."[8] An implied definition of forgiveness emerges in Blustein's account. Forgiveness here is about overcoming emotion; its grounds are basically affective. In this, Blustein departs only slightly from much of the Western tradition in its considerations of forgiveness, as I argued in Chapter 3: forgiveness is, in the West, usually and most often understood as the overcoming of emotions, typically hostile ones. Blustein here follows and modifies what he reads as a deep association of forgiveness with sentiment in the "orthodox or standard account" of the

Anglo-American philosophical tradition, one based largely (though as I argued in the previous chapter, somewhat mistakenly) upon Bishop Joseph Butler's sermons on forgiveness of 1729.[9] According to Blustein's reading of Butler, "forgiveness is said to involve the overcoming of some type of angry or hostile emotion."[10] The idea of forgiveness in its conventional usage therefore "marks a change in how the offended feels about the person who committed the injury, not a change in the actions to be taken" in response to that offense.[11]

As I argued in Chapter 3, however, Bishop Butler's articulation of the relation of forgiveness to affect is deeply interrelated with complex issues of law and sovereignty. If Blustein and others are largely correct in tracing this affective genealogy to Butler and in regarding "standard" forgiveness as construed largely as the overcoming of anger, rancor, bitterness, or resentment, I believe both he and the tradition he cites oversimplify Butler's sermons on forgiveness and resentment, with the result that they misappraise his opinion of anger and neglect his defense of state-sponsored violence. What crucially distinguishes Blustein from others of this philosophical tradition, though, is his insistence that retributive and hostile emotions are not the only feelings that follow wrongdoing. Other sentiments—sadness or despair, for example—are at least as, if not more, likely to arise in the wake of wrongdoing and can be more painful and damaging to victims than feelings of vengeance might ever be. Psychological trauma is complicated, Blustein rightly notes, and introduces complex and volatile emotions in its wake.

Blustein wants therefore to complicate the moral and emotional picture we have inherited from the English eighteenth century in order to better accommodate our reckoning with the affective dimensions of past wrong. Negative affects like anger, sadness, or resentment are not, for Blustein, bad in and of themselves but can become damaging when they cause persisting or intractable problems in personal and public life. The question of which emotions should be overcome by our gestures of forgiveness becomes therefore a very practical one for Blustein. Those emotions that either forestall individual healing or prevent justified interpersonal reconciliation are the ones that a victim "needs to forget by rendering memories of wrongdoing difficult to access" through "various techniques of emotional regulation."[12] There is a difference, in other words, between what Blustein calls "remembering and remembering well."[13] Besides accuracy, what distinguishes Blustein's good memories from bad ones is the degree to which present harm is controlled or kept at bay by the selectivity of our remembering. In Blustein's conclusions, then, we can hear echoes of Griswold's reading of Butler, or of Butler himself:

affect is bad when it prevents justified reconciliation or personal healing. But who gets to decide when reconciliation is just and how wounds should be healed? Blustein's admirably pragmatic aim is to avoid harm. When memory keeps us from pursing helpful ends—healing or reconciliation for example, if we can bracket these as neutral terms—forgetting is required.

In this we find Blustein coming to common ground with conversation partners from both the continental philosophical and theological traditions. In *Memory, History, and Forgetting*, Paul Ricoeur also negotiates the narrow path between remembering and forgetting by suggesting that to remember well is to evade the recollection of certain bad memories.[14] Ricoeur addresses memory as a constructive, rather than replicative, act. Memories do not re-produce the past, they reconstruct it; and so although we aspire toward and assume our memories' accuracy, no memory can entirely recapture the past, and our memorial acts are always interpretive and therefore engaged in pro-cesses of selection, construction, and forgetting. But in this, writes Ricoeur, memory is uniquely poised to spur action. Since it presents the past out of which we understand ourselves to arise and to which we therefore react, memory is concerned with "the exchanges that give rise to retribution, repara-tion, absolution." Meanwhile, "forgetting develops enduring situations"—stable ones, in other words, peaceful ones not disrupted by cycles of retribution and repair. These cyclical and reciprocal retaliatory actions are "prevented from continuing by forgetting" (Ricoeur, *Memory, History, Forgetting*, 502).[15] In other words, the patterns of retributive violence and emotion Arendt de-scribes can be halted for Ricoeur only by some failure, either willful or unwit-ting, of memory, a failure that can intercede between the inevitable and cyclical stages of action and reaction. Calling the past forward to memory perpetuates the past's effects; leaving it uncalled and undisturbed can there-fore allow its acts to evade reaction, response, or retaliation. To halt reciprocal violence, Arendt appeals to the miracle of beginning; Ricoeur here inserts memory—or the lack of it. When past wrongs are removed from recollection, predictably retributive feelings and their follow-on acts of vengeance do not need to arise in response to what is forgotten. Forgetting therefore can and should serve an "optative" function, insofar as it may promote hope and hap-piness when properly deployed (505). For Ricoeur, to remember well is to remember skillfully; it is hopefully to integrate forgetting into our recollec-tions such that we can remember pleasantly—with remembering or memory here being understood as the interplay between full recollection and selective forgetting.

This failure of memory for Ricoeur is, importantly, not simple erasure or oblivion. There is a "forgetting through effacement" but also a "forgetting kept in reserve" (503). The mere decay and loss of the past through degeneration of the mind's activities is different therefore from the leaving aside of a past that could be brought forth but isn't. Whereas the movement toward erasure, or effacement, is often the "threat" against which "we conduct the work of memory," this is not the productive sort of forgetting as remembering-well that Ricoeur endorses when considering forgiveness (426). This different and forgiving sort of not-remembering has to do with the availability of particular memories to consciousness, such that "we cannot simply classify [this] forgetting . . . among the dysfunctions of memory alongside amnesia, nor among the distortions of memory affecting its reliability" (426). The forgiving sort of forgetting—the leaving aside of memories so that they may harmlessly molder in the storehouse of the mind—designates for Ricoeur "the *unperceived* character of the perseverance of memories, their removal from the vigilance of consciousness" (440). Like Blustein, Ricoeur is concerned to discern the relationship of selective memory to both personal healing and public reconciliation. Memory—with forgetting as an integrated corollary to recollection—becomes then a form of care. "In memory-as-care," Ricoeur writes, "we hold ourselves open to the past, we remain concerned about it." If so, Ricoeur wonders, then would there be "a supreme form of forgetting, as a disposition and a way of being in the world, which would be insouciance, carefreeness?" (505). In other words, if memory cares, then forgetting must be carefree. But in that case, forgetting risks carelessness or indifference too. Under "the pain of slipping back into the traps of amnesty-amnesia," Ricoeur thus reasons that forgetting cannot "constitute an order distinct from memory, out of complacency with the wearing away of time. It can only arrange itself under the optative mood of happy memory" (505). That is, forgetting is not actually indifferent carelessness; rather, it is the form of memorial care concerned with happiness. It is in preserving and balancing this happy memory, this optative mood, against knowledge of the past's real wounds that forgiveness poises itself as a way for caring for ourselves in time. Between remembrance and oblivion, Ricoeur's forgiveness remembers (and forgets) well. It cares about the past, but it also admits irrevocability and so leaves the past to itself for the sake of, out of concern for, the present. This form of memory consists "in inscribing the powerlessness of reflection and speculation at the head of the list of things to be renounced"; in other words, the first thing forgetting forgets is the powerlessness of reflection to alter the past. The renunciation of this knowledge pushes "the barrier of forgetting . . . back a few degrees" for the sake of the "small pleasures of happy memory" (503). Put differently, it recalls those memories that cannot be repaired as simply irreparable, but only inasmuch as that recollection may be made with care, only insofar as it might be incorporated into a happiness that can afford its forgetting to be relinquished only by degrees. Forgiving forgetfulness here does not erase the past. It simply declines to recall enough of that past to spur the affect that might occasion retributive feelings, which would inevitably then lead to vengeful actions.

Miroslav Volf's 2006 book *The End of Memory*, based on lectures presented in 2002, follows Ricoeur's argument quite closely, but within a deliberately theological frame and with eschatologically optative conclusions.[16] Volf also sees human memory as a constant interplay between the practical impossibility of total recall and the everyday reality of selective, often unintended, forgetting. Memory "always only approximates the remembered event. . . . [It] involves a mixture of truthful description and imagined construction" (Volf, *End of Memory*, 48–49). In the case of wrongdoing, however, the stakes of this interplay become much more complicated. To "remember a wrongdoing" for Volf is "to struggle against it" (11). Like Blustein and Ricoeur, Volf worries that too much memory will perpetuate cycles of pain or of violence, either slowing individual healing or preventing interpersonal reconciliation. When remembered wrongly, the past "metastasizes into the territory of the future, and the future, drained of new possibilities, mutates into an extension of the painful past" (81). The issue of the past's pain is central here. When we remember wrongs, questions of accuracy and affect come into complicated relation. Wrongdoing hurts, and the emotional pain of past wrong becomes a part of the past that our remembering works to recall. Therefore, any "emotionless recollection makes for a significantly altered memory"; any memory of suffering that cannot recall the depth or scale of its pain will then "inevitably involve forgetting" (23). But if the memory of wrongdoing is also the struggle against wrongdoing, then these issues of affect expose exactly what Volf argues we should be struggling against. For Volf, as for Blustein and Ricoeur, it turns out that what we seek to manage by selectively forgetful recollection are the hostile or painful emotions we no longer wish to feel but that tend to arise with our memories and then spur retribution, forestall reconciliation, or frustrate healing.

Volf treads carefully in this argument. Like Ricoeur, he understands that casting the past into oblivion can trouble human identity and morality.

Wholesale erasure is therefore no simple solution. Volf admits that "the letting go of memories of wrongs strikes us as immoral, unhealthy, dangerous"
(143). Forgetting wrong "whitewashes perpetrators"; it undermines our identity because "memories of evils suffered are deemed essential" to who we are,
and "the absence of the memory of misdeeds leaves no deterrent for future
perpetrators" (143). It's also important to note that Volf writes out of a personal experience in which historical memory has been deployed toward violent ends. But ultimately all these concerns are only finite and temporal for
Volf. The relevance of all these critiques is limited because their resolution is
eternal, realized in the eschaton.

In a way that both assumes but expands upon Ricoeur's notion that forgetting can be a form of caring for ourselves as beings with both pasts and
futures, the basic problem for Volf comes down to the relevance of past suffering to human identity. We are composed of our histories, Volf acknowledges:
part of who we are is what we have suffered. If forgiveness is forgetting, he
rhetorically wonders, then don't we risk losing ourselves? Doesn't our eschatological redemption then become a sort of annihilation? While admitting the
importance of individual history in our particular subjectivities, Volf argues
that we can leave the past unremembered only if and when we recognize the
fundamental source of and basis for identity elsewhere. Forgetting, for Volf, is
"not a flight from the defective or the unbearable. It is a byproduct of the attachment to the perfectly Good" (141). Forgetting suffering isn't merely an
erasure. Rather, on Volf's account the "forgetting of evil is in the service of
remembering the good, and remembering the good is the consequence of being engrossed in God" (141). For Christian theology, who we are is not only or
primarily what we have suffered; it is that we are created, loved, and redeemed
by God. This good is the whole and sum of our identity; the evil of our individual suffering is ancillary and can be safely sloughed off by forgetting without any risk to our basic identity. The waters of Lethe wash away the dross
while Eunoë restores us fully to ourselves. When our eschatological identities
(and importantly, those also of our enemies) are grounded in this love, then
(according to Volf) the memories "of wrongs, rather than being deleted, will
simply fail to surface in [our] consciousness—they will *not come to mind*"
(145). Note the similarity to Ricoeur's argument here: what's at stake isn't the
past's erasure; it is its irrelevance to the future we hope to or have realized.
Under these "conditions the absence of the memory of wrongs suffered is
desirable" (148).[17] Forgetting the past is, in fact, simply remembering who we
mostly fundamentally and basically are: beloved of God.

This all sounds quite comforting theologically, but it evinces an optimism that I believe too often colors much of the Christian tradition and that this book as a whole aims to interrogate through the particular problem of forgiveness. Because Volf's real worry, I think, is not over whether our identities are finally grounded in God's love for us rather than in the history of our sufferings, but in how happy we will get to be in the eschatological future we have hoped for:

> [Could] we imagine a world of perpetual remembrance as a world of love? We could imagine it as a world of the kind that struggles and suffers. All the blessed would then share in that extraordinary divine love, which loves despite knowing human beings' petty but often nasty transgressions and great crimes against each other and sins against God. But could we imagine such a world as one of felicity? Is it conceivable as a world of *joy*, and the world of joy *in one another* on top of it, which is what a world of love is said to be? I will not claim it is impossible; but it seems to me rather implausible. (212)

I wonder why Volf is troubled by either the possibility or plausibility of felicity. I concede that the terms are slippery here: Is felicity the same thing as joy? Is either the same as happiness? In any case, what Volf seems concerned to protect is an eschaton largely characterized by positive affect. What he argues for is a happy ending. By the lights of our tradition and our scripture, though, we must recall that God is not happiness or joy or ease or bliss or felicity; God is love. The first world Volf here describes, the one that loves amid struggle, suffering, and transgression, seems largely recognizable as divine, if not plausibly happy on human terms. Indeed, it recalls Julian of Norwich's visions of divine love and her preference for the face of an anguished Christ over any blissful vision of heaven. The "extraordinary divine love" Volf lauds here, a love that loves "despite knowing"—that is, despite fully remembering—our petty and nasty transgressions: this is the character of the divine love into which Volf himself argues we are summoned, upon which our own identities are actually and fundamentally grounded, into which we will finally be embraced, but which Volf finds too unpleasantly grim to accept as eternal. As Julian and Jankélévitch have already argued, it is precisely when and because love *does* recall all our wrongdoings that it marks itself as unconditional and limitless and even divine. As Julian's vision of Jesus says to her, "If I could suffer more, I would suffer more."[18] For Volf, meanwhile, what most demands protection is the imagination of "an eternity characterized by joyous mutual love," and he reads in that phrase the promise of a certain sort of happiness (193).

Paradisal eschatology is not unfamiliar within the Christian tradition, of course, and this is a book about forgiveness, not a book of eschatological speculation, whatever the relative plausibilities of our imagined ends. But Volf's concern to preserve a specific form of felicity in the eschaton seems to me to raise a few specific worries with regard to forgiveness. The first comes from another of Volf's works, *Exclusion and Embrace*, in which he argues that "the practice of nonviolence requires a belief in divine vengeance," because we must allow victims of wrongdoing in this world to retain hope for God's consuming wrath to fall upon their enemies in the world to come.[19] In short, Volf eschatologically displaces the compensating pleasures of retribution (critiqued in Chapter 1) into the eternal future. He also critiques the arrogance of any theology that presumes God's love should preclude wrathful violence, while suggesting that any person who disagrees with him should lecture in a war zone, as he has. As previous chapters have indicated, following Walter Benjamin and Butler, violence is never a neutral term, and divine violence in particular is a demanding theoretical and theological category worthy of reflection. But as I have argued, divine violence seems most concerned with upending the systems of ethical balance and relational compensation on which notions such as retributive justice and retaliatory wrath are so uncritically established.

My second worry is more pastoral in nature, since the promise of vengeance presumes that the injured may be comforted only by violence or, when that is inadvisable in the present, by the imagination and promise of it in the future. As Blustein and others have shown, in fact, posttraumatic affect is complex and not always angry, and vengeance enacted and exacted often worsens traumatic response.[20] In response to Volf one might point to the many courageous peace-builders—such as John Paul Lederach (see Chapter 3)—who have, in fact, spent lifetimes in war zones inviting enemies into imagining God's love for one another while also patiently navigating the affective complexity of violence and its aftermath.[21] People less courageous than Lederach, perhaps theologians like myself, might very well regard teaching nonretaliatory Christian ethics in such venues uncomfortable and thus find ourselves avoiding those speaking engagements. But one scholar's avoidance of the difficult or the dangerous does not alone provide ground for a sound eschatological argument.

Last, and perhaps most germanely, I worry that Volf's concern to assume an identity between something called joy and another thing called felicity or happiness, and his concern to protect the prospects for that future happiness—whether political or eschatological—too often trickle down into our everyday understandings of forgiveness. That is, forgiveness is too often understood as merely an instrument of affective transformation, as a way to restore either ourselves or others to happiness or contentment. This leads not only to misreadings of the moral tradition we have inherited, but also to forms of forgiveness that can prove difficult for victims to bear, to forms of forgiving that forestall exactly the individual healing and corporate reconciliation these authors are so concerned to protect. Take for example the philosophical legacy of Joseph Butler, which Blustein and others have recognized as framing forgiveness fundamentally as an emotional labor, as the moral task of overcoming resentment. This is, of course, an overreading of Butler's argument. As described in Chapter 3, the eighth and ninth sermons of 1729, titled "Upon Resentment" and "Upon Forgiveness of Injuries," take Jesus's exhortation from the Sermon on the Mount that we love our enemies as their text (Matt 5:43–44). These are sermons about the nature of love, and we find few affective assumptions or preoccupations about happiness there. Butler's conclusion is decidedly *not* that forgiveness means to overcome resentment. On the contrary, he argues (especially in the first sermon) that "resentment is natural and just" in the wake of wrongdoing.[22] His moral purpose is not to rail against resentment as such, but to denounce the fact that "custom and false honor are on the side of retaliation and revenge" when our putatively natural resentments arise.[23] Indeed, Butler's primary concern is to discourage those "abuses" of resentment that become "excessive" and that then flower into "malice or revenge."[24]

In Chapter 3 I went to great lengths to show that Butler's concern to preserve the Crown's right to punish allowed affect to be smuggled back into his model of forgiveness. Yet it's clear that for Bishop Butler, to overcome resentment does not mean to cease feeling it. Rather, it means to cease acting unilaterally with violence as a result of it. Resentment in itself is not a moral wrong; revenge that takes resentment as its justification may be. Butler rejects the customary marriage of resentment to revenge, yet he wants to preserve the moral anger we experience in response to wrongdoing without it necessarily giving way to retaliatory acts of vengeance. Indeed, when we pay close attention to Ricoeur and Volf, we see how easily feelings of resentment are assumed almost necessarily to spur retributive action. Both Ricoeur and Volf are trying to insert an amnesiac, perhaps Arthurian, break between affect and action. But for Butler "resentment is not inconsistent with good-will." His sermons on Christian love assert that "we may love our enemy, and yet have resentment against him for his injurious behavior towards us." Butler insists, therefore, that "to forgive injuries, is the same as to love our enemies."[25] This must be emphasized because it so sharply contradicts what has become the conventional wisdom about forgiveness: the forgiveness Butler proposes is decidedly not about overcoming anger or any other hostile emotion in itself as an emotion. It is about resisting the acts toward which our anger or despair may tempt us. As noted in Chapter 3, Butler does not set resentment against either forgiveness or love, or (more properly) against forgiveness as an act of love. Though the Western tradition has tended to assume this antagonism in his wake, Butler is not primarily concerned with negative affect, whether at the interpersonal or political level.

Volf and others do affirm victims' anger in response to wrongdoing in considered ways, so I do not want to overstate the departure they are making from Butler.[26] But Volf's insistence upon a "felicitous" eschaton finally grounds his argument for forgetting in crucial ways. Recent theorizations of memory's relationship to forgiveness depend deeply on a contemporary anxiety over affect, a particular fixation on moral sentiments, and most of all an unwillingness to decouple resentment from acts of retaliatory revenge. When bad feelings can be gratified only by an act of vengeance, forgetting becomes the sole human tool available for curtailing violence. It is feeling that must be overcome, rather than the action such feeling urges. Sadness and anger must be replaced by felicity and joy, or else give way to violence. But attending here again to Butler's careful defense of resentment, we see his pastoral sympathy toward victims in their pain, a sympathy which anticipates current critiques of forgiveness, since the wronged in Butler's sermons remain absolutely entitled to their anger. Butler's theology of forgiveness seeks to advance a more pressing moral concern, beyond the question or character of moral sentiments. For Butler, forgiveness is a form of love, and love bears a diversity of feelings. As Julian and Jankélévitch show, the deepest love remembers even our worst wrongs. On a human scale, then, a remembering love must admit a variety of emotions, including anger, bitterness, resentment, and sadness. This is why it is a moral possibility with respect to those who remain our enemies. The questions Butler poses for us, then, are these: What does felicity have to do with love? Is that the nature of the love that, on the Christian account, finally grounds us? And what would become of a love that fails to remember? If forgiveness is truly a form of love, can we ever really forgive and forget?

HOW BAD IS THE SCAR?

Toni Morrison's widely acclaimed and influential 1987 novel *Beloved* seems to confirm fears like those of Blustein, Ricoeur, and Volf.[27] *Beloved* recounts the story of a traumatized family in the years after the Civil War. Sethe, the central character, escaped slavery at a plantation named Sweet Home in Kentucky before the war and has settled in a Cincinnati African American community, along a street called Bluestone Road. She lives there with her daughter Denver and also with the ghost of her unnamed daughter. Sethe killed this child when her former slave owner, schoolteacher, found them in Ohio and arrived to kidnap them and claim them as property. Rather than allow her unnamed daughter to be returned to Sweet Home, Sethe fled to a woodshed at first sight of schoolteacher, took a handsaw to her daughter's throat, and then attempted to crush her sons' skulls before she was restrained. The trauma of that violence—not just the slaying of her daughter but also the vivid memories of the torture, rape, and abuse they all escaped at Sweet Home—has shattered her family. The father of Sethe's children was unable to escape Sweet Home because, after being forced to watch Sethe raped, his psyche crumbled. He is last seen staring blankly by a churn with butter smeared all over his face. Sethe's mother-in-law, Baby Suggs, a charismatic spiritual leader among the community at Bluestone Road, seems to perseverate on apology following the murder, saying "I beg your pardon" repeatedly and at awkward times, eventually taking to her bed to ponder color for the rest of her life. Sethe's sons, Howard and Bugler, having watched their sister (now called Beloved, to match the lone word on her gravestone) murdered and having survived their mother's attempt at murdering them, run away when Beloved's ghost begins shattering mirrors and leaving handprints in their birthday cakes. Only Denver, who was newborn at the time of the killing, remains with Sethe at 124 Bluestone Road, but the pair are outcasts from their community and they live without any significant support, relationship, or friendship from others.

The novel opens when another former slave from Sweet Home, Paul D, arrives at 124, unaware of Sethe's Cincinnati history. His presence begins to stir up Sethe's Sweet Home memories. Sethe is ambivalent about these memories, indeed about memories in general. We are told that she works to remember as little as possible of her life before Bluestone Road, to avoid recalling her past pain in the present. Despite her best efforts, however, her brain is "devious" (Morrison, *Beloved*, 6). While engaged in her daily tasks and preoccupied with chores, all of a sudden she might see "Sweet Home rolling . . . out before her eyes" (7). Most hauntingly, these uninvited memories present the landscape in all its "shameless beauty," a beauty that hides the horror of her own and her loved ones' suffering on the plantation. To be clear, especially with respect to the arguments of Ricoeur and Volf above, the beauty of these rolling hills in Sethe's memory is terrible precisely for the trauma it aims to hide.

Memories carry danger for Sethe. The pain that accompanies these memories' occasioning events, as well as the pain of their recurrence in memory, is excruciating, and Sethe avoids that anguish however and whenever she can. But she has only limited control over her "devious" brain. Not only will it cause her to remember what she would rather forget, but memory here also alters the quality of her unsolicited thoughts in painful ways. The natural beauty of that land, which comes to her in waves, innocuously presents itself to her memory as the whole of Sweet Home. But these beautiful memories paradoxically remind her of images she cannot call to mind, awful images of lynched young boys hanging from the most "beautiful sycamores in the world" (7). The movement of memory for Sethe here is complex and not nearly as straightforward as the simple alternatives of erasure and selection that Ricoeur has suggested. It "shames" Sethe that her mind's eye will retrieve only the trees, but not the boys (7). She does not want to remember the image of those boys, but neither does she want to erase their goodness and dignity and worth as human children by forgetting them. Her selective memory in fact betrays her because she paradoxically recalls what she cannot bear to remember, precisely because she cannot bear to remember it. However much she wills herself to remember differently, to remember better, her mind displaces the children with the sycamores every time, and she cannot "forgive her memory" for that (7). In other words, what her memory occludes for the sake of beauty or calm only serves further to remind her of these children. They remain profoundly worthy of her memory, but she cannot bring herself to see the horror of them swinging from the trees. The comforting selectivity of image in her memory—its insistence on lovely, rolling hills at the expense of recalling the real lives lost on the limbs of those trees—is unforgiveable to Sethe.

Despite this unforgiveable selectivity, however, Sethe regards her primary labor to be the work of restraining and limiting her memory. As a parent,

Sethe regards her first responsibility toward her daughter Denver as the work of keeping her child from the "past that was still waiting for her" (51). Note the twisting of tense here; the past waits to meet Denver in her future. When Paul D moves in to 124, Sethe hopes his support will create the space for her to remember all she cannot forgive her memory for forgetting, because if the full and awful picture of those memories cause her to collapse, a companion will be there to lift her up (21). But Paul D has memories too, ones he has stuffed into the securely fastened "tobacco tin" of his heart, a tin he will allow nothing to pry open, especially not in the company of Sethe (133). In the quiet of dawn we're told that Sethe kneads Paul D's knees, as if she is "working dough" in the early light of morning, beginning all her days with the difficult, routine labor of "beating back the past" (86).

It's important, then, that *Beloved* begins with an exorcism. When Paul D arrives at the home Sethe shares both with Denver and with Beloved's poltergeist, he responds with rage and shouts down the ghost. He bashes furniture, hollers, and screams, drowning out the house's shouts and telling the ghost that Sethe has had enough (22). Despite being assured by Sethe that the ghost isn't "evil, just sad," Paul D takes Sethe into his arms and then banishes that sadness from 124 (10). Grief and pain are what Paul D aims to exorcise, though we should note again that what Sethe hopes from Paul D when he holds her is not forgetting but the chance just to trust "things and remember things" while a companion stands ready to catch her if she falls (21). She does not seek to forget but instead to find a place from which to remember safely. Yet even after the harrowing events of the novel, Paul D remains primarily concerned about the ways that the past can impair the future, or in Miroslav Volf's words, the way the past "metastasizes into the territory of the future, and the future, drained of new possibilities, mutates into an extension of the painful past."[28] "We got more yesterday than anybody," Paul D tells Sethe at novel's end. "We need some kind of tomorrow" (322). The past is for leaving behind, and the future is where that happens.

To be clear, it's not fair to align Paul D too exactly with Volf here. Paul D doesn't strive for unmitigated felicity; he just wants to beat back enough trauma to get through the day. And for a while, he does. After the exorcism, the house falls silent. Then, a few weeks later, a nineteen- or twenty-year-old woman, about the age Denver's dead sister would be had she lived, appears on a tree stump near 124. Sethe, Denver, and Paul D take her in. Denver immediately recognizes this woman as the materialized ghost of her sister, and the text does not disabuse its reader of this suspicion. The young woman has limited language and appears abnormally attached to Sethe. She cannot articulate any history but says that "in the dark" her name is Beloved (88). Beloved hates Paul D, progressively alienates him, and gradually but indirectly pushes him first out of Sethe's bed and then out of Sethe's home, until Paul D is sleeping in a backyard shed where Beloved finally steals to him and, seemingly contrary to Paul D's desires, has sex with him. Beloved wants endlessly to hear Denver's stories of Sethe's escape from Sweet Home, but Denver doesn't have a personal recollection of her birth, and so she reconstructs a memory from the pieces of her story that she has been given secondhand by Sethe. As in *Gilead*, stories and selves cannot be given in isolation. Tales are told in relation. The full picture of events cannot be compiled alone but requires the sharing of perspectives, memories, and stories. And the novel presents this collective, imagined reconstruction as a direct narration. Sethe's own stories, meanwhile, serve as a form of nourishment for Beloved. As the novel's narrator observes, storytelling feeds and nourishes Beloved. In the same way that Denver learns to ply Beloved with sweets and treats, Sethe discovers the deep satisfaction Beloved takes from stories (69). Like Nola with her stacked cakes and forced smile, Beloved seeks sweetness only. Thus, along with Denver, the reader slowly comes to the supernatural conclusion these circumstances suggest: that the sad ghost Paul D chased off at the beginning of the story has returned now in the flesh, singular and hungry and resentful.

In fact, though, for much of the novel Sethe has no such supernatural suspicions. Unlike Denver, Sethe does not intuit a haunting, despite the young woman's name and her extreme and obsessive devotion. At first she explains Beloved's odd behavior as most likely a posttraumatic reaction to sexual slavery. Sethe, terribly aware of the risks of young black women like Beloved, simply assumes that Beloved had been "locked up by some white man" and has somehow escaped (140). Her odd behavior, Sethe seems to reason, is a natural consequence of the sexual trauma she has survived. A similar thing had happened to another member of the Bluestone Road community, a woman named Ella who will play a significant role later in the novel. Ella, Sethe recalls, was imprisoned by a man and his son for a year and tortured in unimaginable ways. All Beloved's odd behavior, her animosity toward Paul D and her strange obsessiveness, Sethe attributes to this or to a similar trauma. But after Paul D has gone, Sethe overhears Beloved humming a tune she recognizes as one she hummed to her dead baby, and the broken pieces in Sethe's brain abruptly settle "into places designed and made especially for them" (207). Immediately and entirely, Sethe sees Beloved as her dead and resurrected daughter.

Once this epiphany befalls Sethe, things at 124 Bluestone Road begin to fall apart. Sethe reciprocates Beloved's obsession, and they become entangled in a shared and insatiable exchange of deep need and pain. Most of all, Sethe hopes that Beloved will be able to relieve her of the memories she wants to leave behind. In one of the few first-person passages in the novel, Sethe speaks directly to Beloved, saying, "I can forget it all now": all the terror and trauma of their past, the awfulness of her initial act and all the chaotic sadness of the subsequent haunting (217). For years, Sethe tells Beloved, she thought the ghost of her dead daughter was mad, but her return in the flesh has proved to Sethe that she must not be angry anymore, that now all may be forgotten. Except, Sethe remains desperate to know one thing, to indulge in the evidence of one dreadful recollection: "How bad is the scar?" (217). The gift Beloved brings to Sethe is the possibility that the past can be forgotten. But this forgetting invites other gifts: first, the knowledge that Beloved is no longer angry, that some anger has been appeased. And second, a wish to see the wound. Note, too, how different this desire is from the relief of safe memory Paul D promised upon his arrival at 124. Because the past has been restored, Sethe expects that this restoration will lead to an affective transformation. Now neither sad nor mad, Beloved has returned; or rather, her return is a sign that Beloved does not (or does no longer) bear Sethe any anger or sadness, any negative affect. Sethe's one need, to see the scar she made on her daughter's neck, suggests an ambivalent relationship to the memory she claims she wants to forget, one that I explore below. Even a healed scar testifies to a wound, and in so doing summons memory. Be that as it may, for now I observe how Beloved's need for stories as a sort of metaphorical nourishment becomes absolutely literal in the novel. Beloved must be fed, with sweets and devotion both, and Sethe gives all she has to Beloved now that she is able to offer some amends. Just as the ghost has materialized, the ghost's needs have become material too, and Sethe withholds nothing from Beloved's desire. Beloved and Sethe abandon all practical concern. They become codependently obsessed with attending to one another, "Sethe happy when Beloved was; Beloved lapping devotion like cream" (286). When this devotion leads Sethe to lose her job, Sethe declines to pursue another, instead committing all of her newly available time to entertaining Beloved, "who never got enough of anything" (282). Beloved is insatiable, eating Sethe's songs and stories as well as the batter from her mixing bowl and the cream from her milk. Sethe surrenders everything to Beloved until she has been consumed, until she is "licked, tasted, eaten by Beloved's eyes" and has given this risen ghost her very self (68). But Beloved can taste only sweetness; the bitterness and pain of their past must be replaced by sugar and cream. And the bigger Beloved gets, the smaller Sethe becomes. As Beloved grows, Sethe wastes away; as Beloved's eyes grow wide and bright, Sethe's droop and dull with sleeplessness. Beloved eats up Sethe's very life; she becomes swollen and tall with it (295). And while Beloved grows fat on Sethe's devotion as Sethe starves, Sethe continually pleads with Beloved "for forgiveness," listing all her reasons for the killing, wishing she could trade places with the child, offering her own life in exchange for a single of Beloved's tears. Nonetheless, for all of Sethe's sweetness and cream, for all her devotion and stories, despite all her repeated pleas for forgiveness, Beloved will not grant it (284). She remains a needful, hungry, unforgiving ghost.

This destructive relationship of obsession and possession into which Sethe and Beloved have devolved represents almost exactly the worry Blustein, Ricoeur, Volf, and Paul D have expressed. If Beloved is a ghost of the past come alive in the present, then here precisely are all those dangers made flesh. Sethe's inability to let go of the past forestalls both healing and forgiveness. Sethe ruminates so deeply upon her pain that it has taken up a body and a residence in her home. Having abandoned all hope for her future, Sethe no longer cares what the next day will bring. Her only goal is to sweeten this enfleshed memory, to fill it up and make it happy. To recall Volf yet again, her past has metastasized into her future, and her future has become a mere extension of her past. We should note, however, what this past is hungry for, what it feeds on and how it grows. What consumes Sethe's body and memory is the need to feed Beloved's greed for sweets: sugary treats and happy stories, both. Beloved will not taste bitterness, and Sethe won't offer it.

The worry is real and the past has come to haunt the present in ways that perilously threaten it. Sethe seems ready, then, for another exorcism. Denver, growing alarmed at her mother's decline, eventually reaches out to her neighbors and the community of women on Bluestone Road. Some believe Beloved is a ghost, some deny it, but it is the previously mentioned Ella who is more convinced than any of the other women that Sethe is in immediate need of rescue. Ella resents the pretentions of a past that claims for itself the right to take "possession of the present" (302). For Ella, the past—her own traumatized one not least—is meant for leaving behind. And one that refuses to be left there might need stomping out. The women of the Bluestone Road community gather at the telling time of 3 p.m. on a Friday to advance as one upon 124. Before they depart, they ask Ella if they may pray. Ella assents to this reverent delay but adds that afterwards, they need to "get down to business" (302). And so the women come to 124 praying and singing and kneeling, building "voice upon voice" until their common cause crests as a "wave of sound" that breaks "over Sethe" where she shudders like the "baptized in its wash" (308). Denver's new white employer, Mr. Bodwin, is also coming down the road as the rescue party of women arrives. Literally consumed by memory, Sethe mistakes Mr. Bodwin for schoolteacher and rises in rage in an attempt to relive her past differently. She takes up an ice pick and tries to alter her past, to murder the white man instead of her beloved daughter this time, but the rising women surround and restrain Sethe. These women bear her bodily in their arms, just as Paul D had done after his first exorcism. And in this melee of song, prayer, and community, Beloved vanishes.

The notes of this climactic scene ring a Christian tune. The baptismal imagery is explicit, as are the prayers and devotions of the women who come to enact the community's forgetting by force. Important, too, is that the exorcism occurs on a Friday at three in the afternoon, the day and time of Jesus's death. But what—or who—is killed here at this meaning-laden hour? If it is only a harmful past that has been put back and suppressed, why the reference to Calvary? How can or does Beloved stand for or displace a sacrificed Christ in this scene?

REMEMBRANCE AND REMEMORY

As I have suggested above, and as much of this book has argued from various theoretical and theological angles, I believe forgiving love bears an unsettling but undeniable resemblance to grief—indeed, I have argued that love and loss are inseparable. But I want to explore this tension around the particular question of memory further, because I think it helps clarify what has been at stake since we encountered the forgetting fog of Ishiguro's *The Buried Giant*, what assumptions operate in our considerations of forgiveness, and how we should frame the various discussions of healing and resurrection to follow. To begin doing so I think further about *Beloved* and in particular about the relationship between Sethe and Beloved. It's important to specify this relationship as my focus, I believe, because if *Beloved* is in some ways a novel about forgiveness, it also is one that deliberately constrains the scope of its reflections to the moral demands and moral injuries of those forced to live and act under conditions of abject brutality. In other words, the novel does not even begin to suggest any forgiveness for schoolteacher, and my consideration of Sethe and Beloved and of the whole community of Bluestone Road should not be read to do so either. This is not to say that forgiveness is ever irrelevant or impossible, only that my reflections on repentance, violence, necessity, and nonretaliation from Chapter 2 are probably far more apt when considering the grave sins of schoolteacher than the ideas of memory, redemption, satisfaction, and resurrection that I explore here with respect to Sethe and Beloved.

In addition to the hope that Beloved's return will absolve Sethe of the need ever again to remember, Sethe also believes that the return of her child will afford her the chance to explain. Early in the novel, before Beloved's enfleshed return, Sethe laments that her daughter was only two years old when she died, too young to talk or understand much of anything, let alone the grim calculus of Sethe's dilemma (Morrison, *Beloved*, 5). When Denver wonders whether perhaps the ghost doesn't even want to understand, Sethe considers this but insists that she could make her reasoning clear to her dead daughter if only the child would return (5). This is in utter contrast to her relationship with the other families on Bluestone Road, to whom she feels no obligation whatsoever to justify herself or explain her actions. Even though immediately after the murder Baby Suggs (Sethe's mother-in-law) will neither endorse nor renounce "Sethe's rough choice," the rest of the community is decidedly less ambivalent (212). At Beloved's funeral they refuse to eat Sethe's food or enter her house; they just share their cold condolences in Sethe's yard and eat the food they have brought along themselves. Sethe in return refuses to touch their food and forbids Denver from doing so too. The Bluestone Road community ostracizes Sethe for years because you "can't just up and kill your children" (301). But for Sethe this animosity is mutual; she has no interest in either their approval or their condemnations and feels no urge to explain. Even when Paul D leaves 124 after learning of Sethe's past, his criticisms of Sethe do not cause her moral confidence to waver in the least. Her children, she states firmly, were neither captured by schoolteacher nor returned to Sweet Home. The clear and obvious evil of enslavement admits no argument. "It ain't my job to know what's worse," Sethe contends, but to know "what is and to keep them away from what I know is terrible" (194). This Sethe did, using the only means available to her, and she has no patience for others' questions or criticisms.

We might read here the impossibility of justification I described in Chapter 2, even perhaps a case of divine violence that upends and undermines the

possibility of any ethical deliberation since it exposes the absolutely and violently immoral frame within which Sethe's rough choice has to be made. To
suggest that any choice might be justified or even justifiable would be to
honor the system of hatred and violence that has consigned her to that choice.
But I don't want to reduce Sethe's act to an abstraction. Once her brain clicks
in to those specially meant-for places and she comes at last to believe in
ghosts, Sethe triumphantly announces that she doesn't have to explain anything to her daughter, since Beloved already "understands it all" (216). However she disdains her neighbors' judgment, that old urge to make it all clear to
her dead daughter never goes away, and Sethe finds that she cannot but explain herself to the young woman, even all the while insisting that her expli-
cations are unnecessary. The girl's return in the flesh, after Paul D has banished
her ghost, serves as proof for Sethe of a love, a loyalty, and an understanding
in her daughter that will demand no rationale or explanation from that child's
mother. In the same brief first-person passage cited above, Sethe says that she
will indeed explain it all to Beloved, even though there is no need, but only
just to tell her, "How if I hadn't killed her she would have died and that is
something I could not bear to happen to her" (236). Beloved's return obviates
the need for explanation; she wouldn't have returned if she didn't understand.
And yet, Sethe still feels a compulsion to confirm this understanding, to
prove that her rough choice was justified. This leads her to make those desperate and repeated pleas to Beloved for forgiveness that I noted above. Over
and again, Sethe begs Beloved to be forgiven, again offering her own life in
exchange for any of Beloved's suffering, were it possible (284). The compensatory schemes of punishment and penance I considered in the first half of this
book echo again here in Sethe's pleas for pardon. Just before Sethe's rescue,
Sethe is constantly trying to compensate "for the handsaw," while Beloved
never relents in "making her pay for it" (295). And the impulse belongs to
Sethe as much as to Beloved. Denver notices that even when Beloved is
dreaming or distracted, Sethe will sidle over and mutter "some justification"
in Beloved's ear, disrupting the peace for the sake of an impossible explanation. Sethe's requests for forgiveness become as relentless as Beloved's denials
of them, until it appears to Denver that Sethe doesn't "really want forgiveness
given; she want[s] it refused" (297). And Beloved is happy to oblige.

Sethe seeks desperately for her act to be justified and wants that justification to warrant forgiveness, but at the same time she also intuits that any justification will misapprehend the terrible stakes of her rough choice. It will
obscure the sinful, racist frame that consigned her to it. She therefore needs the

warrant for her forgiveness to be both articulated and repudiated. Her impulses work against one another. She wants Beloved's return not only to offer a better ending to her tragic story, but also to redeem the details of that story, to justify the events of it, through its ending. Her urge for a good ending leads her back to the impossible temptation of justification; it makes her believe that the past can be restored, and even if the facts of it cannot be changed, at least they can be made right instead of wrong. In an echo of a simili-forgiveness Jankélévitch criticizes (see Chapter 1), Sethe believes she will be forgiven if she can persuade herself and Beloved there is nothing to forgive. All will be well, to borrow Julian's phrase, if it wasn't wrong in the first place. But to believe she wasn't wrong amounts to a forgetting that Sethe can only reject, not least because it forgets the conditions that forced her choice, like the sycamores crowding out the boys. And so she asks for a forgiveness she cannot accept.

In his 2014 book *The Ethics of Everyday Life*, Michael Banner begins his own reflections on forgiveness by attending to the mourning practices of a small village of Orthodox Christians in Greece. The names of the dead there, he notes, are always appended with the adjective "forgiven," as in "Maria, the forgiven one."[29] Banner suggests that perhaps we would better think of forgiveness as an adverb rather than a noun—that forgiveness is primarily a practice of remembering "forgivingly." In fact, Banner asserts, "with certain warrant and some understatement," that Christianity itself "is a practice of remembering."[30] Implied also in all this—in a way I endorse—is the notion that forgiveness's remembering bears a strong likeness to mourning, that these related and difficult maneuvers of memory have much in common, since they each reckon with an irrevocable past and seek bravely to meet only that present and future world that a broken past has left us.

If we look again for just a moment at the novels that have occupied us so far, we find that each narrative revolves around its own respective failures of grief, its refusals of mourning. In *The Buried Giant*, the primary betrayal between Axl and Beatrice has been Axl's forbidding Beatrice to visit their dead son's grave. The literal practices of grief and mourning are what have been wanting in their love. Only when they embrace this grief do they come at last to a grim forgiveness, a forgiveness realized in yet another grief: the loss of Beatrice's life and the end of the companionship they hold so dear. In *Gilead*, John Ames begins a letter to his surviving son and discovers the history of his and his town's failures. He learns what he has lost and expands his private grief over the son he must leave behind into a general recognition of his complacency in the face of racism. In *LaRose*, the difficult atonement that the

Ironses offer the Raviches in accordance with traditional ways does seek to address loss honestly and directly, but this practice is set in a colonial framework whereby the Ojibwe past has been systematically suppressed and the bones of the family matriarch remain lost and unburied.

In *Beloved* also, mourning and grief are rejected in ways that have damaging consequences. At her daughter's funeral, of course, Sethe's neighbors refuse her food or to step within her home, and Sethe pridefully reciprocates their chilliness. A breach thus opens in the community that, though restored in the novel's final pages, haunts Sethe's lonely life before the final, climactic exorcism. But there are also hints that Paul D's attempt to quell some of 124's sadness gives rise to much of what follows. When Paul D first walks through the quavering pool of red light that haunts Sethe's entryway, he is doused so thoroughly in a wave of grief that he becomes overcome by the urge to cry (Morrison, *Beloved*, 11). Paul D doesn't know the story of Sethe's trauma. All he feels is a consuming sorrow that he turns out of the house by shouting and throwing furniture around. But Sethe and Denver never ask for the sadness to be put out. In fact, we rather have a sense of their collective peace with it. Sethe assures Paul D when he walks in that the ghost isn't angry, just sad. She becomes convinced of its anger only when it returns and demands sweetness. Another time, long before Paul D's arrival, Denver enters the house to see Sethe evidently at prayer and an empty white dress kneeling peaceably at her mother's side, with its sleeve encircling Sethe in a "tender embrace" (35). When Denver asks her mother what she was praying for as she knelt beside the empty dress, Sethe replies that she doesn't really pray anymore, she just talks about time. "Some things go," she tells Denver. "Pass on." Other things, she says, "just stay" (43). Sethe says she used to believe that the unpredictable presence and absence of the past were only her "rememory," but now she realizes that some part of her past still remains "real. It's never going away" (43). Reflecting upon this, Denver reasons that if the past still waits somewhere, then "nothing ever dies"; to which Sethe responds, looking directly in her daughter's eyes, "Nothing ever does" (44).

I don't want to constrain the poetry of this exchange by clumsily mapping it onto the abstract ideas I've explored in earlier chapters, but part of what I read Sethe as expressing here is the subtlety Jankélévitch was at pains to explain about the irrevocability of the past, even when its effects can be mitigated. What cannot, for Sethe, "pass on" is the death of her daughter, and this is what consumes her kneeling talk. It's important, also, that she terms this sort of encounter with her daughter a "rememory" rather than a memory or a remembrance. This ghost asserts its own pastness, its irrevocability; its persistence in the present exists as a fact that cannot be undone by anything that arises today or tomorrow. It is confined to the past, to rememory, even when that rememory rises up into the present again and again.[31] What it manifests in the present, in other words, is its own irreversibility. But when the past does appear to be reversed, when Beloved returns as a woman to 124, Sethe proclaims that she doesn't "have to rememory" anymore (226). Memory has broken into an embodied present, and Sethe is done with her praying talk. She no longer needs to reckon with her irrevocable past, because her present has already revoked it in flesh and in blood. One might even suggest that instead of the rememory Sethe no longer needs, she now re*members*, with all the corporal connotations of that word's etymology duly emphasized. That once irrevocable and immaterial ghost embraced Sethe tenderly in its sadness; this flesh-and-blood and resurrected specter now chokes Sethe in the clearing, consumes her peace, and wastes her almost entirely away (113).

Grief and mourning continue to be renounced at the end of the novel, too. Paul D especially repeats his exhortation that Sethe abandon them. This explains why the sad, strong, supportive Sethe, the Sethe who never before sought to avert her eyes from trouble, the Sethe we meet when we begin this novel, so poorly resembles the frail, helpless, disconsolate woman we know when the novel ends (275). For all the efforts of these characters to stamp down the past, even after all Sethe's ghosts have been exorcised, Sethe is no better; she is worse. Even Paul D must admit that something has gone from 124 Bluestone Road. It is not just Beloved or the mournful red light that are now missing. Though Paul D cannot quite conceive of what has departed from the home, he senses that he is being watched from outside by some glaring "thing that embraces while it accuses" (319). What Paul D aimed to exorcize at the beginning of this novel was not only a ghost, but a sadness. What I believe the novel reveals is that when Sethe's sorrowful rememory has been obscured by resurrection and banished by exorcism, it returns and rises into violence rather than ceding to the promised peace of a forgetful oblivion.

RESURRECTING MEMORIES

At the beginning of *Beloved*, Sethe's home is haunted by a poltergeist. When Paul D shouts its memory out of the house, 124 calms. But then they meet the strange woman on the stump. Before long it is hard for both readers and characters of the novel not to see this woman as Sethe's resurrected daughter, a corporeal form of the tragic past Paul D has chased away. But despite all the narrative momentum of the novel, there are clues she might not be a risen ghost. Sethe is among the last to be convinced. Stamp Paid, the man who saved Sethe on her arrival to Cincinnati, who brought the infant Beloved blackberries before her death, and who encourages Ella to respond to the crisis, asks Paul D who he thinks Beloved might be. Paul D replies that Beloved reminds him of something that he believes he ought to remember (276). Beloved resembles a memory he thinks he's meant to have. But Stamp Paid then recalls that a white man who had held a girl captive for years in a cabin nearby was found dead about the time of Beloved's appearance. The girl he'd imprisoned and tortured was never found. Stamp speculates that perhaps Beloved is this lost girl (277). Of course, this was Sethe's first intuition too, not just Stamp Paid's. But all these intuitions die away as Beloved's specter rises, as Sethe's memories come eventually to consume her.

But what if these original suspicions were correct? If Beloved is a real child rather than a resurrected specter, a child who—like Ella—has been sexually enslaved by a white man for years, if she is a woman who has escaped and ar-rived at 124 seeking rescue and human relationship, then the reference the text makes to Calvary in the final moments of Beloved's story will come into har-rowing relief. If Beloved is a running woman rather than a risen apparition, we might be forced to arrive at some unsettling conclusions. The central horrors of this novel are Sethe's handsaw and Beloved's scar, the sacrifice of a beloved child in order to spare that child from slavery. But if Beloved is not Sethe's long-dead daughter but a traumatized woman seeking safety, then the sacrifice of the beloved child is unwittingly repeated in the final moments of this novel. As Elizabeth House notes in a critical essay that first articulated this reading, "emotional ghosts of hurt, love, guilt, and remembrance haunt those whose links to family members have been shattered" just as palpably as do polter-geists. Griefs and traumas "ranging from the atrocities of slavery to less hid-eous pains, must be remembered."[32] On this realist reading, the reference to crucifixion in the Friday timing of the climactic exorcism and the Christian imagery of a baptismal wash attending that exorcism both become clear and troubling. The memory of Beloved has not been suppressed into safety; it has instead become the instrument of a new sacrifice. Beloved has not been cast out into nothingness; she has been erased, obscured, discarded, and displaced by a memory. Ella—herself a victim of a similar history—cannot recognize the woman who arrives as a person in need. All she sees is a supernaturally personified past that must be "stamped down" and rejected. Sethe—despite her initial recognition—cannot hold on to her hunch about a newly escaped slave in desperate need. Instead, she projects her own traumatic memories upon the body of that need. Denver cannot see Beloved for who she truly is; she just wants to welcome home the banished ghostly companion who has been her only friend since childhood. Stamp Paid—even though his first suspicions are correct—can't see her, and Paul D can't see her either. The memory of that other child is so present that it shifts their vision, makes them see the past in the present. Like Sethe mistaking Bodkin for schoolteacher, they all see Beloved through a scar. When the women of Bluestone Road rise to confront Beloved, they call her a devil-child and suspect demonic trickery because they are surprised by how unafraid they are as she appears in their collective vision (308). Despite their worst imaginings and fearful suspicions, she is beautiful. She appears before them, "thunderblack and glistening" and her belly taught and round as if pregnant. They corporately and mentally exclaim: "Jesus" (308). But in the fit of their vision, Beloved's beauty appears demonic to them, poised to threaten instead of pregnant with possibility, and this beautiful woman disappears without a trace into all that uprising.

Beloved is an indisputably important novel, and a vast critical literature has accrued around it during the three-and-a-half decades since its publication, much of it explicitly concerned with how theology might understand the righting of past wrongs. Some of these readings are compelling and powerful, but in many cases they discern a redemption in the novel's conclusion that may not be quite warranted if we accept House's reading. Christina Bieber Lake, for example, reads Beloved as a demonic character, while recognizing an opportunity for exorcism through communal narration in the novel's conclusion.[33] John J. Allen, in a recent article, makes a similar argument, stating that the "act of communal narration becomes a means for transcending the past in order to reclaim power for the future."[34] Joshua Pederson, meanwhile, follows Delores Williams's womanist critique of atonement theology to discern in *Beloved* a depiction of the dangers of substitution and surrogacy, while also suggesting an escape from it in Paul D's final affirmation to Sethe, "You your own best thing" (322).[35] And L. Gregory Jones offers a brief reading of *Beloved* in his book *Embodying Forgiveness* that sees the novel as raising the possibility of redemption and new life even in the most horrifying circumstances. Because "human beings are called to become holy by embodying . . . forgiveness through specific habits and practices that seek to remember the past truthfully, to repair the brokenness, to heal divisions, and to reconcile and renew relationships," he argues, "forgiveness ought not simply or even primarily be focused on the absolution of guilt." Instead, he says, "it ought to be focused on the reconciliation of brokenness, the restoration of communion."[36] *Beloved* is introduced as an example of this possibility even in the most harrowing of circumstances, especially insofar as community is rebuilt in the novel's climactic scene. As I have argued in my previous chapters, I take forgiveness to be a posture of nonretaliation rather than of either an absolution of guilt or a restoration of relationship. Indeed, I think there are dangers in confusing these things under a single notion of forgiveness. And I also worry that there may be especially insidious dangers when redemption and new life are read as depending upon these overlapping accomplishments, because the urge to live anew might cause us to identify redemption where it does not yet exist, or not in the forms we hope to see.

Something more complex is going on in *Beloved* than can be accommodated by these theological readings or by the claims of Jeffrey Blustein, Paul Ricoeur, and Miroslav Volf, careful and thoughtful though this work may be. At first glance we might believe all their fears clearly confirmed: witness here memory rearing up so vividly that the present can only helplessly replicate its forms, see the damage that remembering too much can do. And though their worries are indeed justified, and this is partly what I'm suggesting has happened in *Beloved*, we must read a bit deeper also—because the Bluestone Road community has made their tragic mistake precisely in an attempt to do what Blustein, Ricoeur, and Volf have suggested. When they arrive at 124, they are trying to push Beloved back, to purify the past in their baptismal wash. Their exorcism is an attempt to forget, to erase or obscure an embodied remembrance. The women are trying to expunge harmful memories, to feed the past sweets, or at least to suppress it with white beans and rabbit meat and raisin loaves left at the edge of the yard for their starving neighbors. They seek even to overwhelm that past with their singing and marching this Friday. The problem, though, is that acts of memory and forgetting are never so simple, since each (Ricoeur is right to note) is always already bound up in the present. Our memories are not discrete, either from one another or from our immediate experience. They do not sit singly in our minds or in our histories, untouched by and untethered to the memories that surround them. Rather, they fold into and frame one another. Put simply, where we have been is the only intelligible frame we have for recognizing where we find ourselves now and where we might next be going. Memories, whether harmful or happy, frame our understanding of the world we encounter. Blustein, Ricoeur, and Volf are right—this does present a challenge to us when we directly engage the memory of past wrongs. But it's not a problem we can escape through either sweetness or suppression. Since the past cannot but frame both our present and our future, when we ignore that past we also risk repeating it, sacrificially. These abused and wounded people cannot recognize an abused and wounded woman in need of aid. Instead, they see a ghost, they enflesh a memory. When we erase or obscure what we have done or what has been done to us, we also risk hiding from ourselves what we are presently doing, and to whom. We may think we are exorcising a ghost when in fact we are banishing a young woman into the river alone, erasing a suffering we are able and obliged to see. We might believe we are witnessing resurrection when in fact we are replicating sacrifice.

I have more to say about death and resurrection, and about Jesus's death and resurrection in particular, momentarily. For now, however, I address directly the particular problem of memory *Beloved* has posed in the wake of Blustein, Ricoeur, and Volf. If we cannot safely and fully forget, but remembering frustrates healing or reconciliation, then what way forward remains? I suggest that, despite the dangers, the only option we have is to remember. Because what is wrong in *Beloved* is not really a failure of forgetting; it's a failure of remembering. To remember the past, I suggest, is to regard it as *past*. This is different from forgetting it (either through erasure or selection), which is not to regard it at all. Nor is it to suggest that the present does not remain haunted by the past, as 124 quite obviously is when this novel opens. The carceral state and the legacy of Jim Crow offer evidence enough that chattel slavery continues to haunt the United States today. To remember rightly, then, would neither be to suppress what we would rather forget nor to ignore how our world remains shaped by our traumas. Rather, it would be entirely to embrace that past as both memory and rememory, as both irrevocable and retrievable. It would be to recognize the past as unavoidably relevant in our present, but as a ghost or a specter rather than a revenant. It would be to regard past wrongs as irreparable and unavailable for alteration, whether by sacrifices, exorcisms, rituals, or retaliation, but it would be nonetheless to insist upon regarding them. In other words, to remember rightly would be neither to erase nor to elide, neither to suppress nor to stamp down. It would be to grieve.

ATTENDING AN EMPTY TOMB

I've suggested so far that Sethe's willingness to live with loss is what Paul D exorcizes from 124 upon his arrival, and that a fantasy of restoration is what alters the sight of all these characters so that they recognize a dead child raised again rather than a living woman frightfully drawn to death. People who "die bad don't stay in the ground," they reason, even "Jesus Christ Himself didn't," so they interpret the appearance of this woman out of the water as a form of resurrection rather than as an opportunity for rescue (Morrison, *Beloved*, 221). But this resurrection goes bad, and so they must exorcise this ghost once again, even if she is not a ghost at all. And thus a new victim is made in the woman's disappearance.

The associative links made between *Beloved*'s climactic passage and Good Friday are, I think, terribly important and speak difficult truths to us about the way Christians have typically regarded the death and triumphant resurrection of Jesus Christ. My reading of *Beloved* raises the question of whether what Christians take to be a resurrection is instead a repetitive tendency toward sacrifice. The Christian tradition has been only too willing throughout its long history to disappear all sorts of others for the sake of its heavily policed vision of Christ. Like Ella or Stamp Paid or Sethe, we have often been so desperate to see the Jesus who haunts us, the Christ we think we must remember, that we have looked past the real need standing vulnerable and beautiful before us in our midst. We have exorcised human persons in order to make our remembrances more real, and all in an attempt to overcome the pain of our broken past.

In fact, there is good evidence from within the Christian theological tradition that the first concern of any theology of resurrection should not be to proclaim a triumph or a miraculous resolution of past wrongs, but instead to invite disciples into a rigorous relationship with loss, to insist upon their attendance at a persistently empty tomb. It has become, Donald MacKinnon writes, "almost a convention of Christian practice to read [the Gospels] as if they were orientated towards a happy ending, as if the resurrection-faith which gave them birth was powerful to obliterate memory of the somber events which they describe."[37] In fact, the proclamation of resurrection should occasion more complicated, less straightforwardly happy conclusions. As MacKinnon continues, whatever the resurrection may be, we must affirm that "it is not a descent from the cross postponed for thirty-six hours. It is not the sudden dramatic happy ending which the producer of a Hollywood spectacular might have conceived."[38] This is not primarily or not only because the apparition stories in the Gospels remain inconsistent and even dreamlike, with Christ disappearing from sight, appearing through locked doors, manifesting to some and not to others in the same crowd. The fact that Jesus's "commerce with [his disciples] is elusive and restricted" does not necessarily undermine the credibility of these apparitions so much as guard his witnesses "against the mistake of supposing that they [have been] witnesses of a reversal, and not of a vindication, of those things which had happened."[39] The danger for those disciples, and for us as disciples, is to believe that the trauma of Good Friday is simply undone by resurrection. The resurrection decidedly does not reverse the death, MacKinnon writes; it vindicates it. The Christian expectation of a reversal merely mimics the mocking cries of the crowds at Golgotha: "Come down from the cross and we will believe."[40] Thus, for MacKinnon, it is "sheer nonsense to speak of the Christian religion as offering a solution to the problem of evil."[41] To understand resurrection as resolution, replacement, reversal, or restoration would be "totally to misunderstand both the difficulty and the consolation of its treatment."[42]

What, then, is the consolation that resurrection promises?—especially if, as MacKinnon insists, the faithful disciple cannot "avert his attention from the element of sheer waste, the reality of Christ's failure."[43] Sheer waste and the reality of failure here are the point, not the platitude familiar to conventional devotion to the cross. Rowan Williams suggests that what matters most is the community of people who respond to resurrection. The resurrection apparitions, he writes, are not "simple manifestations of an apotheosized Jesus." These apparitions are grounded not in the reliability or credibility of any individual report but in the "continuing existence of the community" that is caught up in this "concrete, shared human history of hope, betrayal, violence and guilt" and is redeemed in that history, too.[44] What is important about the New Testament accounts of Jesus's resurrection appearances has as much to do with the future toward which this fraught and fractured community of discipleship has been called as it does with the past from which they are seeking to recover. "To see the risen Jesus," Williams says, "is to see one's own past and one's own vocation, to 'see' the call towards a new humanity."[45] Into the place of Christ's sheer waste and failure comes the community that arises after him and in which his death is vindicated. Williams is clear to distance his own argument from a sort of Bultmannian demythologization of resurrection, which would say: because Christ has not *literally* risen, because his resurrected body is *only* a myth, we should interpret the community of his followers therefore as his risen body. Williams acknowledges some temptation to assent to this sort of intellectualization, but he resists what he regards as too simple a rationalization by marking as crucial the "confusing jumble of incompatible stories" between the empty tomb and the established community.[46] In other words, this demythologization would amount to its own kind of happy ending; it would provide a firm and secure meaning we might posit to resolve our guilt, a consolation we might advance to stanch our grief. When we turn away from the tomb and the confusion of its aftermath and turn too quickly toward the established community as the replacement for what we have lost, we risk rushing headlong into a different version of the same restorative triumphalism MacKinnon has criticized. All we can say for certain of this period of grief, loss, and confusion in the wake of Jesus's death is that its resurrection appearances "were fundamentally experiences of restoring grace."[47] That is, those who had betrayed Jesus became convinced, despite their grief, loss, guilt, and confusion, that they remained beloved of God in the sign of these apparitions. In other words, faced only with the fact of their own sin and betrayal, this new community found a way to arise into the experience of being forgiven, even if that arising was to remain crucially mired in defeat and bewilderment. There simply is, for Williams, no "hope of understanding resurrection outside the process of renewing humanity in forgiveness."[48] There is no relationship to resurrection that is not also a relationship to failure and to loss. So this new humanity is one always implicated in the work of forgiveness. No simple transaction or balancing of ethical accounts, for Williams "forgiven-ness is precisely the deep and abiding sense of what relation—with God or with other human beings—can and should be."[49] Not unlike Judith Butler's conception of nonviolence explored in Chapter 2 of this book, it is the posture of a community committed to a particularly interdependent and mutually vulnerable sort of relation, one that positions itself toward a new humanity. As Butler states, this community would set itself toward an "impossible world," one beyond the "horizon of our present thinking" that could avoid the simple binaries of total war or perfect peace while bravely facing the "open-ended struggle required to preserve our bonds against all that in the world which bears the potential to tear them apart."[50] This community of forgiven-ness, as Williams might describe it, would concern itself with "the affirmation of this life, bound up with yours, and with the realm of the living: an affirmation caught up with a potential for destruction and its countervailing force."[51] Forgiveness among the community of Christ's followers, past or present, should therefore according to Williams remain "a stimulus, an irritant," a sign of the community we await and are called to become, and an echo of that original grief out of which the conviction of forgiveness first arose.[52] This makes our commitment to the community one that is fundamentally forward facing while still framed by the past. Once we "grasp that forgiveness occurs not by a word of acquittal but by a transformation of the world of persons, we are not likely to regard it as something which merely refers backwards."[53]

And indeed, those theologians—especially of the womanist tradition—who have most closely and persuasively read *Beloved* have wrestled with the theological complexity of the novel in a way that speaks directly to what is, I think, at stake in any useful Christian ideas about resurrection. In their respective engagements with *Beloved*, both Emilie Townes and M. Shawn Copeland focus on Baby Suggs's sermons to her community. Before the death of Sethe's daughter, before Baby goes to bed to contemplate color and begs everyone's pardon, she routinely retreats with her community into a clearing and there calls them with eloquent and unapologetic tenderness to love themselves in whole and in part, as individual bodies and as one corporate body too. She exhorts them in rapt poetic language to be loved, to be beloved (Morrison, *Beloved*, 122ff.). Following Baby Suggs's exhortation, Copeland argues that the possibilities for "resurrection of soul—individual or personal, communal or collective—lie in self-knowledge, self-affirmation, and love—daring to love self, to love others selflessly. For, the most radical, the most sacred act of subjectivity—divine or human—is enfleshing love."[54] Townes invokes Baby Suggs's sermons in a similar spirit in her essay "To Be Called Beloved."[55] But in each author's work, this enfleshing love is fraught and intersubjective. It is not just about individual or simple restoration but rather calls us to wrestle with the real challenges of the past and of otherness in community. To be restored to wholeness, Townes writes, is to "remember our fleshiness"; it is to lose too simple a sense of one's self; it is "to recognize that dualistic oppositions such as self-other, egoism-altruism, theory-practice, individual-community, and mind-body are interactive and interdependent."[56] As such, even Baby Suggs's altogether true sermons can offer no simply redemptive solution to pain. As Copeland observes in a complication of Townes's reading, we cannot recall Baby Suggs's sermons without also remembering that what happened to her and her family causes her to collapse into "marrow weariness" and to retire to a bed from which she never again arises (Morrison, *Beloved*, 180).[57] Any theology of resurrection must reckon with this failure to rise, however it wants to read the ghost or body of Beloved. But Baby Suggs's marrow weary collapse need not imply that she has entirely abandoned her teachings on love, as has been suggested.[58] It does perhaps suggest, however, as we have seen Vladimir Jankélévitch state earlier in this book, that love may be as strong as death but no stronger. In any case, however, what is clear from *Beloved* and from Copeland's and Townes's readings is that

"Morrison offers us no comfortable conclusion, no pious affirmation of faith, no simplistic dismissal of grotesque suffering."⁵⁹ The Christian theology of resurrection offers no easy salve to suffering, no simple explanation for what happened to Jesus, and no reductive personal prospect for individual restoration, redemption, or reclamation. Resurrection cannot solely be about what happened to Jesus; it must also be about what "happened to the disciples," what has happened to us, and how we might live both their experience and ours into a shared and dangerous future.⁶⁰ Jesus's appearances to his friends and companions after his death are "transformative encounters with the risen Lord" that "re-form the disciples' grasp of just who Jesus is" and also their sense of whom they ought to become.⁶¹

A forgiveness formed by this relationship to resurrection, then, will not be just about reckoning past wrong, but also about living into better forms of the future. It is about becoming the new community into which we have been called. It is about practicing resurrection. Thus, as Timothy Jackson argues, the Christian commitment to resurrection can reveal that "death cannot rob charity of its meaningfulness, come what may."⁶² I have more to say about making loss meaningful a bit later in this chapter, but here I emphasize Jackson's reluctance to attach any heavenly happy endings to the resurrection story, Volf's eschatological retaliations and aspirations notwithstanding. If it is worthwhile to live into this new model of community, then this must be for its own sake, not in exchange for some heavenly reward. Insofar as we read resurrection as removing "the sting of Jesus's unexpected and 'shameful' death, it tempts us today to ignore or belittle the cross."⁶³ And indeed, Jackson sees this temptation toward ignoring or belittling the losses and traumas of our past as running through even the earliest written accounts of Jesus's resurrection. The shorter and most likely earliest ending of the first Christian Gospel, the only Gospel that deliberately names its own story as good news, ends abruptly with an empty tomb and the women who came to care for Jesus's body fleeing in fear (Mark 16:5–8). So, Jackson asks, shall we end with this note of emptiness and terror, or shall we also "include the highly didactic and likely redactional 16:9–20," which gives a happier ending?⁶⁴ According to Jackson, there may be some moral consequences in tacking on the consolations of those last twelve verses. An "insistence on immortality as the necessary consequence of or rationale for forgiveness quickly dilutes *agape* by entangling it in economies of exchange."⁶⁵ Resurrection, says Jackson, is not the immortal reward for the costly work of forgiveness. If the "cross cannot be accepted on its own terms," then we will have diminished the significance not of its triumph, but of its devastation. As Emilie Townes has written, "we must live our lives not always comforted by the holy, but haunted by God's call to us to live a prophetic and spirit-filled life."[66] Or, as Shelly Rambo elaborates, when we read the resurrection story as one in which "life emerges victoriously out of death" with a linear and unproblematic simplicity, we might "gloss over the realities of pain and loss, glorify suffering, and justify violence."[67] Attending to the empty tomb demands something more than mere triumphalism. It means regarding that tomb as inescapably empty, being haunted by the absence we find there, refusing the rushing urge to compensate for its painful lack, and attending to grief, loss, and confusion in the hope of discerning a fleeting apparition of love.

This is all fair enough with respect to Jesus, but it either fails to describe what goes wrong with the community at Bluestone Road or it hides what has historically gone wrong with the Christian community. The Jesuit sociologist and occasional theologian Michel de Certeau explores the implications of resurrection and gives a clue to their dangers in noting a particular feature of the tomb's emptiness: that it summons forth both institutional witness and writing. Christianity for Certeau sets itself on an irrefutable absence—the missing body of Jesus Christ, the empty tomb that is at once both the scandal and the condition for its own possibility. The "initial privation of body" opens space for the establishment of "institutions and discourses that are the effects of and substitutes for that absence: multiple ecclesial bodies, doctrinal bodies, and so on."[68] The theologian's question "How can a body be made from the word?" raises for Certeau the "haunting question of an impossible mourning: 'Where art thou?'"[69] Indeed, Certeau observes, this deep mourning is the basic foundation of and beginning for any experience of or narrative for resurrection. Already at the "evangelical beginnings," Mary Magdalene stands before the empty tomb and laments, "I do not know where they have put him" (John 20:13). Or, as the angel says to Mary in the Gospel of Matthew, "He is not here; he is risen" (Matt 28:6). Christ's absence and his resurrection are manifestations of the same event. There is a twofold significance to Certeau's argument here. First, the loss of the body gives rise to substitutes for what is missing. Institutions and practices and testaments arise in the absence of what has gone. Jesus Christ had to "be present so that his disappearance might become the sign of a different future."[70] But the danger for Certeau would be to imagine these future substitutes too simply as replacements for what has been lost. What is necessary is the mystics' persistent question, a question that presumes enduring absence, longing, and loss: Where art thou?

This is especially important with respect to those early evangelical beginnings and the written Gospel accounts, to the grief-stricken middle between the empty tomb and the church that Rowan Williams has noted, and to the choice Timothy Jackson has commended between the shorter and longer endings of the Gospel of Mark. For Certeau, all Christian language "begins with the disappearance of its 'author.'"[71] In other words, Jesus's erasure makes witness to him possible. The space of the empty tomb is the space into which we move when we give account of Christ. Jesus "*effaces himself* to give faithful witness to the Father who authorizes him, and to 'give rise' to different but faithful communities, which he makes possible"; therefore, the "empty tomb is the condition of possibility for spiritual knowledge."[72] This means, then, that Christian discipleship is a continuing practice of loss, an incessant insistence on what is and remains forever missing, a relentless mystical inquiry: Where art thou? Christian discipleship means holding both halves of the angel's good news at the tomb tethered inseparably together: it means confessing "he is not here," even in the same breath that we proclaim "he is risen." Every Christian, therefore, every Christian "community, and Christianity as a whole is called on to be the *sign of that which is lacking*." This lack, Certeau insists, is not some "wide region to conquer or to be filled in." On the contrary, this lack is the "*limit* by means of which every witness publicly confesses his relation" to a Christ whose absence clears space and makes "room for others." Because Christ is no longer here, we can recognize the movements of God in the "unforeseeable and unknown spaces which God opens elsewhere and in other ways."[73] I want to call attention to Certeau's insistence that the lack is not some region to conquer or to be filled in, especially in light of my discussion of Milbank's ontology of atonement in Chapter 3. The Christian has "access to Jesus only through texts which, in talking of him, narrate what he awakened and hence describe only their own status as writings," and this mediated textual access opens new possibilities, gives way to the new humanity for which Williams and Jackson hope.[74] There is an optimism to Certeau's insistence on loss here, but the loss and its endurance remain both crucial and indisputable. The call to follow Jesus "comes from a voice which has been effaced, forever irrecuperable, vanished into the changes which echo it back, drowned in the throng of its respondents," even if this throng of respondents are all children of God who, because of Christ's forgiving absence, can assume new forms and enter new spaces.[75] Christianity thus moves through history in novel ways, among new peoples, across fixed boundaries, precisely because it remains unbound to an immovable original. The emptiness of the tomb makes room for others and beckons writing. In the Gospels, an "initial non-site (the empty tomb) in a sense gives rise to the function of the text."[76] Were the historical Jesus still walking among us, giving an account of himself, there would be little need for these accounts to arise into the absence his departure has left behind. Because the tomb is empty, space is made for a witness to be given and for writings to be written.

What Certeau suggests but understates here, though, are the dangers of this movement, dangers that *Beloved* exposes.[77] The empty tomb may indeed occasion this optimistic movement and give rise to the new communities and futures for which Williams and Jackson hope. But as soon as we abandon that place of grief, loss, and confusion, as soon as we lose the mystics' relentless question, that unending "Where art thou?," as soon as we convince ourselves that Christ has been finally and forever found, we cease the progressive movement away from a lost origin and stop turning in grief toward new life. That is, finding Jesus should mean confirming his loss yet again and thus being called always toward relentless and restless searching. He is *not* here. He is risen. What's needed is the insistence upon a perpetually unsatisfied desire, a deep longing (like Julian's) that can turn away from the temptation of replete satisfaction, sufficient compensation, or even simple replacement. Again, this shows the practical and political dangers of a theology (like Milbank's) that recognizes loss as ultimately recovered in the plentitude of God's being, as well as the promise of a theology (like von Speyr's) that discerns diremption and loss as basic to the Trinitarian life. What's needed for the community to move from grief and confusion to resurrection, paradoxically, is the refusal to recover from loss, an insistent commitment to mourning. As soon as we become convinced that we have recovered from our loss or that the one we have lost has triumphantly returned, as soon as we believe that the missing body has been replaced and revivified, we stop searching, stop risking, stop grieving, and we stifle the movement toward new life. As Certeau concedes, "there is no life without new risks in our actual situation."[78] The resurrection community, ironically, is the one that incessantly mourns what it has lost and what it cannot possibly recover.

This is all to say that I read Beloved as an important but decidedly and necessarily ambiguous Christ figure in Toni Morrison's novel. The Good Friday associations of her eventual disappearance expose the dangers I have just teased out as operative within the work of Certeau, Williams, and Jackson. It is because the adult Beloved is recognized as the replacement for or restoration of a long-dead child that the Bluestone Road community becomes unable to recognize her for who she truly is, unable to see this vulnerable woman in her own singularity and thus respond to her with the care she deserves. As I've suggested, this is a persistent problem in Christian history and in Christology. Our fierce allegiance to the Christ we believe we have seen through our scars, to the Christ we believe we have found and whom we therefore refuse to lose yet again, not only prevents us from expanding our communities, solidarities, and visions, but it also facilitates ignorance, exclusion, and violence against those who do not fit the limits of our witness. And the colonialist white supremacy that established both the transatlantic slave trade and the United States on the violence of that trade, the racism that indeed grounds and forces Sethe's rough choice, is a direct outgrowth of this exclusionary violence.[79] Beloved is, I think, a Christ figure who can invite Christians into a more honest and conflicted relationship with Christendom. When we attend to her disappearance, as a child, as a ghost, or as an adult, we might be encouraged to turn back toward the grief, loss, and confusion our history demands.

But in saying all this, I also fall into exactly the trap I have been at so many pains to avoid. Having called Beloved a Christ figure, I must also immediately and insistently reject this reading. If I do believe that I ought to read Beloved as a figure for Christ, this also means that I must let go of that reading as soon as I offer it, or else risk erasing and effacing Beloved once again with my own vision of whom I wish and insist that she might be. She functions as a Christ figure only insofar as I insist that she is *not* Christ, but Beloved. He is not here. He is risen. I must admit the tomb remains empty and attend directly to Beloved and to her singular and irreplaceable loss. Resurrection requires an insistence on loss, a refusal to turn away from the perpetual emptiness of the tomb and from the intractable mourning that emptiness occasions.

WRITING RESURRECTION

Williams, Jackson, and Certeau all see testimony, narrative, and writing arising in the emptiness Jesus leaves behind in his tomb. Again, with the possible exception of Jackson, this reference to writing is mostly auspicious, and we can see the valorization of writing or narrative interpretation in other approaches to forgiveness as well. As noted earlier in this book, forgiveness has been a topic of interest to thinkers in the continental tradition for some time, and repeatedly for Julia Kristeva. Kristeva approaches the problem of forgiveness from a psychoanalytic frame and sees in it a therapeutic possibility. For Kristeva, forgiveness is about taking what is unspeakable in the unconscious and putting it into words, words that are summoned by the analytic relationship. Because there is another who intends to listen, I articulate my broken past for that person, and that articulation makes it psychically manageable. Along with so many others cited so far, Kristeva doesn't believe that forgiveness can undo or "cleanse actions"; rather, it introduces the one who perpetrated those actions to "an other who does not judge but hears [one's] truth in the availability of love, and for that very reason allows [one] to be reborn."[80] The presence of that attending and loving other is crucial, since the relationship is what occasions the articulation. But the act of articulation and expression implies a will to make meaning. As Kristeva continues, forgiveness "at the outset constitutes a will, postulate, or scheme: *meaning exists.*"[81] But the meaning is a narrative or therapeutic construction; it arises only because suffering has confounded meaningfulness. Much like the empty tomb, the persistent lack of meaning is what calls forth the work of meaning-making. And to be clear, meaning here is a form of doing, of making. It is an act of construction that mimics the movements of literature. Forgiveness, for Kristeva, is "an acting out, a doing, a *poeisis,*" but it makes that meaning in a space that has been utterly emptied of significance through suffering. As such, forgiveness is conditioned by—it bears "as a lining"—the "erosion of meaning, melancholia, and abjection." By including erosion, melancholia, and abjection, Kristeva says, forgiveness "displaces them; by absorbing them it transforms and binds them."[82] Forgiveness is therefore for Kristeva always involved in transforming and translating abjection into meaningfulness, suffering into significance, and thus resembles a writing that "causes the *affect* to slip into the *effect.* . . . It conveys affects and does not repress them."[83] It is more like rememory than remembrance; it is living meaningfully alongside sorrow instead of requesting and refusing that the past be justified by the present. A felt brokenness is put into words and made meaningful. Thus, for Kristeva, forgiveness is simply interpretation. And therapeutic interpretation is also "a pardon: a rebirth of the psychical apparatus."[84] It is the psyche learning to find meaningfulness again, "with and beyond the hatred that bears desire, which religion is and is not aware of and from which it defends itself."[85] Here hatred is set at odds with interpretation, but hatred is also essential to the abjection that lines pardon and so it spurs interpretation too. Pardon's interpretive ambition is simply "to make psychical rebirth possible" from within the abject hatred and emptiness of injury.[86] As my last chapter revealed, I believe there is room for rancor and bitterness, though perhaps not for hatred, in religion's forgiveness, and I don't find Kristeva entirely persuasive here on religion's ambivalence toward hateful desire.[87] Nonetheless, a "postmoral" and Freudian framing of forgiveness here seems to apply Certeau's empty tomb to the psyche. The loss of meaning opens space for the making of it. All that is required is a loving attendant to midwife that meaning into speaking.

Following Arendt, Kristeva therefore notes "the meaning of the Greek words for 'forgiveness' in St. Luke: *aphiemai, metanoien,* and *hamartanein,* to dismiss, release, change one's mind, return, retrace one's steps, lapse."[88] As with so many of the thinkers I have discussed, forgiveness in this case is thus not about undoing, resolving, replacing, or compensating for the past. The making of meaning is about summoning the new, a psychic rebirth, and giving rise to "a new, subjective, and intersubjective configuration" through "grace and forgiveness."[89] Thus for Kristeva forgiveness does bear significant therapeutic value: "To give meaning to suffering and begin the associative speech that will transform malady and death into a narrative of life, a new life: this is how the value of analytical interpretation as pardon can be defined. If you prefer, you can call this experience a healing. An endless one."[90]

It's important not to romanticize Kristeva's therapeutic forgiveness here. If forgiveness on this account is a healing, it is one that neither finally resolves nor undoes suffering. This is the significance, I think, of its endlessness. As she has suggested, each act of meaningful narrative construction presumes a space of utter emptiness, lined by abjection, a meaninglessness out of which meaning might arise; and this abjective frame cannot be entirely explained away by our interpretation since it is the condition for any meaningful explanation that is given. And so the experience of forgiveness may be healing, but it never reaches its culmination or end.

As I have said, what here resembles the mapping of Certeau's empty tomb onto the individual psyche (or perhaps, inversely, Certeau's psychoanalytic framing of the empty tomb) is useful and gives an interesting account of how and why forgiveness might relate to writing: forgiveness is a making, a doing, a *poeisis* of meaning. Or I might better say meaningfulness rather than meaning, because I want to avoid any sense that our accounts will make final and fully redeeming sense of our losses and our wounds. What our forgiveness should aspire toward is a meaning that is both habitable and yet includes all that we still grieve, a meaning we can live with for now but that will need reworking and rewording in the future. I note, too, how the Butlerian confessional frame I reviewed in Chapter 2 echoes here in Kristeva, as meaningfulness is shown to arise intersubjectively and also requires repeated revisitation and revision in relationship. But I also believe this reading needs to be supplemented by others in order adequately to frame the challenge *Beloved* sets before us, because the form of healing at which Kristeva arrives seems so singularly impossible for Sethe or Paul D or Beloved, and the abjection in which they are mired seems so resistant to redemption by meaning.

Consider Morrison's own account of her inspiration and motivation in writing *Beloved*. She notes that the extant slave narratives in our literary history explicitly silence, mute, or hide the traumatic horrors of enslavement. The primary objective of their writing was not honest expression but abolition, the persuasion of white readers rather than the prophecy of Black witness, and so writers kept care not to shock the sensibilities of their white audiences too much. This is the danger of Kristeva's intersubjective frame: the only account one can give is the one that will be received. In order "to make [their suffering] palatable to those who were in a position to alleviate it," Morrison observes, the authors of these early narratives of enslavement "were silent about many things, and they 'forgot' many other things."[91] Kristeva might contend therefore that no forgiveness, no intersubjective meaning-making, remains possible. But this is exactly what Morrison regards as her task in writing a novel such as *Beloved*. In seeking fictionally to "find and expose a truth about the interior life of people who didn't write it," Morrison fills in the archival blanks and parts the historical veil by endeavoring a literary "recollection that moves from the image to the text. Not from the text to the image."[92] Without the words of the witnesses, Morrison must imagine, she must put text to images and generate faithful fiction. This fiction is faithful in the sense that its imagination is honest; it bears fidelity to what is missing and seeks to speak for it. This means speaking what cannot be said and writing what cannot be known—a fictional narration that seeks at once to restore what has been lost while also enacting the impossibility of its restoration.[93] For Morrison writing is not just "thinking and discovery and selection and order and meaning"; it is also "awe and reverence and mystery and magic."[94] Any account of the past that will be fully faithful, any writing that aims more honestly to remember the past, must reckon with what is absent and with what has been excised. *Beloved* is indisputably a book about forgiveness, but the novel is not primarily about a therapeutic technique or a particular approach to healing. Rather, in signaling what cannot be said precisely through saying it, in reminding its reader of what is missing through the movement of its imagination, it expands a technique for healing into an act of public, political, and religious significance.

To explain how this might be, I need to return again to Jacques Derrida and to perhaps his least discussed and most difficult consideration of forgiveness, the essay "Literature in Secret."[95] In this essay, Derrida considers both the Noahic and the Abrahamic covenants of the Hebrew Bible, as well as Kierkegaard's analysis of Abraham and also Franz Kafka's posthumously published letter to his father, in order to posit the notion of the secret as essential to what we regard as literature. The essay's primary aim is to describe the nature of the literary, but the reader discovers that for Derrida literature cannot be understood without also understanding the impossibility and secrecy of forgiveness. As Charles Barbour puts it, what Derrida wants "to propose is that both the experience of forgiveness and the experience of literature revolve around something like a secret."[96]

For Derrida, what makes a piece of writing literary is that its meaning is not entirely available, that it is in some way unknowable and bears a secret. But it bears that secret publicly; as literature, the text announces that it has a meaning waiting to be excavated, and so it gives away part of its secret by signaling that it has something to hide. For Derrida, every text that takes a public space or invites public reception, every text that is generally legible but whose "content, sense, referent, signatory, and addressee are not fully determinable . . . can become a *literary* object" (Derrida, "Literature in Secret," 131). To be clear, this means that any text can become literary, for what text is there whose content, referent, signatory, and addressee are fully determinable, which might not be read or interpreted by some indeterminable and future other? This is quite a different standard for meaning-making than Kristeva's abjection. What makes a piece of writing literature is not anything inherent in the form or beauty of the writing itself, nor the utter eradication or abdication of some meaning that preceded it, but simply the fact that the writing bears a secret, that some aspect of it—content, referent, signatory, addressee—is no longer determinable. Derrida calls the fact that no piece of writing can fully determine its own significance *destinerrance*—a necessary errancy between every text's origin and its intended significance or semantic destination.[97] In other words, because no text is fully determined or determinable, every text is available to literary interpretation and so to be or become literature. For Derrida, each literary text bears a secret that it partially reveals and that in turn coyly calls for the interpretation that would uncover its half-kept secret.

What does any of this have to do with forgiveness? Derrida claims that forgiveness forgives only the unforgivable. In those earlier essays, discussed in Chapter 1, this paradox followed a Jankélévitchean logic. That which might be overlooked or undone, that which in other words is clearly forgivable, does not merit the irrational miracle of forgiveness. But here Derrida expands on this idea of impossibility in crucial ways. As Barbour explains, Derrida means that I forgive another, or ask forgiveness of another, only when "I in some sense presume their position," that is, when I "presume that I know that they feel guilty, and thus need to be forgiven, or . . . presume that I know they feel generous, and are thus capable of forgiving."[98] This entails a fundamental "reduction of their otherness, or an unforgivable violation or invasion of the secret that constitutes them as other."[99] This is to say that when I ask or offer forgiveness, I risk an interpretation of the other's irreducibly singular interiority, I imply a knowledge of their unknowably secret alterity, and impose a sense of myself upon them. Like Christ obscuring Beloved or Beloved obscuring Sethe's daughter, I erase the irreducible secret of the other in my urge to recognize and read them. Thus, in his characteristically oracular rhetoric, Derrida states that we must ask forgiveness for asking forgiveness, that we must be forgiven for offering it, that forgiveness endlessly replicates itself in human relationships since we are fundamentally unknowable to one another and yet we speak and act with knowing confidence. Forgiveness is made impossible by "the fact that one cannot forgive, ask, or grant forgiveness without this specular identification, without speaking in the other's stead and with the other's voice" (Derrida, 137). By "specular identification," Derrida means that we identify with the other—that is, we impose our own identity upon the other—through speculation. Forgiveness is speculative because we imagine and impose what we think we know about ourselves onto others. Thus, instead of bringing offense to a tidy conclusion, instead of "dissolving or absolving it, forgiveness can then only extend the fault." Where it hopes to redeem or resolve, it instead "can only import into itself this self-contradiction . . . allowing it to survive in an interminable agony" (126). Derrida suggests something similar to what we saw in Kristeva, but he wants here to emphasize the complex politics of interpretation rather than the dynamics of our psychically constructed meanings. In the interpersonal, therapeutic context of Kristeva's psychoanalysis, we might call interpretation pardon and vice versa, and it might even be experienced as significant healing (though it can never fully escape the melancholy from which it emerges). But Derrida wants to draw our attention to the politics of interpretation. If forgiveness is in fact interpretation, then it is an act of interpreting another who always remains secret from me. The meaningfulness my forgiveness endeavors will be the one I have imposed to some degree upon the other.

Derrida reads the irreducible singularity of the encounter with the unknowable other as originating in the ancient covenants of the Hebrew Bible. Consider Noah and God's destruction of creation through a flood. We read in scripture that God comes to regret the devastation he summons. If this is the case, Derrida asks, then to whom or from whom or for whom might God seek forgiveness in the aftermath of this catastrophe, especially if one can only "ever ask someone else for forgiveness," when one identifies "sufficiently with the other, with the victim"? (142). How could there possibly be a specular identification between God and Noah? The promise never again to wreak destruction functions to expose the secret of God's remorse; or, rather, we interpret the covenant thus and impose our own reading upon a God whose mystery forever eludes us, an interpretation that must demand forgiveness of us since God is unknowable. Or consider Abraham and the command to sacrifice Isaac. In this case, writes Derrida, the secret has less to do with the content of God's command to offer sacrifice than with the "pure singularity of the face-to-face with God, the secret of this absolute relation" (154). Abraham's most essential secret, Derrida claims, is not that God commanded an awful sacrifice but that God has spoken at all, that there has occurred this pure singularity of an encounter with the unknowable. Abraham cannot reveal this secret because it is so absolutely singular, utterly unrelatable and indescribable. It cannot be put into words; the experience confounds identification and speculation by its nature. The content of the secret, that terrible command, is ultimately insignificant, because what gives the secret its secrecy is not what God has asked, but *that* God has asked. "In short," then, "the secret to be kept would have, at bottom, to be without an object, without any object other than the unconditionally singular covenant, the mad love between God, Abraham, and what descends from him" (155–56). To remain a secret, this command and covenant would need to remain inexpressible, incommunicable. And yet, out of this indescribably secret singularity, this unutterably singular secret, arises all of Abrahamic religion and three vast scriptural traditions. This absolutely irreducible, impossibly unidentifiable event is written, published, promulgated, and preached. It "is sealed but necessarily betrayed by the inheritance that confirms, reads, and translates the covenant. By the testament itself" (156). The story is given, the testament is written, and a literary tradition of reading subsequently follows that conforms to the unforgivable contours of forgiveness: I risk an interpretation and claim to uncover a secret that recedes from my reading even as I give it, and that persistently, perpetually demands yet another reading, and another, and another. My reading, like my forgiveness, "betrays [the secret] in the double sense of that word: it is unfaithful to it, breaking with it at the very moment when it reveals its 'truth' and uncovers its secret" (157). As soon as I find Christ, he eludes me: Where art thou? As soon as I name Beloved, she vanishes. Literature can thus "but ask forgiveness for this double betrayal. There is no literature that does not, from its very first word, ask for forgiveness" (157).

Literature is congruent with forgiveness because each exposes a secret it describes but cannot uncover. Their common secrecy "does not consist in hiding *something*, in not revealing the truth, but in respecting the absolute singularity, the infinite separation of what binds me or exposes me to the unique, to one as to the other, to *the One as to the Other*" (122–23). This infinite separation echoes language in Weil, von Speyr, and von Balthasar, but Derrida's concerns are not primarily metaphysical. I must give an account to the other; I must receive the other's account. But, as Judith Butler has observed, these accounts will always be inadequate and thus require revision; they are mired in failure and thus require the possibility of forgiveness. This failure, according to Derrida, is a feature of "all readings, all interactions, all engagements, perhaps all relations and experiences in general." As Barbour concludes, we are "always breaking our oath," always "violating the secret that holds us together while holding us apart." We cannot avoid "assuming that we know what we can never possibly know." Thus we need constantly "to be forgiven, and we always need to forgive others. And in asking and in granting forgiveness, we are always, and constantly, perpetrating the unforgivable."[100]

The themes of the preceding chapters—grief as the ground for justice, failure as the ground for moral relation, estrangement as the ground for love—emerge in concert here. We might also see these secrets and violations operating in the proclamations of the Gospel narratives. Tell no one who I am, Jesus instructs his disciples over and again, tell no one what you have seen.[101] And yet we have all these Gospel narratives, these evangelical proclamations of forgiveness, this proliferation of stories that seek to describe exactly who Jesus is. Despite Jesus's clear command that we keep his secret, our endless interpretations inevitably arise—as Rowan Williams argues—in the midst of our grief, guilt, betrayal, and confusion at the fact of his loss, and these incessant interpretations perpetually and repeatedly demand forgiveness. The Gospel writings aim to explain and uncover a secret that keeps receding, they open the tomb to reveal it as empty, they relentlessly raise the question, "Where art thou?" The stories represent the search for answers, and that search unremittingly continues. He is not here. He is risen. In their unending search for closure, each form of these stories asks us to identify and then ask forgiveness for our interpretation. Each Christ we write is a betrayal that demands forgiveness, a forgiveness only the absconding Christ can offer. Every Christian witness, every theology, every theological reading of literature, even these secular fictions that I have read but that operate within a Christian cultural history, all these expose the secret of a singularity and then seek forgiveness for that exposure.

This is not to baptize secular fictions for the cause of Christ. I do not claim that these novels are clandestinely Christian theologies. That is not their secret. Rather, I seek here only to expose even the most foundational and canonical Christian writings as betrayals and impossibilities too. In revealing their witness, they conceal their revelation. Yet, they could not but be written, and read, and rewritten, and read again. *Beloved* once again uncovers both the risk and necessity of writing in the wake of unspeakable loss. The novel's final pages are especially disturbing on this reading, and they come into starker and more dramatic relief if we think of Beloved not as a ghost haunting Sethe and Denver and Paul D and Stamp Paid but as a vulnerable young woman in need of their help. The final two pages of the novel serve as a kind of epilogue, a commentary and a lament over the erasure we have just witnessed. Resisting the invocation of the name Beloved until the novel's final word, the narrator tells us that the young woman who appeared at 124 becomes "disremembered and unaccounted for" over time (Morrison, *Beloved*, 323).

Although we have called this victim, whether woman or ghost, by the name Beloved throughout the novel, the narrator reminds us that her name has never in fact been revealed. Beloved was the sole word on a gravestone, and it is the name the grown woman assumes when she arrives at 124, but that word is the mark of an incomplete mourning rather than of a person. This nameless person—whether a very young child or a fully grown woman—has a claim on us, but none of us will claim her. She waits to be loved while we forget. She has moral worth despite our urge to erase her. Our laughter swallows her away, because we cannot square her need for love and weeping shame with our need to put her away from our collective memory. And so we forget her "like a bad dream" (323). We are told that all who knew her, both the tellers of tall tales and the people who shared a home with her and loved her, come to forget her through either their willful intention or the eventual and wise impulse to move forward. But the peace of all this forgetting comes with a price. In crafting and curating our stories so that we might set our best path toward an aspirational future, we unwittingly edit out the most wounded and vulnerable victims among us. This "girl who waited to be loved" fragments into pieces and is swallowed away (323). And throughout this concluding, tragic, and poetic reflection upon this beloved child twice sacrificed, these two wounded people erased into each other and out of memory, the narrator repeats as if in chorus, "It was not a story to pass on. . . . It was not a story to pass on. . . . This is not a story to pass on" (323–24). Passing on, of course, recalls Sethe's conversation with Denver about prayer and death and can infer at least three meanings, all of which hold here. This story is not one to ignore, and neither is it a story we want to tell again to others. We can neither pass on it nor pass it on. But it is also a story that refuses to die, that refuses to pass on, whatever we do. Our forgetting cannot kill it, even if it is killed. Memory rises up and lives, even where we do not recognize it as memory. The only responsible way forward is to name what we have forgotten, to give a name to the one whose name is unremembered. The only way forward is to remind ourselves of what remains unrecovered, to speak of what is still unspeakable, to tell the secret we do not know, even if that naming continues to obscure what we cannot recall, and so requires forgiveness. We cannot say it and we cannot decline to say it. We cannot pass it on, we cannot pass on it, and it does not pass on. All we can offer is a failing answer and an appeal for forgiveness in that offering; all we can do is stir the resolve to speak and seek forgiveness again and again. We must say the name that hides a history in order to bring the fact of its hiddenness forth. We must speak without hope of absolution for the secret we have revealed because whatever we say, however long we ask "Where art thou?," the one we have effaced will, like Christ, be "in agony unto the end of the world."[102] She will be crying shame and waiting to be loved. Beloved.

Epilogue

ON LITERARY FORGIVENESS

W. H. Auden wrote often of the role and power of the arts or, more properly, of their limits. In works such as "In Memory of W. B. Yeats," "Musée des Beaux Arts," and "The Sea and the Mirror," Auden considered the place of art in human life and attempted to describe both what it could and could not do, what it would or would not represent, what it might or might not change. One thing he insisted dramatic art in particular could not do was show forgiveness. This argument emerged both in his unpublished correspondence and in his published essays. Auden was a great admirer of Hannah Arendt in general and of *The Human Condition* in particular, for example, but he disagreed with her characterization of forgiveness as an act of retaliatory restraint, taken in the public square, which could occasion a new beginning. This was mostly because Auden—like so many others—believed forgiveness to be largely an event of inward affective transformation. For Auden, forgiveness was a practice of charity, but charity was more an interior state than it was an outward act. He argued this directly in personal correspondence with Arendt and expanded upon this argument in his essay "The Prince's Dog," contending that dramatic forgiveness—in Shakespeare's late comedies specifically—could not strictly be performed on the stage since forgiveness was a feeling, and it was impossible dramatically to represent a change of feeling.[1] Forgiveness, because essentially interior, could not "be unambiguously made into a dramatic act."[2]

Auden's disagreement with Arendt distinguished pardon from forgiveness. Pardon, Auden claimed, was the official and regulatory corollary of punishment; forgiveness, meanwhile, was the interior and affective opposite of spitefulness. This was why forgiveness had no place in Arendt's public, since action must be public and forgiveness was necessarily private. On Auden's terms, only official pardon—not forgiveness—could really qualify as an action. Forgiveness, though unconditional for Auden in its pure and charitable form, therefore could arrive at dramatic representation only by implication, in the repentance and apology of those forgiven. Since the affective experience of overcoming vengeance could publicly manifest only as restraint exercised against retribution—as doing nothing, in other words—it had no dramatic form unless requested and granted in the words of the play and its players.

One result of Auden's argument was that it severely limited the genius of Arendt's Jesus, whose teaching on forgiveness could be relevant only in personal, rather than in political, matters. And since Arendt (as noted in Chapter 3) was suspicious of love as a political action precisely because she (like Auden) regarded it primarily as an inward affective state rather than an outward relation to others, she granted Auden's point to a significant degree and abandoned her language of forgiveness.[3] As this book has attempted to show, I think this was a mistake for both Auden and Arendt, a mischaracterization of Jesus's teachings on forgiveness that was hampered in the end by an inadequate notion of love. But there are hints in Auden's essay and elsewhere in his poetic work that the grace of retributive restraint has more moral and dramatic significance than he allows in his anxiety to preserve the interiority of charity. Though he will not call it forgiveness (as I do), there is a discernible grace accompanying nonretaliation that remains uniquely available to poetic depiction. And whatever Auden's concerns about dramatic representation, this really was Arendt's point in her description of Jesus's forgiving genius: it is when retaliation is already predetermined that restraint—doing nothing—gains moral significance. Indeed, when violent reprisal is assumed, the refusal of retaliation can be quite dramatic indeed. Forswearing vengeance appears as an action in human affairs when the revenge we anticipate is a foregone conclusion. Perhaps more than Auden would allow, forgiveness as a habit of loving restraint does have immense moral significance as well as political and dramatic potential. And as a final word in this book of literary moral theology, I briefly consider one of Auden's most well-known and important poems of war as exemplary of how literature can stir forgiveness and forgiveness literature.

In the famous work "The Shield of Achilles," Thetis looks over the shoulder of Hephaestos as he casts and decorates the renowned shield of her famed warrior son, that man of rage, Achilles. But instead of the heraldic scenes of martial valor she expects to see painted there, Hephaestos renders scenes of industrial blight and human abuse instead. This is a poem written—like *The Human Condition*—after two world wars and unspeakable genocide, and it exhibits the exhaustion of modern art before all the failed propagandas that have historically called art into service. There is no glory to be shown here. The only thing the creaky craftsman Hephaestos can depict is the reality of warfare and the horror that awaits Achilles in battle. When he is finished painting the scabbed and broken scenes on the warrior's shield, Hephaestos "hobble[s] away" while Thetis "crie[s] out in dismay" at what he has wrought on the doomed Achilles's shield.[4] Instead of heraldic scenes of martial glory suitable for a hero's shield, Hephaestos has hammered out images of desolation and loss. Thetis cries out because the violence of war is unrelenting. Act and retaliation will inevitably escalate until even her all-but-invincible son is destroyed. The final scene Hephaestos has painted upon the shield, the one that crowns his work and causes Thetis to exclaim in anguish, is of a child who would never know "Of any world where promises were kept, / Or one could weep because another wept."[5]

It is a grim conclusion to a poem that gives the lie to martial glory, a lie so often sung in lyrics like this. But the scene that causes Thetis at last to cry out and its line—"weep because another wept"—is not just a tender rhyme to complete the couplet it concludes. It refers, in fact, to a moment in the life of this Achilles, who would not live long. *The Iliad* begins by singing Achilles's rage, and the poem is one that follows the increasingly brutal and reciprocal flow of gruesome retaliation. As Simone Weil observes, *The Iliad* is an epic almost entirely governed by exactly that "automatic, natural reaction to transgression" Arendt has named as vengeance, to the cycle of retributive violence that so often and so naturally governs human affairs.[6] Elsewhere Weil refers to this inevitable violence, this nearly chemical certainty of action and reaction in human affairs, as gravity, or necessity, or force.[7] But in *The Iliad*, briefly, miraculously, dramatically, this cycle is broken by what Weil refers to as a moment of grace, and what she describes as the most sublime expression of love in the epic. With Achilles's lover Patroclus dead at Trojan hands, and Priam's son Hector rotting on the field where Achilles has slain him, Priam comes to Achilles's tent. Prostrate, the great king clutches "Achilles' knees, kisse[s] his hands," the "terrible, manslaughtering" hands that have lain waste to "so many of [Priam's] sons."[8] But instead of kicking the old man away, Achilles trembles at the sight of "godlike Priam" and, recalling his own father in the figure of the enemy king, feels an urge to weep that overcomes his rage.[9] Achilles takes Priam by the arm, and each man is consumed by memory, Priam for his son Hector while "huddled in tears at Achilles' feet," and Achilles for his own "father and then too for Patroclus."[10] One weeps because another wept. After this encounter in Achilles's tent, a truce is briefly called and the dead on both sides are buried and duly mourned. This moment of peace and grace, quite dramatic indeed, "can cause to vanish the thirst to avenge a slain son or friend; by an even greater miracle, it can close the gap between benefactor and suppliant, victor and victim."[11] It is, for Weil, the "purest triumph of love."[12]

Weil is susceptible to hyperbole in her rhetoric, so I wouldn't suggest that grief can anywhere stop a war or that weeping could so easily broker peace. And this may be Auden's point in his poem: these noble moments of truce are no longer poetically or actually possible; world war and genocide have desiccated them entirely. But surely this is Weil's and Arendt's point also, the meaning of the miracle they describe: when vengeance seems inevitable, as necessary as gravity, human beings still really do retain the grace and freedom to risk a new beginning in spite of everything. Auden thought this grace unrepresentable because it was inward. But perhaps it is only that such graces are not representable anymore in the tidy resolutions of Shakespearean comedy. This is the hidden secret of Auden's poem, the literary secret of forgiveness: Hephaestos's shield is a lie, but not for the reasons Thetis wishes. There is no martial glory. War is still and always will be hell. The dead remain yet dead. But even in the midst of war, Achilles can still weep, the man of rage can still be moved to tears by his enemy Priam's weeping. What retributive restraint, what loving one's enemy, what forgiveness looks like in Achilles's tent is grief. In The Iliad, the man of rage and the godlike king remember all they have lost and will never, ever recover. So the enemies pause, weep, eat, and keep their peace, and it couldn't be more dramatically rendered.

It matters which stories we tell, and how we tell them. Like Hephaestos, we must speak the dreadful truth about our histories and what they have wrought. We must name with terrible candor the violence, brutality, racism, colonialism, and extermination that have been perpetrated upon us and perpetrated in our name. In their difficult meditations on forgiveness, Kazuo Ishiguro, Marilynne Robinson, Louise Erdrich, and Toni Morrison bravely name them. Whatever forms of confession or forgiveness we foster should help us raise our voices and raise them well. And we must speak knowing there can be no compensating erasure of our pains, whether through forgetting or through the glory we assign to martial vengeance. We must speak as if into an empty tomb, wary of hearing only the fading echoes of our anguish. But even once we have spoken these unspeakable things, we still have something more that we can say. Forgiveness raises its voice with the courage to speak but keeps on speaking, just as poetry claims no final word, only an ageless echo of imagination, even if from empty tombs. We are everywhere estranged, and yet always have more to say. Like Priam and Achilles weeping at the wastes of war or Mary weeping at Jesus's tomb, when we attend with loving courage to all we have lost and cannot regain, we might manage to build a peace we can barely imagine upon the ruins we reveal.

Notes

INTRODUCTION

1. Collier and Brown: Mark Berman, "'I Forgive You.' Relatives of Charleston Church Shooting Victims Address Dylann Roof," *Washington Post*, June 19, 2015, https://www.washingtonpost.com/news/post-nation/wp/2015/06/19/i-forgive-you-relatives-of-charleston-church-victims-address-dylann-roof/; Simmons: Elahe Izadi, "The Powerful Words of Forgiveness Delivered to Dylann Roof by Victims' Families," June 19, 2015, https://www.washingtonpost.com/news/post-nation/wp/2015/06/19/hate-wont-win-the-powerful-words-delivered-to-dylann-roof-by-victims-relatives/.

2. Benjamin Wallace-Wells, "The Hard Truths of Ta-Nehisi Coates," *New York Magazine*, July 12, 2015, http://nymag.com/daily/intelligencer/2015/07/ta-nehisi-coates-between-the-world-and-me.html.

3. Many of these scholars and their work will be considered throughout this book, as well as many others who reject forms of unconditional forgiveness that Charleston exemplifies. The more notable examples are Charles Griswold, *Forgiveness: A Philosophical Exploration* (New York: Cambridge University Press, 2007); David Konstan, *Before Forgiveness: The Origins of a Moral Idea* (New York: Cambridge University Press, 2010); Maria Mayo, *The Limits of Forgiveness: Case Studies in the Distortion of a Biblical Idea* (Minneapolis: Fortress, 2015); Regina Schwartz, *Loving Justice, Living Shakespeare* (New York: Oxford University Press, 2016); Martha Nussbaum, *Anger and Forgiveness: Resentment, Generosity, Justice* (New York: Oxford University Press, 2016).

4. David von Drehle, "How Do You Forgive a Murder?," *Time*, November 12, 2015, http://time.com/time-magazine-charleston-shooting-cover-story/. Quotation from audio clip "Hear Anthony Thompson Talk About What Comes Next," accessed June 19, 2018.

5. Waltrina N. Middleton, "I Don't Forgive the Man Who Murdered My Cousin DePayne at Mother Emanuel," *Christian Century*, June 16, 2020, https://www .christiancentury.org/article/first-person/i-don-t-forgive-man-who-murdered-my-cousin-depayne-mother-emanuel.

6. "We can probably say that moral questions have always arisen when moral norms of behavior have ceased to be self-evident and unquestioned in the life of a community" (Theodor W. Adorno, *Problems of Moral Philosophy* [Stanford, CA: Stanford University Press, 2001], 16).

7. These objections arise with especially compelling urgency in feminist and womanist theologies. See, for example, Delores S. Williams, *Sisters in the Wilderness: The Challenge of Womanist God-Talk* (Maryknoll, NY: Orbis Books, 2013), and Rita Nakashima Brock and Rebecca Ann Parker, *Proverbs of Ashes: Violence, Redemptive Suffering, and the Search for What Saves Us* (Boston: Beacon, 2001).

8. For a thorough examination of several traditional atonement theologies, see F. W. Dillistone, *The Christian Understanding of Atonement* (London: James Nisbet, 1968).

9. See especially John Milbank, *Being Reconciled: Ontology and Pardon* (New York: Routledge, 2003).

10. See, for example, Matt 16:13–20 and Matt 18:15–22.

11. Anthony Bash acknowledges the confusions of the New Testament in *Forgiveness and Christian Ethics* (New York: Cambridge University Press, 2010). Maria Mayo, while recognizing these inconsistences and diagnosing an unhelpfully anachronistic and therapeutic hermeneutic in contemporary readings of scriptural forgiveness, also probably too entirely dismisses the New Testament's problematizations of punishment and conditional forgiveness. See Mayo, *Limits of Forgiveness*. David Konstan also provides an illuminating study of ancient moral understandings in *Before Forgiveness* and likewise uncovers a modern psychological bias in our readings of scriptural forgiveness. But he also limits the options for what the New Testament might suggest, I think, even as he successfully argues that it could not have imagined our modern forms of forgiveness.

12. Mark Jordan, *Blessing Same-Sex Unions: The Perils of Queer Romance and the Confusions of Christian Marriage* (Chicago: University of Chicago Press, 2005), 120–21.

13. Both Karl Barth and Hans Urs von Balthasar use spatial metaphors of distance when describing the saving work of the incarnation. Barth refers to "the way of the Son of God into the far country," while von Balthasar's "mission of the Son" in the Theo-Dramatic is depicted as an extended journey and descent into hell. See Karl Barth, *Church Dogmatics IV.1, Sections 57–59* (New York: T&T Clark, 2010), 150–203, and Hans Urs von Balthasar, *Theo-Drama IV: The Action* (San Francisco: Ignatius Press, 1994), 317–51.

14. See Timothy Gorringe, *God's Just Vengeance: Crime, Violence, and the Rhetoric of Salvation* (New York: Cambridge University Press, 1996), for an exhaustive and illuminating study of the intersections of atonement theology and penal practice in the modern West.

15. See, for example, Lewis B. Smedes, *Forgive and Forget: Healing the Hurts We Don't Deserve* (San Francisco: HarperOne, 2007); Colin Tipping, *Radical Forgiveness* (Boulder, CO: Sounds True, 2009); and Adam Hamilton, *Forgiveness: Finding Peace Through Letting Go* (Nashville: Abingdon, 2012).

16. Everett L. Worthington Jr., "Understanding Forgiveness of Other People: Definitions, Theories, Processes," in *Handbook of Forgiveness*, ed. Everett L. Worthington Jr. and Nathaniel G. Wade (New York: Routledge, 2019), 11–21.

17. Miroslav Volf offers a more modest, even momentary form of reconciliation through the metaphor of embrace, for example. Miroslav Volf, *Exclusion and Embrace: A Theological Exploration of Identity, Otherness, and Reconciliation* (Nashville: Abingdon, 1996).

18. The South African Truth and Reconciliation Commission famously blurred the boundaries between political reconciliation and interpersonal forgiveness, its important accomplishments notwithstanding.

19. I discuss more about the conditions typically attached to forgiveness throughout this book, and especially in Chapter 3.

20. In *Exclusion and Embrace*, Volf suggests that we might also refrain from violence in order to leave room for God's vengeance at the eschaton. This sort of restraint would be based upon honoring righteous anger more than loving one's enemy, and so I find it less theologically and morally persuasive than what I have suggested here; but I can recognize with Volf that the realities of complex trauma will likely afford multiple motivations for retributive restraint in situations of actual postconflict peacemaking. I discuss this further in Chapter 4.

21. See, for example, David Aers, *Salvation and Sin: Augustine, Langland, and Fourteenth-Century Theology* (Notre Dame: University of Notre Dame Press, 2009); Sarah Beckwith, *Shakespeare and the Grammar of Forgiveness* (Ithaca, NY: Cornell University Press, 2013); Richard Hughes Gibson, *Forgiveness in Victorian Literature: Grammar, Narrative, and Community* (New York: Bloomsbury Academic, 2015); Jan Frans van Dijkhuizen, *A Literary History of Forgiveness: Power, Remorse, and the Limits of Forgiveness* (New York: Bloomsbury Academic, 2020).

22. See Rowan Williams, "Poetic and Religious Imagination," *Theology* 80 (1977): 178–87.

23. My project, then, falls very much within the tradition of constructive (rather than systematic or dogmatic) theology. Constructive theology "is a method of doing Christian theology that takes seriously theological and church tradition as well as modern critiques of that tradition being something universal, eternal, or essential; it employs traditional themes and loci of theology in order to formulate useful, inclusive, fallible guidance for living as Christians in the contemporary world, against descriptions of a systematic theological system that pretend to unveil any true essence or essential reality of Christianity; and takes as its mode a goodfaith engagement with parallel academic disciplines, often religious studies; an activist/crisis confrontation; or, ideally, both" (Jason A. Wyman Jr., *Constructing Constructive Theology: An Introductory Sketch* [Minneapolis: Fortress, 2017], xxx).

24. Maurice Blanchot, "Literature and the Right to Death," in *The Work of Fire*, trans. Charlotte Mandel (Stanford, CA: Stanford University Press, 1995), 300–344.

CHAPTER 1. RETALIATION

1. Kazuo Ishiguro, *The Buried Giant* (New York: Knopf, 2015).

2. James Wood, "The Uses of Oblivion," *New Yorker*, March 16, 2015, https://www.newyorker.com/magazine/2015/03/23/the-uses-of-oblivion.

3. There are, of course, scriptural citations that can be brought to the defense of God's forgetting, Isa 43:25 standing as a powerful example. Nonetheless, the argument and arc of this book contends that a love which requires forgetting will be weaker than one which can love in full knowledge of wrong. See Chapter 4 for further discussions of this.

4. Friedrich Nietzsche, *On the Genealogy of Morals and Ecce Homo*, trans. Walter Kaufmann (New York: Random House, 1967), 61.

5. The French reads, "Of doing evil for the pleasure of doing it."

6. Jeffrie G. Murphy, *Getting Even: Forgiveness and Its Limits* (New York: Oxford University Press, 2003), 17.

7. Murphy, *Getting Even*, 17.

8. Murphy, *Getting Even*, 31.

9. These trends in criminal justice are well-documented; for a start, see Michelle Alexander, *The New Jim Crow: Mass Incarceration in the Age of Colorblindness* (New York: New Press, 2010).

10. Robert Solomon, *A Passion for Justice: Emotions and the Origin of the Social Contract* (Reading, MA: Addison-Wesley, 1990), 272–73, 273–74.

11. Trudy Govier, *Forgiveness and Revenge* (New York: Routledge, 2002), 4–5.

12. Solomon, *Passion for Justice*, 272.

13. Solomon, *Passion for Justice*, 272.

14. Solomon, *Passion for Justice*, 272.

15. Govier, *Forgiveness and Revenge*, 2.

16. Govier, *Forgiveness and Revenge*, 2, viii.

17. Govier, *Forgiveness and Revenge*, viii.

18. Jean Hampton, "The Retributive Idea," in *Forgiveness and Mercy*, by Jeffrie G. Murphy and Jean Hampton (New York: Cambridge University Press, 1988), 111–61.

19. Hampton, "Retributive Idea," 125.

20. Hampton, "Retributive Idea," 126.

21. Hampton, "Retributive Idea," 128.

22. Hampton, "Retributive Idea," 133.

23. Hampton, "Retributive Idea," 137.

24. Govier, *Forgiveness and Revenge*, 11.

25. Martha Nussbaum, *Anger and Forgiveness: Resentment, Generosity, Justice* (New York: Oxford University Press, 2016), 5, 6.

26. James Cone, quoted in "Blood at the Root: In the Aftermath of the Emanuel Nine," by David Remnick, *New Yorker*, September 21, 2015, https://www.newyorker.com/magazine/2015/09/28/blood-at-the-root.

27. Govier, *Forgiveness and Revenge*, 12.
28. Nussbaum, *Anger and Forgiveness*, 24.
29. Nussbaum, *Anger and Forgiveness*, 25.
30. Nussbaum, *Anger and Forgiveness*, 21–22.
31. Nussbaum, *Anger and Forgiveness*, 24.
32. Charles Griswold, *Forgiveness: A Philosophical Exploration* (New York: Cambridge University Press, 2007), 29.
33. Nussbaum, *Anger and Forgiveness*, 5.
34. Martha Minow, *Between Vengeance and Forgiveness: Facing History After Genocide and Mass Violence* (Boston: Beacon, 1998), 13.
35. Judith Herman, *Trauma and Recovery: The Aftermath of Violence—From Domestic Abuse to Political Terror* (New York: Basic Books, 1997), 189.
36. Herman, *Trauma and Recovery*, 189. It must also be noted that Herman immediately follows this critique of the revenge fantasy with a similar excoriation of the fantasy of forgiveness. But the forgiveness Herman assumes seems to resemble the erasure, unearned reconciliation, and forced equanimity the present book aims to critique and leave behind.
37. Friedrich Nietzsche, *Thus Spoke Zarathustra* (New York: Cambridge University Press, 2006), 111.
38. Although the atomic bombs are largely credited in American popular culture and conventional wisdom for saving hundreds of thousands, even millions, of American lives, the historical evidence shows the contrary. The United States did not regard a ground invasion as necessary and had abandoned plans for it already in early 1945. Postwar surveys proved that Japan would have had to surrender even had the bombs never been used. And the number of Americans estimated by officials to have been "saved" by the atomic bombs inflated rapidly in popular discourse during the months after the war, as discomfort with the effects of the bombs became more widely expressed in the United States. See Paul Ham, *Hiroshima Nagasaki: The Real Story of the Atomic Bombings and Their Aftermath* (New York: Thomas Dunne, 2014), esp. 468ff.
39. See Carl Schmitt, *Political Theology: Four Chapters on the Concept of Sovereignty*, trans. George Schwab (Chicago: University of Chicago Press, 2005).
40. Ted A. Smith, *Weird John Brown: Divine Violence and the Limits of Ethics* (Stanford, CA: Stanford University Press, 2015), 72.
41. Gillian Rose, *Love's Work: A Reckoning with Life* (New York: New York Review Books, 2011), 123.
42. Rose, *Love's Work*, 123.
43. In English: Vladimir Jankélévitch, *Forgiveness*, trans. Andrew Kelley (Chicago: University of Chicago Press, 2005).
44. See note 7 of the Introduction, above.
45. Jankélévitch phrases this in particularly stark and hyperbolic terms that oversimplify the dilemma of moral warrant and justification, a dilemma forgiveness importantly addresses. Whether or how acts can be justified, the moral significance of our justifications, and the relevance of forgiveness to this problem are central concerns of Chapter 2.

46. John Milbank, in particular, objects to this aspect of Jankélévitch's thought, believing that it undermines, undersells, or misunderstands the redemptive logic and trajectory, even the fundamental ontology, of Christian forgiveness. I discuss further my own worries about Milbank's logic and ontology of forgiveness in Chapter 3.

47. In his book *Forgiveness and Love* (New York: Oxford University Press, 2012), Glen Pettigrove usefully distinguishes forgiveness from reconciliation, debt cancellation, and emotional regulation, distinctions that I fully endorse and that echo some of those Jankélévitch here makes, if from a different philosophical register. However, Pettigrove understands the love that inspires forgiveness as requiring "seeing the other as good," or at least committing to seeing some good in the other (96). A robustly Christian love, I argue, is one that does not depend upon the other's goodness in any respect. The love that inspires Christian forgiveness, like God's love, is fully self-grounding and loves—as Jankélévitch writes—for no other reason than that it loves.

48. Vladimir Jankélévitch, "Should We Pardon Them?," trans. Ann Hobart, *Critical Inquiry* 22, no. 3 (Spring 1996): 552–72.

49. See Chapter 3 for further reflections on resentment, affect, and forgiveness.

50. Jacques Derrida, "To Forgive: The Unforgivable and the Imprescriptible," in *Questioning God*, ed. John D. Caputo, Mark Dooley, and Michael J. Scanlon (Bloomington: Indiana University Press, 2001), 21–51, at 31.

51. Derrida, "To Forgive," 31.

52. Jacques Derrida, *On Cosmopolitanism and Forgiveness* (New York: Routledge, 1997), 32.

53. Derrida, "To Forgive," 33.

54. Derrida, "To Forgive," 33.

55. Jacques Derrida, *Memoires for Paul de Man* (New York: Columbia University Press, 1986), xvi.

56. Gillian Rose, *Mourning Becomes the Law: Philosophy and Representation* (New York: Cambridge University Press, 1996), 121.

57. Rose, *Mourning*, 121.

58. Rose, *Mourning*, 121.

59. Rose, *Mourning*, 35–36.

60. Jacques Derrida, "Force of Law: The 'Mystical Foundation of Authority,'" in *Acts of Religion*, ed. Gil Anidjar (New York: Routledge, 2002), 244.

61. Derrida, "Force of Law," 244.

62. Derrida, *Memoires*, 31.

63. Derrida, *Memoires*, 31.

64. Derrida, "To Forgive," 41–42.

65. Hannah Arendt, *The Human Condition* (Chicago: University of Chicago Press, 1958).

66. Notably, Arendt reads punishment as an alternative to forgiveness that can also cease the reactive dynamic of reciprocal violence. This would require a punishment absolutely and entirely absent of retributive vengeance, a questionable possibility.

67. Elizabeth Burow-Flak, "Genocide, Memory, and the Difficulties of Forgiveness in Card's Ender Saga and Ishiguro's *The Buried Giant*," *Renascence* 71, no. 4 (Fall 2019): 247–67, at 264.

68. Burow-Flak, "Genocide," 264.

69. It may be that the peace of forgetting allowed Axl's heart to be "won back by the years" (*Buried Giant*, 312), as he says, that his forgetting pacified an urge toward vengeance over time. But as Part II of the current book shows, this is not true of the political realm in which Axl lives, where—as Wistan has said—forgetting has only allowed wounds to fester. In that part I explore further whether forgetting or some other restraint might be the best pacifying factor in the long path toward forgiveness.

CHAPTER 2. REPENTANCE

1. Kazuo Ishiguro, *The Buried Giant* (New York: Knopf, 2015).
2. Marilynne Robinson, *Gilead* (New York: Picador, 2006).
3. Marilynne Robinson, *Lila* (New York: Picador, 2020), 80.
4. For another reading of how Ames has fallen short in his ministry through a sort of forgetting, see "'The Prairie Still Shines like Transfiguration': Forgiveness, Theology, and Politics in Marilynne Robinson's *Gilead* Novels," by Jan Frans van Dijkhuizen, in *A Literary History of Reconciliation: Power, Remorse, and the Limits of Forgiveness* (New York: Bloomsbury, 2018), 181–201.
5. Martha Nussbaum, *Anger and Forgiveness: Resentment, Generosity, Justice* (New York: Oxford University Press, 2016), 72.
6. Nussbaum, *Anger and Forgiveness*, 74.
7. Michel Foucault, *On the Government of the Living: Lectures at the Collège de France 1979–1980*, trans. Graham Burchell (New York: Palgrave Macmillan, 2012).
8. Foucault, *Government of the Living*, 103.
9. Foucault, *Government of the Living*, 133.
10. Foucault, *Government of the Living*, 152.
11. Foucault, *Government of the Living*, 201.
12. Foucault, *Government of the Living*, 209.
13. Tertullian, *Ante-Nicene Fathers, Volume 3: Latin Christianity: Its Founder, Tertullian* (New York: Christian Literature Publishing, 1885), 664.
14. Tertullian, *Ante-Nicene Fathers*, 664.
15. Tertullian, *Ante-Nicene Fathers*, 664.
16. Readers interested in the way Foucault excavates these ancient meanings and their modern implications for penitential practices should also study David Lambert's *How Repentance Became Biblical* (New York: Oxford University Press, 2016). In it, Lambert expertly tracks how modern preoccupations with interiority and subjectivity have constrained and conditioned our interpretation of penitential acts in ancient sources.
17. Judith Butler, *Giving an Account of Oneself* (New York: Fordham University Press, 2005).
18. Virtue requires a "concept of a self whose unity resides in the unity of a narrative which links birth to life to death as narrative beginning to middle to end" (Alasdair McIntyre, *After Virtue* [Notre Dame: University of Notre Dame Press, 1981], 204).
19. Judith Butler, *Precarious Life: The Powers of Mourning and Violence* (New York: Verso, 2004).

20. Judith Butler, *Frames of War: When Is Life Grievable?* (New York: Verso, 2016), 171.

21. Butler, *Frames of War*, 171.

22. Butler, *Frames of War*, 172.

23. Judith Butler, *The Force of Nonviolence* (New York: Verso, 2020), 15.

24. Walter Benjamin, "The Critique of Violence," in *Reflections: Essays, Aphorisms, Autobiographical Writings* (New York: Schocken, 1978), 277–300, at 288.

25. Benjamin, "Critique," 288.

26. For another account of failure as essential to ethics, see Lisa Tessman, *Moral Failure: On the Impossible Demands of Morality* (New York: Oxford University Press, 2014).

27. Ted A. Smith, *Weird John Brown: Divine Violence and the Limits of Ethics* (Stanford, CA: Stanford University Press, 2015), 74.

28. Smith, *Weird John Brown*, 76.

29. Benjamin, "Critique," 298.

30. Benjamin, "Critique," 298.

31. Smith, *Weird John Brown*, 76.

32. Smith, *Weird John Brown*, 76.

33. Smith, *Weird John Brown*, 138.

34. Smith, *Weird John Brown*, 138.

35. Dietrich Bonhoeffer, *Ethics*, Dietrich Bonhoeffer Works Vol. 6, trans. Reinhard Krauss, Douglas W. Stott, and Charles C. West (Minneapolis: Fortress, 2005), 299.

36. See Dietrich Bonhoeffer, *Creation and Fall: A Theological Exposition of Genesis 1–3*, Dietrich Bonhoeffer Works Vol. 4, trans. Martin Rüter and Ilse Tödt (Minneapolis: Fortress, 2004).

37. These questions echo in the indigenous American theologian George Tinker's reflections on repentance, reflections that find their own resonance in my considerations of atonement in Chapter 3. See George Tinker, *American Indian Liberation: A Theology of Sovereignty* (Maryknoll, NY: Orbis Books, 2008), 53ff.

38. Clifford Green, "Editor's Introduction to the English Edition," in Bonhoeffer, *Ethics*, 15.

39. Green, "Editor's Introduction," 15.

40. Lee Spinks, "'The House of Your Church Is Burning': Race and Responsibility in Marilynne Robinson's *Gilead*," *Journal of American Studies* 51, no. 1 (2017): 141–62, at 142.

41. It should be noted that Tanabe's philosophical exhortations toward repentance were framed exclusively by the culpability he felt in encouraging a war that ruined his nation. He did not acknowledge or express contrition for the brutal ruin his nation visited upon other nations and peoples in East and Southeast Asia.

42. Hajime Tanabe, *Philosophy as Metanoetics* (Berkeley: University of California Press, 1986), 23.

43. These tendencies toward completion and plenitude are persistent problems in Christian theology. I engage them further in Chapter 3.

44. Tanabe, *Philosophy as Metanoetics*, 4.

45. Tanabe, *Philosophy as Metanoetics*, 4.

46. Tanabe, *Philosophy as Metanoetics*, 4.

47. Tanabe, *Philosophy as Metanoetics*, 5.

48. Tanabe, *Philosophy as Metanoetics*, 5, 25, and 49.

49. Spinks, "'House of Your Church,'" 152.

50. Spinks, "'House of Your Church,'" 152.

51. Gillian Rose, *Love's Work: A Reckoning with Life* (New York: New York Review Books, 2011), 105.

52. Butler, *Frames of War*, 182.

53. Judith Butler, "On the Edge—Judith Butler," lecture, PEN World Voices Festival, New York, April 28–May 4, 2014.

54. Butler, *Force of Nonviolence*, 105.

55. In the sequel to *Gilead*, *Home* (New York: Picador, 2020), Robinson describes events contemporaneous with those of *Gilead* that take place within the Boughton home, and we learn of Robert Boughton's lack of interest in or sympathy for the Montgomery bus boycotts.

56. Several other readers of this novel have noted Ames's failure, to varying degrees, in reflecting upon race in the *Gilead* series. See especially Lisa M. Siefker Bailey, "Fraught with Fire: Race and Theology in Marilynne Robinson's *Gilead*," *Christianity and Literature* 59, no. 2 (Winter 2010): 265–80; Jonathan Lean, "Not at Home in Gilead," *Raritan* 32, no. 1 (June 2012): 34–52; Lee Spinks, "'The House of Your Church Is Burning': Race and Responsibility in Marilynne Robinson's *Gilead*," *Journal of American Studies* 51, no. 1 (2017): 141–162; Jan Frans van Dijkhuizen, *A Literary History of Reconciliation: Power, Remorse, and the Limits of Forgiveness* (New York: Bloomsbury Academic, 2020), 181–201; and Elisa Gonzalez, "No Good Has Come: Marilynne Robinson's Testimony for the White Church," *The Point*, March 24, 2021, https://thepointmag.com/criticism/no-good-has-come/.

57. Spinks, "'House of Your Church,'" 161.

58. Rowan Williams, *Resurrection: Interpreting the Easter Gospel* (Cleveland, OH: Pilgrim, 2002), 30.

59. Williams, *Resurrection*, 31.

60. Hannah Arendt, *The Human Condition* (Chicago: University of Chicago Press, 1958), 247.

61. Søren Kierkegaard, *Upbuilding Discourses in Various Spirits*, trans. Howard V. Hong and Edna H. Hong (Princeton, NJ: Princeton University Press, 1993), 17.

62. Kierkegaard, *Upbuilding Discourses*, 17.

63. Kierkegaard, *Upbuilding Discourses*, 19.

CHAPTER 3. REMISSION

1. Marilynne Robinson, *Gilead* (New York: Picador, 2004), 237.

2. Robinson, *Gilead*, 237.

3. Hannah Arendt, *The Human Condition* (Chicago: University of Chicago Press, 1958), 246.

4. Arendt, *Human Condition*, 242.

5. Arendt, *Human Condition*, 241.

6. Arendt, *Human Condition*, 241.

7. Arendt, *Human Condition*, 243.

8. See Hannah Arendt, "Reflections on Little Rock," in *Responsibility and Judgment* (New York: Schocken, 2003), 193–213; and Kathryn T. Gines, *Hannah Arendt and the Negro Question* (Bloomington: Indiana University Press, 2014).

9. Louise Erdrich, *LaRose* (New York: HarperCollins, 2016).

10. Regina Schwartz, *Loving Justice, Living Shakespeare* (New York: Oxford University Press, 2016), 92.

11. David Konstan, *Before Forgiveness: The Origins of a Moral Idea* (New York: Cambridge University Press, 2010), 15.

12. Konstan, *Before Forgiveness*, 150.

13. Konstan, *Before Forgiveness*, 155.

14. Konstan, *Before Forgiveness*, 171.

15. Maria Mayo, *The Limits of Forgiveness: Case Studies in the Distortion of a Biblical Idea* (Minneapolis: Fortress, 2015), 44.

16. Ashraf H. A. Rushdy, *After Injury: A Historical Analysis of Forgiveness, Resentment, and Apology* (New York: Oxford University Press, 2018).

17. I explore these references to Jesus's resurrection and its implication for forgiveness at greater depth in Chapter 4.

18. Martha Nussbaum, *Anger and Forgiveness: Resentment, Generosity, Justice* (New York: Oxford University Press, 2016), 6.

19. Nussbaum, *Anger and Forgiveness*, 77.

20. Nussbaum, *Anger and Forgiveness*, 78.

21. Margaret Urban Walker, *Moral Repair: Reconstructing Moral Relations After Wrongdoing* (New York: Cambridge University Press, 2006), 158.

22. Nussbaum, *Anger and Forgiveness*, 75.

23. Nussbaum, *Anger and Forgiveness*, 76.

24. Joseph Butler, *Fifteen Sermons and Other Writings on Ethics*, ed. David McNaughton (New York: Oxford University Press, 2017), 76.

25. Butler, *Fifteen Sermons*, 76.

26. Butler, *Fifteen Sermons*, 78.

27. Butler, *Fifteen Sermons*, 78.

28. Trudy Govier, *Forgiveness and Revenge* (New York: Routledge, 2002), viii.

29. Jean Hampton, "Forgiveness, Resentment and Hatred," in *Forgiveness and Mercy*, by Jeffrie G. Murphy and Jean Hampton (New York: Cambridge University Press), 35–87, at 43.

30. Hampton, "Forgiveness, Resentment and Hatred," 83.

31. Hampton, "Forgiveness, Resentment and Hatred," 83.

32. Hampton, "Forgiveness, Resentment and Hatred," 84.

33. Jeffrie G. Murphy, *Getting Even: Forgiveness and Its Limits* (New York: Oxford University Press, 2003), 13.

34. Nussbaum, *Anger and Forgiveness*, 59.

35. Nussbaum, *Anger and Forgiveness*, 59.

36. Nussbaum, *Anger and Forgiveness*, 63.

37. Charles Griswold, *Forgiveness: A Philosophical Exploration* (New York: Cambridge University Press, 2007).

38. Butler, *Fifteen Sermons*, 73.
39. M. Shawn Copeland, *Knowing Christ Crucified: The Witness of African American Religious Experience* (Maryknoll, NY: Orbis Books, 2018), 172.
40. David von Drehle, "How Do You Forgive a Murder?," *Time*, November 12, 2015, http://time.com/time-magazine-charleston-shooting-cover-story/.
41. Walker, *Moral Repair*, 156.
42. Desmond Tutu, in an interview with Bill Moyers, paraphrased by Walker, *Moral Repair*, 156.
43. Nussbaum, *Anger and Forgiveness*, 76.
44. Govier, *Forgiveness and Revenge*, 15, 16.
45. Margaret Holmgren, *Forgiveness and Retribution: Responding to Wrongdoing* (New York: Cambridge University Press, 2012), 176.
46. Holmgren, *Forgiveness and Retribution*, 168.
47. Stephen Cherry, *Healing Agony: Re-Imagining Forgiveness* (New York: Continuum, 2012), 10.
48. Christopher D. Marshall, *Beyond Retribution: A New Testament Vision for Justice, Crime, and Punishment* (Grand Rapids: Eerdmans, 2001), 259.
49. Marshall, *Beyond Retribution*, 259.
50. Marshall, *Beyond Retribution*, 261. Marshall notes Matt 7:1; Luke 6:37; Rom 14:3, 10, 13; Rom 12:19; 1 Cor 4:3–5; 1 Thess 4:6; Heb 10:30; Rev 6:10; and Acts 7:24 as support. Also, given the context of Marshall's critique of retributive punishment, I take "judge" here to signify "the one who imposes sentence" at least as much as "the one who assigns blame." In any case, as Holmgren has shown, the inclination intuitively to collapse these roles together is a conceptual slippage that is useful to attend to.
51. Marshall, *Beyond Retribution*, 262.
52. Marshall, *Beyond Retribution*, 259.
53. Theodor W. Adorno, *Problems of Moral Philosophy* (Stanford, CA: Stanford University Press, 2001), 16.
54. This is a characteristic of much of Erdrich's fiction, and indeed, in some cases she composes a polyphonous first-person narrative construction. Although *LaRose* is written in the third person, Erdrich still approaches the novel's stories from multiple perspectives in time and character.
55. Frank Baum, Aberdeen *Saturday Pioneer*, January 3, 1891.
56. Frank Baum, Aberdeen *Saturday Pioneer*, December 20, 1890.
57. Beth H. Piatote, "Genealogies of Violence and Animations of Indigenous Law in Louise Erdrich's *LaRose*," in *Violence and Indigenous Communities: Confronting the Past and Engaging the Present*, ed. Susan Sleeper-Smith, Jeffrey Ostler, and Joshua L. Reid (Evanston, IL: Northwestern University Press, 2021), 33–50, at 46.
58. It is important to note that Nola's family also bears its own history of violence, one documented earlier in Erdrich's trilogy. Nola's maternal family is caught up in the gruesome murders and subsequent lynchings that occur in the first book of the trilogy, *The Plague of Doves*, and her mother murders her father, an abusive cult leader, in that novel too.

59. For some comments on the relationship between divine and human forgiveness, see my brief discussion of Rushdy, *After Injury*, above at note 16.

60. Understandings of Jesus's death in the modern Christian West have been dominated by Reformation understandings of atonement as articulated by John Calvin and Martin Luther, themselves indebted to Anselm. Alternative interpretations of Jesus's death in political, feminist, liberationist, and womanist theology are indeed notable, not least for their common dissatisfaction with the dominant, substitutionary model. See especially Delores S. Williams, *Sisters in the Wilderness: The Challenge of Womanist God-Talk* (Maryknoll, NY: Orbis Books, 1993); JoAnne Marie Terrell, *Power in the Blood? The Cross in the African American Experience* (Maryknoll, NY: Orbis Books, 1998); Rita Nakashima Brock and Rebecca Ann Parker, *Proverbs of Ashes: Violence, Redemptive Suffering, and the Search for What Saves Us* (Boston: Beacon, 2001); and M. Shawn Copeland, *Knowing Christ Crucified: The Witness of African American Religious Experience* (Maryknoll, NY: Orbis Books, 2018), among many others.

61. For indigenous American perspectives, see Clara Sue Kidwell, Homer Noley, and George E. Tinker, *A Native American Theology* (Maryknoll, NY: Orbis Books, 2001), 163ff. For some other perspectives, see especially Serene Jones, *Trauma and Grace: Theology in a Ruptured World* (Louisville: Westminster John Knox, 2009); Shelly Rambo, *Spirit and Trauma: A Theology of Remaining* (Louisville: Westminster John Knox, 2010); Deanna Thompson, *Crossing the Divide: Luther, Feminism, and the Cross* (Minneapolis: Fortress, 2004); and James H. Cone, *The Cross and the Lynching Tree* (Maryknoll, NY: Orbis Books, 2011).

62. John Milbank, *Being Reconciled: Ontology and Pardon* (New York: Routledge, 2003).

63. Milbank, *Being Reconciled*, 68.

64. Milbank does still want to preserve the language of the sovereign exception in the case of Christ's death for reasons that lie outside the interests of this book, with heavy reference to Giorgio Agamben's *homo sacer*. In short, Milbank sees Christ as the one cast out of the rule of law, whether the law of Israel, Rome, or the mob. See especially chaps. 5 and 6 of *Being Reconciled*, 79–104.

65. Milbank, *Being Reconciled*, 100.

66. Milbank, *Being Reconciled*, 53.

67. See especially Timothy Gorringe, *God's Just Vengeance: Crime, Violence, and the Rhetoric of Salvation* (New York: Cambridge University Press, 1996), and James Samuel Logan, *Good Punishment? Christian Moral Practice and U.S. Imprisonment* (Grand Rapids: Eerdmans, 2008).

68. Paul S. Fiddes, *Past Event and Present Salvation: The Christian Idea of Atonement* (Louisville: Westminster John Knox, 1989), 71.

69. Fiddes, *Past Event*, 70–71.

70. Fiddes, *Past Event*, 71.

71. Fiddes, *Past Event*, 75.

72. Fiddes, *Past Event*, 70.

73. Paul S. Fiddes, "Sacrifice, Atonement, and Renewal: Intersections Between Girard, Kristeva, and Balthasar," in *Sacrifice and Modern Thought*, ed. Julia Meszaros and Johannes Zachhuber (New York: Oxford University Press, 2013), 48–65, at 53.

74. Fiddes, "Sacrifice," 53.

75. Fiddes, *Past Event*, 72.

76. Fiddes, *Past Event*, 79.

77. Milbank, *Being Reconciled*, 61.

78. Julian of Norwich, *Revelations of Divine Love*, trans. Barry Windeatt (New York: Oxford University Press, 2015), 100.

79. Julian of Norwich, *Revelations*, 91.

80. Julian of Norwich, *Revelations*, 69.

81. Julian of Norwich, *The Shewings of Julian of Norwich* (Kalamazoo, MI: Medieval Institute Publications, 1994), 66.

82. Rowan Williams, *Holy Living: The Christian Tradition for Today* (New York: Bloomsbury, 2017), 171.

83. Williams, *Holy Living*, 171.

84. Julian of Norwich, *Revelations*, 68.

85. Williams, *Holy Living*, 172.

86. Williams, *Holy Living*, 172.

87. Williams, *Holy Living*, 172.

88. Julian of Norwich, *Revelations*, 89.

89. Julian of Norwich, *Revelations*, 75.

90. Julian of Norwich, *Revelations*, 74.

91. Julian of Norwich, *Revelations*, 143.

92. Noted in Williams, *Holy Living*, 171.

93. Julian of Norwich, *Revelations*, 65.

94. Julian of Norwich, *Revelations*, 42.

95. It's also not unique to Julian among medieval mystics. Hadewijch, for example, writes eloquently and repeatedly on the longing estrangements of love.

96. Adrienne von Speyr, *The Farewell Discourses: Meditations on John 13–17*, trans. E. A. Nelson (San Francisco: Ignatius Press, 1987), 336.

97. Adrienne von Speyr, *The Word Becomes Flesh: Meditations on John 1–5*, trans. Sr. Lucia Wiedenhöver and Alexander Dru (San Francisco: Ignatius Press, 1994), 58.

98. Hans Urs von Balthasar, *Theo-Drama: Theological Dramatic Theory, IV: The Action*, trans. Graham Harrison (San Francisco: Ignatius Press, 1994), 323.

99. von Balthasar, *Theo-Drama*, 324.

100. See the thirteenth revelation of Julian of Norwich, *Revelations*, 74ff.

101. Gillian Rose, *Love's Work: A Reckoning with Life* (New York: New York Review Books, 2011), 142.

102. Rose, *Love's Work*, 142

103. Rose, *Love's Work*, 142–43.

104. Rose, *Love's Work*, 143. The French reads, "God reveals himself in his withdrawal."

105. von Balthasar, *Theo-Drama*, 325.

106. von Balthasar, *Theo-Drama*, 325.

107. Simone Weil, *Waiting for God* (New York: Harper Perennial Modern Classics, 2009), 74.

108. Weil, *Waiting for God*, 72.

109. Weil, *Waiting for God*, 75.
110. Howard Thurman, *Sermons on the Parables* (Maryknoll, NY: Orbis Books, 2018), 138.
111. Thurman, *Sermons*, 139.
112. Thurman, *Sermons*, 138.
113. von Balthasar, *Theo-Drama*, 349.
114. Timothy P. Jackson, *The Priority of Love: Christian Charity and Social Justice* (Princeton, NJ: Princeton University Press, 2003), 144.
115. Jackson, *Priority of Love*, 155.
116. Jackson, *Priority of Love*, 155.
117. Jackson, *Priority of Love*, 144.
118. John Paul Lederach, *The Moral Imagination: The Art and Soul of Building Peace* (New York: Oxford University Press, 2005), 5.
119. Lederach, *Moral Imagination*, 55.
120. Lederach, *Moral Imagination*, 56.
121. John Paul Lederach, *Journey Toward Reconciliation* (Scottdale, PA: Herald Press, 1999), 164.
122. Lederach, *Journey Toward Reconciliation*, 164.
123. Kidwell, Noley, and Tinker, *Native American Theology*, 110.
124. See Brian Burkhart, *Indigenizing Philosophy Through the Land: A Trickster Methodology for Decolonizing Environmental Ethics and Indigenous Futures* (East Lansing: Michigan State University Press, 2019), esp. chaps. 4 and 6.

CHAPTER 4. RESURRECTION

1. Louise Erdrich, *LaRose* (New York: HarperCollins, 2016), 371.
2. Martha Minow, *Between Vengeance and Forgiveness: Facing History After Genocide and Mass Violence* (Boston: Beacon, 1998), 1.
3. Minow, *Between Vengeance and Forgiveness*, 2.
4. Minow, *Between Vengeance and Forgiveness*, 6. Minow's book is an incredibly fruitful study of real-world responses to mass violence, but conceptually she associates forgiveness with forgetting in a way that I explore and question.
5. John Milbank, *Being Reconciled: Ontology and Pardon* (Routledge: New York, 2003), 44.
6. Milbank, *Being Reconciled*, 44.
7. Jeffrey M. Blustein, *Forgiveness and Remembrance: Remembering Wrongdoing in Personal and Public Life* (New York: Oxford University Press, 2014), 10.
8. Blustein, *Forgiveness and Remembrance*, 4.
9. Blustein, *Forgiveness and Remembrance*, 18.
10. Blustein, *Forgiveness and Remembrance*, 18.
11. Minow, *Between Vengeance and Forgiveness*, 15.
12. Blustein, *Forgiveness and Remembrance*, 10.
13. Blustein, *Forgiveness and Remembrance*, 101.
14. Paul Ricoeur, *Memory, History, Forgetting*, trans. Kathleen Blamey and David Pellauer (Chicago: University of Chicago Press, 2004).

15. In these claims Ricoeur is deeply and self-consciously indebted to Hannah Arendt; see Chapter 2 for more on Arendt's influential account of forgiveness.

16. Miroslav Volf, *The End of Memory: Remembering Rightly in a Violent World* (Grand Rapids: Eerdmans, 2006).

17. In the original this sentence is emphasized with italics, an emphasis I think is unnecessary here.

18. Julian of Norwich, *Revelations of Divine Love*, trans. Barry Windeatt (New York: Oxford University Press, 2015), 68.

19. Miroslav Volf, *Exclusion and Embrace: A Theological Exploration of Identity, Otherness, and Reconciliation* (Nashville: Abingdon, 1996), 304.

20. Judith Herman, *Trauma and Recovery: The Aftermath of Violence—From Domestic Abuse to Political Terror* (New York: Basic Books, 1997), 189.

21. In Costa Rica, while negotiating peace during the Nicaraguan conflict, Lederach was stoned, beaten with a two-by-four, and Sandinistas attempted to disappear his three-year-old daughter. He reflects on the spiritual and pastoral challenge of recognizing God's love for one's enemies in light of these events in chap. 2 of *The Journey Toward Reconciliation* (Scottdale, PA: Herald Press, 1999), 29–42. See his book *The Moral Imagination: The Art and Soul of Building Peace* (New York: Oxford University Press, 2005) for reflections on empowering distrust, anger, and patience in postconflict peace-building.

22. Joseph Butler, *Fifteen Sermons and Other Writings on Ethics* (New York: Oxford University Press, 2017), 76.

23. Butler, *Fifteen Sermons*, 76.

24. Butler, *Fifteen Sermons*, 78.

25. Butler, *Fifteen Sermons*, 78.

26. Volf at times writes with pastoral wisdom and personal eloquence on these issues, especially in *The End of Memory* but also in his earlier volume *Exclusion and Embrace*.

27. Toni Morrison, *Beloved* (New York: Vintage, 2004).

28. Volf, *End of Memory*, 81.

29. Michael Banner, *The Ethics of Everyday Life: Moral Theology, Social Anthropology, and the Imagination of the Human* (New York: Oxford University Press, 2014), 182.

30. Banner, *Ethics of Everyday Life*, 175.

31. There is an extensive critical literature around the meaning of rememory. See especially Caroline Rody, "Toni Morrison's Beloved: History, 'Rememory,' and a 'Clamor for a Kiss,'" *American Literary History* 7, no. 1 (Spring 1995): 92–119. Rody's exploration of rememory is excellent and instructive, but my own interest here is to pair Rody's reading with Elizabeth House's interpretation of Beloved's ghost, cited below, and to distinguish the empty dress kneeling peacefully beside Sethe from the woman who moves into her house and consumes Sethe later in the novel, using rememory to characterize that distinction.

32. Elizabeth B. House, "Toni Morrison's Ghost: The Beloved Is Not Beloved," *Studies in American Fiction* 18, no. 1 (Spring 1990): 17–26, at 24. I have offered this reading of Beloved elsewhere but did not there attribute the first articulation of this interpretation to Professor House because of my own inadequate research. See my essay

"Imagination" in *The Cambridge Companion to Literature and Religion*, ed. Susan Felch (Cambridge: Cambridge University Press, 2016), 103–15.

33. Christina Bieber Lake, "The Demonic in Service of the Divine: Toni Morrison's *Beloved*," *South Atlantic Review* 69, no. 3/4 (Fall 2004): 51–80.

34. John J. Allen, "On White Theology . . . and Other Lies: Redemptive Communal Narrative in Toni Morrison's *Beloved*," *Literature and Theology* 35, no. 3 (September 2021): 285–308, at 287.

35. See chap. 5 in Joshua Pederson, *The Forsaken Son: Child Murder and Atonement in Modern American Fiction* (Evanston, IL: Northwestern University Press, 2016), 71–86).

36. L. Gregory Jones, *Embodying Forgiveness: A Theological Analysis* (Grand Rapids: Eerdmans, 1995), xii.

37. Donald MacKinnon, *Borderlands of Theology and Other Essays* (Eugene, OR: Wipf & Stock, 2011), 101.

38. MacKinnon, *Borderlands*, 95.

39. MacKinnon, *Borderlands*, 95.

40. MacKinnon, *Borderlands*, 96.

41. MacKinnon, *Borderlands*, 92.

42. MacKinnon, *Borderlands*, 93.

43. MacKinnon, *Borderlands*, 103.

44. Rowan Williams, *Resurrection: Interpreting the Easter Gospel* (Cleveland: Pilgrim Press, 2002), 109.

45. Williams, *Resurrection*, 109.

46. Williams, *Resurrection*, 108.

47. Williams, *Resurrection*, 109.

48. Williams, *Resurrection*, 109.

49. Williams, *Resurrection*, 45.

50. Judith Butler, *The Force of Nonviolence* (New York: Verso, 2020), 65.

51. Butler, *Force of Nonviolence*, 65.

52. Williams, *Resurrection*, 45.

53. Williams, *Resurrection*, 45.

54. M. Shawn Copeland, "Enfleshing Love: A Decolonial Theological Reading of *Beloved*," in *Beyond the Doctrine of Man: Decolonial Visions of the Human*, ed. Joseph Drexler-Dreis and Kristien Justaert (New York: Fordham University Press), 91–112, at 93.

55. Emilie Townes, "To Be Called Beloved: Womanist Ontology in Postmodern Refraction," *Annual of the Society of Christian Ethics* 13 (1993): 93–115.

56. Townes, "To Be Called Beloved," 113.

57. Copeland, "Enfleshing Love," 104.

58. See, for instance, Eddie S. Glaude Jr., *In a Shade of Blue: Pragmatism and the Politics of Black America* (Chicago: University of Chicago Press, 2007), 42.

59. Copeland, "Enfleshing Love," 104.

60. M. Shawn Copeland, *Knowing Christ Crucified: The Witness of African American Experience* (Maryknoll, NY: Orbis Books, 2018), 154.

61. Copeland, *Knowing Christ Crucified*, 154–55.
62. Timothy P. Jackson, *The Priority of Love: Christian Charity and Social Justice* (Princeton, NJ: Princeton University Press, 2003), 163.
63. Jackson, *Priority of Love*, 163.
64. Jackson, *Priority of Love*, 163. For a complementary reading of the Gospel of Mark, see part 2 of Serene Jones, *Trauma and Grace: Theology in a Ruptured World* (Louisville: Westminster John Knox, 2009).
65. Jackson, *Priority of Love*, 163.
66. Emilie M. Townes, *Womanist Ethics and the Cultural Production of Evil* (New York: Palgrave Macmillan, 2006), 161.
67. Shelly Rambo, *Spirit and Trauma: A Theology of Remaining* (Louisville: Westminster John Knox, 2010), 143.
68. Michel de Certeau, *The Mystic Fable, Volume One: The Sixteenth and Seventeenth Centuries*, trans. Michael B. Smith (Chicago: University of Chicago Press, 1992), 81.
69. Certeau, *Mystic Fable*, 81.
70. Michel de Certeau, "How Is Christianity Thinkable Today?," in *The Postmodern God: A Theological Reader*, ed. Graham Ward (Malden, MA: Blackwell, 1997), 142–55, at 151.
71. Certeau, "How Is Christianity Thinkable?," 145.
72. Certeau, "How Is Christianity Thinkable?," 145.
73. Certeau, "How Is Christianity Thinkable?," 150.
74. Michel de Certeau, "The Weakness of Believing: From the Body to Writing, a Christian Transit," in *The Certeau Reader*, ed. Graham Ward (Malden, MA: Blackwell, 2000), 214–23, at 227.
75. Certeau, "Weakness of Believing," 227.
76. Certeau, "Weakness of Believing," 234.
77. I've written elsewhere on the potential risks of reading Christianity's relentless movement so optimistically, especially in a colonial context. See "Christ, Identity, and Empire in *Silence*," *Journal of Religion* 101, no. 2 (April 2021): 183–204.
78. Certeau, "How Is Christianity Thinkable?," 155.
79. For more on how Christian theology framed colonial white supremacy and patriarchy, see Sylvia Wynter, "Unsettling the Coloniality of Being/Power/Truth/Freedom: Towards the Human, After Man, Its Overrepresentation—An Argument," in *CR: The New Centennial Review* 3, no. 3 (Fall 2003): 257–337; and Willie Jennings, *The Christian Imagination: Theology and the Origins of Race* (New Haven: Yale University Press, 2011).
80. Julia Kristeva, *Black Sun: Depression and Melancholia* (New York: Columbia University Press, 1989), 205.
81. Kristeva, *Black Sun*, 206.
82. Kristeva, *Black Sun*, 207.
83. Kristeva, *Black Sun*, 217.
84. Julia Kristeva, *Hatred and Forgiveness*, trans. Jeanine Herman (New York: Columbia University Press, 2010), 193.
85. Kristeva, *Hatred and Forgiveness*, 193.

86. Kristeva, *Hatred and Forgiveness*, 193–94.

87. As noted in previous chapters, I take anger, rancor, and bitterness to be affective states that can exist alongside loving actions. I take hate, the wish for another's suffering and annihilation, to be the opposite of love.

88. Julia Kristeva, *Intimate Revolt: The Powers and Limits of Psychoanalysis*, trans. Jeanine Herman (New York: Columbia University Press, 2002), 16.

89. Kristeva, *Intimate Revolt*, 16.

90. Kristeva, *Intimate Revolt*, 24.

91. Toni Morrison, "The Site of Memory," in *Inventing the Truth: The Art and Craft of Memoir*, ed. William Zinsser (New York: Houghton Mifflin, 1995), 85–102, at 91.

92. Morrison, "Site of Memory," 94.

93. Morrison's approach here resembles the method of critical fabulation developed and employed by Saidiya Hartman: "The intention here isn't anything as miraculous as recovering the lives of the enslaved or redeeming the dead, but rather laboring to paint as full a picture of the lives of the captives as possible. This double gesture can be described as straining against the limits of the archive to write a cultural history of the captive, and, at the same time, enacting the impossibility of representing the lives of the captives precisely through the process of narration" ("Venus in Two Acts," *Small Axe* 12, no. 2 [June 2008]: 1–14, at 11).

94. Morrison, "Site of Memory," 92.

95. Jacques Derrida, "Literature in Secret: An Impossible Filiation," in *The Gift of Death: Second Edition and Literature in Secret*, trans. David Wills (Chicago: University of Chicago Press, 2008), 119–58.

96. Charles Barbour, *Derrida's Secret: Perjury, Testimony, Oath* (Edinburgh: Edinburgh University Press, 2017), 139–40.

97. It bears noting that Derrida believes this idea of literature to depend in some significant degree upon democracy. "Put crudely, for Derrida, literature and democracy mean that people have a right to say anything, in private but also in public, and a right not to be compelled to give an account of what they say—simply to let their words circulate without having to be traced back to some intention, origin or inward truth" (Barbour, *Derrida's Secret*, 114).

98. Barbour, *Derrida's Secret*, 144.

99. Barbour, *Derrida's Secret*, 144.

100. Barbour, *Derrida's Secret*, 145.

101. Mark 1:34, 3:12, 5:43; Luke 4:41, 5:14, 8:56; Matt 8:4, 9:30, 12:16, among others.

102. MacKinnon, *Borderlands*, 96.

EPILOGUE

1. See W. H. Auden, "The Prince's Dog," in *The Dyer's Hand* (New York: Vintage, 1989), 182–208.

2. Susannah Young-ah Gottlieb, *Regions of Sorrow: Anxiety and Messianism in Hannah Arendt and W. H. Auden* (Palo Alto, CA: Stanford University Press, 2003), 5.

3. Correspondence from Hannah Arendt to Wystan Auden, 14 February 1960, Correspondence, General, 1938–1976, n.d., Auden, W. H., 1964–1975, The Hannah Arendt Papers at the Library of Congress, The Library of Congress, Washington, DC.

4. W. H. Auden, *The Shield of Achilles* (New York: Random House, 1955), 37.

5. Auden, *Shield of Achilles*, 37.

6. Hannah Arendt, *The Human Condition* (Chicago: University of Chicago Press, 1958).

7. See Simone Weil, *Waiting for God* (New York: Harper Perennial Modern Classics, 2009), and *Gravity and Grace* (Lincoln: University of Nebraska Press, 1997).

8. Quoted in Simone Weil, *The Iliad, or the Poem of Force*, trans. James P. Holoka (New York: Peter Lang, 2006), 47.

9. Weil, *Iliad*, 47–48.

10. Weil, *Iliad*, 48.

11. Weil, *Iliad*, 63.

12. Weil, *Iliad*, 63.

Index

Arendt, Hannah: on action, 59–65; agent
of, 61; on forgiveness, 62–65, 124,
182, 229; forgiver of, 64; on freedom,
61–62; *The Human Condition,* 59,
124, 229; on humans, 60; Jesus of,
230; on love, 124–25, 156, 230; on
punishment, 240n66; on respect,
125; on restraint, 140; on revenge,
62; on self-sufficiency, 61; on
sovereignty, 60–61
atonement: divine, 125; John Paul
Lederach on, 176; Julian of Norwich
on, 163–68; in *LaRose,* 127, 148–56;
spacial metaphor of, 168–70;
theories in Christian theology, 157
atonement theology: of Christian
forgiveness, 6, 156–57; Delores
Williams's womanist critique of,
207; Jesus as a substitute in
Christian, 158, 174; Julian of
Norwich's contribution to Christian,
163–65
Auden, W. H.: on forgiveness, 230; "In
Memory of W. B. Yeats," 229; love
for, 230; "Musée des Beaux Arts,"
229; "The Prince's Dog," 229; "The
Sea and the Mirror," 229; "The
Shield of Achilles," 231–32
Auschwitz, 51
authenticity, 83–85

Banner, Michael, 203
baptism, 85
baptismal redemption, 85–86
Barbour, Charles, 222
Baum, Frank, 149
beginning, forgiveness as a, 64, 182
Being Reconciled (Milbank), 158–60
Beloved (Morrison): chattel slavery in,
194, 206; Christ figure in, 217–18;
critical literature on, 207–8, 213;
exorcisms in, 196, 199–200; failure
of remembering in, 209; fantasy of
restoration in, 209–10; forgiveness

in, 199, 202; impossibility of
justification in, 201–3; memory in,
194–95, 208–9; pain in, 195; past and
future in, 196, 199; rejection of grief
and mourning in, 204–5;
"rememory" in, 204–5, 249n31;
themes explored in, 13, 201; violence
in, 194
Benjamin, Walter: divine violence of,
98–102; "The Critique of Violence,"
97–98
Bethge, Eberhard, 101
beyond the law: Arthur as, 40, 41;
forgiveness as, 55–56
bitterness. *See* anger
Black anger, 143
Blustein, Jeffrey, 184–86, 191
Board of Education, Brown v., 115
boarding schools for indigenous
American peoples, 149–51, 171
Bonhoeffer, Dietrich: on action, 102–3;
arrest of, 101, 102; on breaching the
law, 103; on confession and
repentance, 103–4; *Ethics,* 101–2; on
God's love, 102–3
Brown v. Board of Education, 115
Buddhism, Japanese Shin, 104
Buried Giant, The (Ishiguro): Arthurian
fantasy underlying, 23; Arthur's
divine sovereignty in, 40–42;
dilemma in, 25; forgiveness in, 70,
203; grief and mourning in, 13, 203;
irrevocable loss in, 63–64, 70; love
and memory in, 25, 37, 66–67, 70–
71, 74; plot of, 23–26, 36–39;
rejection of death in, 63; retaliation
impulses in, 36; sadness in, 43–44;
self-mortification in, 72–73; themes
explored in, 13, 36, 63–64; vengeance
in, 38–39, 43, 63–64; war in, 40
Burkhart, Brian, 178
Butler, Joseph: Charles Griswold on
forgiveness of, 138–44; David
Konstan on, 128–29; on lawful

fallibility, admission of, 106
fantasy of the absolute, 105
fascism, 104
Father, the. *See* God
felicity, 190–92
Fiddes, Paul, 161–63
financial compensation, law of like for
   like and, 22
financial crimes, compensating, 33–34
finitude, 104–5, 108, 159–60
fire in *Gilead*, 118
Force of Nonviolence, The (Judith Butler),
   96–101
forgetfulness, knowing, 109
forgetting: forcing a, 42; in forgiveness,
   17, 82, 144, 183–84; in *Gilead*, 82,
   109; Jeffrey Blustein on, 184; as
   memorial care, 187; Paul Ricoeur on,
   186–88; punishment as an alternative
   to, 36; reconciliation and, 185–86;
   selective, 50, 186–87; "well," 186–87
forgiveness: affective dimension of, 17,
   125, 128–29, 138, 145, 184–86, 229; as
   an act of retaliatory restraint, 17,
   229; anger and, 132; Ashraf H. A.
   Rushdy on, 130; as a beginning, 64,
   182; in *Beloved*, 199, 202; as beyond
   the law, 55–56; in *The Buried Giant*,
   70, 203; as charity, 229; Charles
   Griswold on, 128, 141, 145; as
   Christian nonretaliation, 10, 21;
   Christian theology of, 14, 83, 184;
   commodification of, 145; conditional
   (nature of), 8, 83, 128, 132–33, 138,
   140; David Konstan on, 128–29;
   death and, 50; divine, 107, 130, 160,
   164, 170–71; divine and human, 156–
   57; dramatic art and, 229; as dyadic,
   128; as an exception to the law, 42,
   56; forgetting in, 17, 82, 144, 183–84;
   as a form of love, 47–48, 50, 193; as a
   freedom, 62–63; Friedrich Nietzsche
   on, 55; in *Gilead*, 75, 80, 81–82, 107;
   as grief, 232; Hannah Arendt on,

62–65, 124, 182, 229; imagination
   and, 10, 13; as interpretation, 223–24;
   Jacques Derrida on, 53–59, 222–25;
   James Cone on, 32–33; Jean
   Hampton on, 135–36; Jeffrey
   Blustein on, 184–86; John Milbank
   on, 158–60, 162–63, 184; Joseph
   Butler on, 129, 133–35, 140, 144, 193;
   Julia Kristeva on, 218–20; Julian of
   Norwich on, 163–64; as justice, 46–
   47; L. Gregory Jones on, 207–8; as
   loving restraint, 230; Martha
   Nussbaum on, 83, 130–33, 136–37,
   145; memory and, 48–50, 184;
   Michael Banner on, 203; as a moral
   problem, 143–44; as mourning, 10,
   18, 54, 64, 93, 108, 203, 232; pardon
   and, 230; the past and, 74, 145–46;
   Paul Ricoeur on, 187–88; as payback,
   130, 135, 145; as a *poeisis* of meaning,
   219–20; "postmoral" and Freudian
   framing of, 220; promise and, 62; as
   resistance and resilience, 32;
   resurrection and, 214; retaliation as
   opposite of, 21; romanticization of,
   55; Rowan Williams on, 212–13; as a
   secret, 222, 225–26; in Shakespeare's
   plays, 129; shortcomings of, 80; sin
   and, 46; spacial metaphor of, 168–
   70; Tanabe Hajime on, 105–6;
   Timothy Jackson on, 175;
   transactional model of, 127–28, 133;
   Trudy Govier on, 135–36;
   unconditional, 7, 46; Vladimir
   Jankélévitch on, 45–53; W. H. Auden
   on, 230; wrong and, 46–47, 50, 107;
   wrongdoing and, 108, 128
Forgiveness (Jankélévitch), 45–50, 53
Forgiveness: A Philosophical Exploration
   (Griswold), 138–41, 144–45
forgiver, Hannah Arendt's, 64
forgiving forgetfulness of the past,
   187–89
forgiving love, 200

Homer, 30
House, Elizabeth, 206
Housekeeping (Robinson), 75
Human Condition, The (Arendt), 59, 124, 229
human suffering, 161
humans: compassion of, 140–41; finiteness of, 102; Hannah Arendt on, 60; interdependence of, 91–92, 96

identity, 189
Iliad, The (Homer), 231–32
imagination, forgiveness and, 10, 13
"In Memory of W. B. Yeats" (Auden), 229
inadequacy, embracing, 105
incarnation, 127
indigenous American communities: boarding schools/cultural reeducation for, 149–51, 171; Frank Baum on annihilating, 149; genocide of, 149–50, 171; sin for, 178
indignation, 140
individualism, Judith Butler's critique of, 96–97
interdependence of humans, 91–92, 96
interpersonal exchange in forgiveness, 128
interpersonal forgiveness, *Gilead* and, 75
interpretation, forgiveness as, 223–24
irrecuperability, Martha Nussbaum on, 33
irrevocability of the past, 34, 36, 49–50, 53, 64–65, 204–5
Ishiguro, Kazuo: *The Buried Giant*, 11, 23–26, 36–44, 63–75; family origins of, 41; *The Remains of the Day*, 23; work of, 12, 23

Jackson, Timothy, 175, 214–15
Jankélévitch, Vladimir: on expiation, 53; on forgiveness, 45–53; *Forgiveness*, 45–50, 53; John Milbank on, 159, 240n46; on pardoning Nazi war

crimes, 51; on prescriptibility, 51–53; on punishment, 51–52; on resentment, 51–52; "Should We Pardon Them?," 51–53; on wrongdoing, 53
Japan, 16, 41
Japanese Shin Buddhism, 104
Jesus: death of, 13–14, 148, 157–58, 159, 210, 246n60; empty tomb of, 214–17; Hannah Arendt's, 230; as mediator, 176; New Testament writings after death of, 13, 161, 211; as a substitute, 158, 174
Jesus of Nazareth. *See* Jesus
John, Gospel of, 215
Jones, L. Gregory, 207–8
Jordan, Mark, 5
judging as separate from sentencing and pardoning, 146
judgment: affective, 139; divine, 99; Margaret Holmgren on, 146–47; third-party, 142, 145
Julian of Norwich: atonement theology of, 164–68; on forgiveness, 163–64; longing of, 167; *Revelations of Divine Love*, 164–67
justice: divine, 157; forgiveness as, 46–47; Joseph Butler on lawful, 140–42, 144; mourning and human, 45; "old form of," 126–27, 148; proxies for, 157; punishment and, 42, 148, 160–61; retaliation and, 21–22; as revenge in Hebrew scriptures and Homer, 30; transactional frameworks of, 146–47
justification: impossibility of, 201–3; of violence, 82, 96–102

knowing forgetfulness, 109
Konstan, David, 128–29, 236n11
Kristeva, Julia, 218–20

Lake, Christina Bieber, 207
Lance, Ethel, 1

language: Christian, 216; failure of,
76–78

LaRose (Erdrich): anger in, 154–55;
atonement in, 127, 148–56;
community sustainment in, 152;
ending, 180–81; grief in, 153; guilt in,
153; healing in, 156; loss in, 151–53,
171–72; love in, 153, 156, 173–74;
retaliation in, 151–52, 171–72; themes
explored in, 13, 125–26, 149, 153;
tragedy in, 126, 170–71; vengeance
in, 172; violence in, 126–27, 149–52,
172–73, 245n58; white colonialism
in, 149, 154–55, 182

law, the: Dietrich Bonhoeffer on
breaching, 103; forgiveness as an
exception to, 42, 56; inadequacies of,
45; Jacques Derrida on forgiveness's
relationship to, 55, 58; retribution in,
31; sovereignty and, 40, 41–42, 55–56

law of like for like. See *lex talionis*
law of talion. See *lex talionis*
law-breaking, forgiving, 103
Lederach, John Paul, 175–76, 249n21
Lethe, waters of, 184, 189
Leviticus, Book of, 22
lex talionis, 22, 27, 28, 33, 36, 106, 109
Lila (Robinson), 77
literature, 219, 222, 225
"Literature in Secret" (Derrida), 222
longing, Julian of Norwich's, 167
loss: Christian discipleship as a practice
of, 216; forgiveness as upsetting the
compensatory economy of, 146;
ineradicability of, 22, 36; of Jesus's
body, 215; in *LaRose*, 151–53, 171–72;
love and, 125, 169; Michel de
Certeau on, 215–16; refusal to
recover from, 217; resurrection and,
215–18; singularity of, 33; as a
transformation to be endured, 108

love: Adrienne von Speyr on, 167–68;
divine, 157, 190 (*see also* God's love;
Revelations of Divine Love [Julian of

Norwich]); forgiveness as a form of,
47–48, 50, 193; forgiving, 200; in
Gilead, 116, 123–24; Hannah Arendt
on, 124–25, 156, 230; hate as the
opposite of, 252n87; infiniteness of
God's, 9, 109, 118; Joseph Butler on,
135, 192; in *LaRose*, 153, 156, 173–74;
loss and, 125, 169; and memory in
The Buried Giant, 25, 37, 66–67,
70–71, 74; of one's enemies, 9, 109,
134, 174, 193; possibilities for
resurrection lying in, 213; a
remembering, 193; as separation,
169–70, 177; for Tanabe Hajime,
105; Timothy Jackson on, 175;
unconditional, 130–32

loving forgiveness, 50, 131
loving restraint, forgiveness as, 230
Luke, Gospel of, 48, 115, 118, 123, 156
luo, 5, 171

MacKinnon, Donald, 210–11
Mark, Gospel of, 156–57, 214, 216
Marshall, Christopher, 147
mastery of another, 32
Matthew, Gospel of, 5, 109, 124, 134, 157,
192, 215
Mayo, Maria, 129–30, 236n11
meaning, forgiveness as a *poeisis* of, 219–
20
memory: in *Beloved*, 194–96, 208–9; in
The Buried Giant, 66–67, 74; as
care, 187; as a constructive act, 186;
divine, 118; erasing, 42; forgiveness
as a form of, 48–50, 184; as
foundational for forgiveness, 184; in
Gilead, 82, 109; happiness and, 183–
88; hatred as a, 42; Miroslav Volf on,
188–89; the past as, 209; Paul
Ricoeur on, 186–87; punishment
and, 26–27, 73; selective, 184–88,
195
Memory, History, and Forgetting
(Ricoeur), 186–88